Studies in the Psychosocial

Series editors
Stephen Frosh
Dept of Psychosocial Studies
Birkbeck, University of London
London, United Kingdom

Peter Redman
Faculty of Arts and Social Sciences
Open University, Milton Keynes, UK

Wendy Hollway
Faculty of Arts and Social Sciences
Open University, Milton Keynes, UK

Psychosocial Studies seeks to investigate the ways in which psychic and social processes demand to be understood as always implicated in each other, as mutually constitutive, co-produced, or abstracted levels of a single dialectical process. As such it can be understood as an interdisciplinary field in search of transdisciplinary objects of knowledge. Psychosocial Studies is also distinguished by its emphasis on affect, the irrational and unconscious processes, often, but not necessarily, understood psychoanalytically. Studies in the Psychosocial aims to foster the development of this field by publishing high quality and innovative monographs and edited collections. The series welcomes submissions from a range of theoretical perspectives and disciplinary orientations, including sociology, social and critical psychology, political science, postcolonial studies, feminist studies, queer studies, management and organization studies, cultural and media studies and psychoanalysis. However, in keeping with the inter- or transdisciplinary character of psychosocial analysis, books in the series will generally pass beyond their points of origin to generate concepts, understandings and forms of investigation that are distinctively psychosocial in character.

More information about this series at
http://www.springer.com/series/14464

Karl Figlio

Remembering as Reparation

Psychoanalysis and Historical Memory

Karl Figlio
University of Essex
Essex, UK

Studies in the Psychosocial
ISBN 978-1-349-95549-7   ISBN 978-1-137-59591-1   (eBook)
DOI 10.1057/978-1-137-59591-1

© The Editor(s) (if applicable) and The Author(s) 2017
Softcover reprint of the hardcover 1st edition 2017
The author(s) has/have asserted their right(s) to be identified as the author(s) of this work in accordance with the Copyright, Designs and Patents Act 1988.
This work is subject to copyright. All rights are solely and exclusively licensed by the Publisher, whether the whole or part of the material is concerned, specifically the rights of translation, reprinting, reuse of illustrations, recitation, broadcasting, reproduction on microfilms or in any other physical way, and transmission or information storage and retrieval, electronic adaptation, computer software, or by similar or dissimilar methodology now known or hereafter developed.
The use of general descriptive names, registered names, trademarks, service marks, etc. in this publication does not imply, even in the absence of a specific statement, that such names are exempt from the relevant protective laws and regulations and therefore free for general use.
The publisher, the authors and the editors are safe to assume that the advice and information in this book are believed to be true and accurate at the date of publication. Neither the publisher nor the authors or the editors give a warranty, express or implied, with respect to the material contained herein or for any errors or omissions that may have been made. The publisher remains neutral with regard to jurisdictional claims in published maps and institutional affiliations.

Cover illustration: Drew Mountain (bw) / Alamy Stock Photo

Printed on acid-free paper

This Palgrave Macmillan imprint is published by Springer Nature
The registered company is Macmillan Publishers Ltd.
The registered company address is: The Campus, 4 Crinan Street, London, N1 9XW, United Kingdom

To my wife, Stina

Acknowledgements

I want to thank the following people, who have helped me with this book.

Geoff Eley has been a generous advisor and correspondent on the historical dimension of and sources for my thesis. Claudia Jerzak, Hedda Joyce and Steffen Kruger have read and commented on parts of the book, clarifying issues concerning German anti-memorial work, guilt and right-wing extremism. I have enjoyed and benefitted from discussions on personal involvement in scholarship with Dave Bell, Matt ffytche and Michael Roper, in our 'Essex Project', and with Roger Frie, in discovering our common interest in psychoanalysis and German history. I have also benefitted from discussions with the German Historical Group, formed by several analysts, historians and philosophers in London with a deep interest in this area. Over many years, as a friend and colleague, Bob Hinshelwood has commented on and discussed various papers and presentations that were predecessors to this book.

I want to express my special gratitude to Stina Lyon, who has contributed to every aspect of my project, from its inception to this book, and to Ronald Britton, who has informed every level of my thinking.

Two published papers were earlier attempts to formulate my thesis, and material from them can be found throughout the book. I want to thank Wiley for permission to draw on 'A Psychoanalytic Reflection on Collective Memory as a Psychosocial Enclave: Jews, German National

Identity and Splitting in German Psyche', *International Social Science Journal*, 62(203–204), 2011, pp. 161–77; and Johns Hopkins University Press for permission to draw on 'Psychoanalysis, Reparation and Historical Memory', *American Imago* 71(4), 2014, pp. 417–44, especially in Chap. 9. Thanks also to Karnac for permission to draw for Chap. 4 on 'The Dread of Sameness: Social Hatred and Freud's "Narcissism of Minor Differences"', in Auestad, L. (ed.) *Psychoanalysis and Politics: Exclusion and the Politics of Representation*, London: Karnac, 2012.

Translations are mine unless otherwise indicated.

'The Ordeal' by Edith Breckwoldt, St Nikolai Memorial, Hamburg, Germany [Photo taken by Karl Figlio]

Plaque reads:
"Kein Mensch auf der ganzen Welt kann die Wahrheit verändern.
Man kann sie nur suchen, sie finden und ihr dienen.
Die Wahrheit ist an jedem Ort."
Dietrich Bonhoeffer

Translation:
No one in the world can change the truth.
One can only search for it, find it and serve it.
The truth is in every place.
[Translated by Joanna O'Neill]

Contents

1	Introduction	1
2	The Internal World	27
3	Psychoanalysis and the 'Social Subject'	45
4	Delusional Enemies	73
5	Solidarity, Catastrophe and Ambivalence	101
6	Conflicts of Remembering: The *Historikerstreit*	119
7	Remembering and Not-Remembering	145
8	The Unconscious Division of Germany	165
9	Reparation	185

10	Remembering, Memorialization and Reparation	207
11	Conclusion	239
References		257
Index		275

List of Figures

Fig. 2.1	Memorial to expellees, Pforzheim (From Margalit, p. 217)	37
Fig. 2.2	Collectivization under the ego-ideal (Freud 1921, p. 116)	39
Fig. 2.3	Drawing by Richard (From Klein 1945, p. 379; Melanie Klein Trust)	42
Fig. 7.1	Kollwitz, Pietà, Neue Wache, Berlin	151
Fig. 9.1	Diagram based on Faimberg 2005	195
Fig. 10.1	Vietnam Veterans Memorial Wall, Washington, DC	209
Fig. 10.2	The three soldiers memorial, Washington, DC	209
Fig. 10.3	Nazi memorial, Hamburg	211
Fig. 10.4	Counter-memorial, Hamburg	212
Fig. 10.5	Heidefriedhof memorial wall, Dresden	228

1

Introduction

Historical Consciousness

Psychoanalysis and history are autonomous fields, but they are varieties of the same species, rooted in the same soil. Both take historical consciousness to be the core of their enquiries because it is the core of being human. For the philosopher, R. G. Collingwood, to be human was to live in historical consciousness. Collingwood (1946/1993) said that the historian raised before his/her mind's eye the scenario under investigation. 'The historical imagination [has] as its task to imagine the past: not an object of possible perception …, but able through this activity to become an object of our thought' (p. 242). Understanding was a function of this imaginative process—based on evidence, but always, necessarily, retrospective: the mind made the evidence into a human situation for the historical actors themselves and for the historian trying to get into it as an internal, mental scene. Indeed, 'Evidence is evidence only when some one contemplates it historically' (p. 247).

The same holds for psychoanalysis. The psychoanalyst understands the patient by raising in his/her mind a scene. This internal scene, as with the historian, is based on evidence, but it is the imaginative, internal, mental scene that creates the moment of understanding. It, too, is always retrospective—Freud called it *Nachträglich*—in the way it exercised its influence on thinking after the fact.

To have a mind is historical consciousness. We are human in having minds that register the impact of the world in scenarios that retrospectively reform the past as they also inform the present and anticipate the future. We live in continuity, not just of the past pushing the present forward, but of the present forming the past into a present state of mind: aware of itself now and as having arrived at now, in a historical consciousness. 'The criterion of [historical truth] is the idea of history itself… which every man possesses as part of the furniture of his mind, and discovers himself to possess in so far as he becomes conscious of what it is to have a mind' (Collingwood, p. 248). It is the leading principle for psychoanalyst and historian alike (Figlio 1998).

Next to their fundamental kinship, the differences that separate the two fields are minor. They seem to boil down to two ideas: (1) that psychoanalysis is based on an enquiry into the thinking and feeling of individuals, and, therefore, cannot legitimately, be extrapolated to social groups; (2) that psychoanalysis studies the mind, subjectivity, but societies have no mind, and are, therefore, not amenable to the methods of psychoanalysis, nor explicable by them. To my mind, both of these objections are mistaken, and one of my aims in this book is to show in what way they are mistaken and how this apparent isolation one from the other can be bridged.

The historian's gathering of historical evidence takes on a subjective dimension, with the subjectivity of the historian entering the subjectivity of the historical actor. The same holds true for the psychoanalyst, except that the subjectivity of the interpreter and of the actor is clear from the start, indeed it is both the source of evidence and the object of scrutiny. And both historian and psychoanalyst can construct in his/her mind a critical use of evidence, even experimental in character.

The kinship between psychoanalysis and history suggests that they should be in dialogue. The arguments against their kinship are not compelling and the yield from a dialogue is compelling. This book is structured around trying to realize this aim. For the historian, evidence is like the remembering—the historical consciousness—of the historical actor and the historian. The same is the case for the psychoanalyst, but, it brings out an additional aspect, which is also true for the historian: that remembering is a form of reparation, and reparation suffers from the same difficulties as does remembering. They are often painful processes, especially if they bring into the present—as they must—experiences that are unbearable. I approach them from two angles: from psychoanalysis, in which reparation is a fundamental concept, certainly in the Object Relations tradition; and from the history of post-war Germany, in which memory of the Nazi period has been a tortured subject since the war.

Memory is not just a cognitive recall, as in a retrieval of a manuscript from an archive; nor is it a facsimile of a situation in the past. It is a creation, a largely unconscious melding of two currents: one of the present, which would include conscious recall; and another of the past, comprising primal, unconscious, affect-laden experiences, which find a route into consciousness through opportunities offered in the present. Such a model is a version of psychic processes, which, as for Freud, are *Nachträglich*; that is, as continually revised retrospectively (Laplanche and Pontalis, pp. 111–14). In this model, psychic processes are compromises between repressed, unconscious experiences, which push through any open channels into consciousness, and continually changing, partly conscious, contemporary scenarios. Memory is the outcome of a moving compromise, based on what of the past can be tolerated in the present.

Memory is also heavily influenced by the social and cultural environment. Individuals belong to groups. Groups consolidate around beliefs held in common. The conditions for belonging to the group include the terms for what can be tolerated as a memory in the present and what must be modified by illusion. In this situation, we remember an illusion that might not appear as such because it has been incorporated into an experience of reality that makes sense today for the group. Memories, infused with illusions, offer a comforting avoidance of painful, external reality—a group version of what Freud (1899) called 'screen memories'.

While memory can fall into, or be pushed into, the past, reparation is a process that continues in the present, with a focus and a purpose: to make good an injury inflicted in the past. Thus, it cannot be put aside as 'past', but is continually renewed as a contemporary indebtedness. As in remembering, there is a version that seeks reality and a version, infused with illusion, which defends against it. One way that memory is continually renewed as reparation is in memorialization. Memorialization can take several forms: monuments and other sites of remembrance; commemorations; archiving, whether in libraries or museums; debates, both popular and scholarly. When I speak of memory as reparation, I shall mainly consider these forms.

The fact that painful memories (and reparation) are avoided does not imply that their retrieval is a sure guide to their reality. Here is an extract from one of Freud's detailed cases, *Wolf Man* (1918 [1914], p. 23).

> A few months after [the] death [of his sister, who was the object of jealousy and of incestuous love, now repressed] he himself made a journey in the neighbourhood in which she had died. There he sought out the burial-place of a great poet, who was at that time his ideal, and shed bitter tears upon his grave. This reaction seemed strange to him himself, for he knew that more than two generations had passed by since the death of the poet he admired. He only understood it when he remembered that his father had been in the habit of comparing his dead sister's works with the great poet's. He gave me another indication of the correct way of interpreting the homage which he ostensibly paid to the poet, by a mistake in his story which I was able to detect at this point. He had repeatedly specified before that his sister had shot herself; but he was now obliged to make a correction and say that she had taken poison. The poet, however, had been shot in a duel.

Wolf Man's memory of his journey occurred in analysis, where its roots and meaning were monitored and interpreted. If he had not been in analysis, his memory might have remained real and painful in its conscious terms. We could only guess at the actual analysis of his memory and how the falsification in it consolidated a defensive avoidance of painful memories. Freud said he assumed that his grief for his sister had been inhibited by his jealousy and incestuous love, and that the interpretation above confirmed this view, which he had begun to doubt. So we are strengthened in conjecturing the following 'rational', repressed account.

> Wolf Man believed that his sister took her life as a repudiation of his shameful treatment of her. In this belief, she accused him of jealous aggression and of prurient incestuous wishes. Because her accusations were the

motive for her suicide, he did not mourn her death, but rebuked her by 'forgetting' her. He did, however, mourn the death of a love object who, though he, too, took his own life, did not incriminate him. In his innocence, Wolf Man could allow his grief to come out freely. The links between sister and poet were his father's comparison of them and 'shot himself'. Remembering her actual death would have brought back the painful memory of his relationship to her.

This clinical vignette demonstrates a form of not-knowing in the presence of all the evidence for knowing. Freud called Wolfman's defence, which was a displacement of affect from its original bond (sister) to an idea onto another idea (poet), 'repression'. There are other forms of not-knowing, principally 'disavowal', which we will explore in the course of the book. I will also argue that similar forms of (not-) remembering have characterized memory of the Nazi period in post-war Germany. Remembering in Germany, as the experience of perpetration, forms a large part of post-war German history and also of this book. One of the forms it takes is commemoration, whether in memorials, anniversary events or public debates. They occur within the post-war drive to make reparation and also to deny the relevance of making reparation

Structure of the Book

Psychoanalysis, clinical and theoretical, forms the spine of the book. With this in mind, I pursue three lines of enquiry, not as chapter headings, but as grounding themes: first, that societies, as well as individuals, remember; second, that remembering is a form of reparation—remembering is an important dimension of the wish to make better—not to expunge, but to recognize reality and to form a better relationship between perpetrators and victims; third, that a dialogue between psychoanalysis and historical research into remembering the Nazi period is essential to both fields, focusing in this case on the Holocaust. The dialogue is intended to throw light on remembering and the avoidance of remembering the Holocaust as reparation and avoided reparation.

I am aware that this proposal is contentious. How could one even conceive of the atrocity of the Holocaust—even have a thought or imagination that came close to it—let alone think—that the injury could be made better? Research and writing about the Holocaust are continually vexed by conflict over an appropriate emotional distance between researcher and topic: too close might confuse understanding with emotional involvement or complicity; too distant might seem professional and scholarly, but too distant adequately to comprehend its topic. Neither would be scholarly and each could draw reproach. The proper, professional role of the historian must not allow 'moralistic' intrusion into scientific research, but objective distance can foreclose on the essence of the enquiry.

The so-called *Historikerstreit* (historians debate) of the 1980s turned on a conflict between conservative historians who sought to 'normalize' German history, by bringing the Nazi period into an intelligible flow of historical understanding and narrative, and others—not necessarily historians—who rejected this stance as a concealed form of apologetics. The problem remains today. Holocaust denial remains a current form of anti-Semitism. In a libel action against Penguin Books and the historian, Deborah Lipstadt, David Irving claimed that they were destroying his reputation as a historian of the Third Reich and suppressing the free speech of historical enquiry, which he pursued in the face of opposition lacking his expertise (Evans 2002; Lipstadt 1994, 2006). The court ruled in favour of the defendants, based on a detailed analysis of Irving's claim to be pursuing the work of the historian as opposed to purveying pro-Nazi prejudice in the form of historical research. The *Historikerstreit* was more subtle, in that no one claimed that the conservative historians lacked expertise, but that, nonetheless, the sought-for normalization of German history was a form of apologetics, an accusation that could not be refuted by claiming that it was a moralistic intrusion from outside, into the profession of history.

Let us turn to the three grounding themes.

Remembering

Historians have debated the role of subjectivity and objectivity in general and in the understanding of German perpetration in the Second World War. In psychoanalysis, one speaks of an internal world. Subjective means 'of the subject', not a wispy, idiosyncratic feeling of a moment withdrawn from 'reality'. 'Objective' means the hard-won recognition and toleration of a world of objects that exist over against appropriation by the subject—won in the struggle with narcissism. 'Narcissism' means the infusion of life—libido—into the self, not just self-importance. Narcissism confronts the object world with its demand to stay alive against the pull of that world, and it also bestows life on its objects by identification. Every external reality is therefore matched by an internal, subjective reality. Projective and introjective mechanisms infuse the object world with subjectivity and orientate the subjective world with objectivity. With this orientation towards a reality that is both internal and external, psychic and perceptual, we can speak of social as well as individual remembering.

We gain the objectivity of observation, experiment and measurement of phenomena by marginalizing subjectivity. We approach an intimation of emotional immediacy by marginalizing objectivity. Thinking embraces both poles in a more moderated way, running from the passion of discovery or of a feeling of certainty that is more or less restrained by evidence; to the logic of systematic observation. In the extreme state of objectivity, subjectivity is unbearable, because the distance between ego and object collapses, threatening the ego with dissolution through the loss of positioning objects in the internal world. Relationship then means the implosion of identity. In the extreme state of subjectivity, objectivity is unbearable, because the distance between ego and object imposes an isolation on an ego, now with no kindred internal objects. In subjectivity, ego and object overlap to the point of confusion; omnipotence is maximal; relationship means total identification. In objectivity, the object world is ego-alien—even inanimate—moralistic and judgemental. These states of mind, with their vulnerabilities, have been clearly described and documented in clinical psychoanalysis (Britton 2015, pp. 65–86; Rosenfeld 1987) Similarly, Steiner (1993) has shown the intense dependence of the ego on the object, along with its permeability to the object and consequent instability for the ego of that needed relationship. A patient in an objective frame of mind might experience an emotionally immediate, subjective interpretation as overwhelming in emotional intensity. A patient in a subjective frame of mind might experience an objective interpretation as an assault. In such states of sensitivity, the ego faces a threat to its very existence, which precludes its functioning as the agent though which the psyche perceives, accommodates or alters the external world. 'Normal' thinking requires a capacity to tolerate the experience of intrusion or detachment. Inside analysis, normality can be sustained by the analyst; outside analysis, it depends on the compatibility between the parties.

Such concepts, now fundamental in psychoanalytic clinical work, even find their way into popular culture. Writing in The Observer (13 November 2016), the political journalist, Andrew Rawnsley, used the technical concept, 'thin-skinned narcissism', to say of Donald Trump, 'Even the most level-headed leadership would struggle to manage [the current] massive geopolitical adjustment. That is why the temperament of Donald Trump, a thin-skinned narcissist prone to react to the slightest provocation by lashing out, so terrifies so many.'

If states of this sort occur in the social world as well, they would profoundly affect the functioning groups and societies. Imagine a society that annulled human sensibilities—the subjectivity of emotions and relationships—because they threatened to collapse the society into an amorphous mass. Imagine a society that annulled an observer's view of it—an objective view—because it could not bear the intrusion into its beliefs that such a view would bring. In my view, groups, and societies more generally, display these polar attitudes, perhaps more intensely than individuals. Social groups tend to consolidate around a leader, an idea, an ideal, and to create other groups to house their sensitivity to complexity while bonding within themselves. Groups, therefore, are likely to react to the confusions of subjectivity and objectivity more quickly and more violently than individuals. They would be more prone to oscillate between acting as if threatened by the objectivity of information and facts, on the one hand, and the fear of falling apart as a stable, coherent culture, on the other.

One casual observation might make the point clear. It is often said that we live in a post-truth world. The swing towards populism in politics across Europe and the United States has been characterized by the rejection of experts, of facts and of information, and also by a sense of cultural collapse into multiculturalism, or, more generally, a sense of insecure borders and of losing one's country, if immigrants were accepted or assimilated, rather than distanced as foreign. These two threats—from experts with their objectivity and from cultural insecurity with its internal dissolution—are examples of the threat from objectivity and from subjectivity. They are the matter of clinical findings and clinical modelling, which can be applied to social groups.

In general, toleration challenges the mind. There is a pressure to divide the mind into an ego separated from self, more broadly, and from the relationship to an object. The fragile, internal, relationships of the ego press for an attack on the object in order to eliminate frustration at breaches in omnipotent self-regard. Memory is an internal object. It, too, can be attacked, falsified by defences. The memory that remains is especially misleading because it is experienced, like all memory, as the foundation of individual and social reality. It is the substance of historical consciousness, and therefore, as Collingwood argues, of having a mind.

Remembering as Reparation

Whether of an individual or of a group, remembering is in relationship to an object—the object of memory but also the memory as itself an internal object. It is a relationship of identification between ego and object, and, again following Collingwood, it is inherently historical: not only in having a history as a matter of record, but in being historical and constantly redone (in Freud's formulation, *nachträglich*). It is a process of continuous reparation, in continually being made better. But 'made better' has more than one sense. It can be a process of greater recognition of reality, taking the form of a benign identification of ego with object. It can also, however, take another form, in which memory is subjected to domination by the ego. In this case, a malignant form of identification controls the object in a demeaned state. In psychoanalysis, the former is called introjective identification, which supports reparation between an ego embedded in the reality of the object in its own right; in the latter case, we speak of projective identification, though which the object is denigrated in support of an illusory, grandiose ego.

The word 'reparation', in both German and English, has historically been associated with compensation for losses in war, a compensation imposed upon the loser by the victor. But along with the idea of compensation, there is a different aspect: making good in the process of compensation, retiring a debt, redeeming one's standing. The German language, and with it Freud, captures these meanings in several concepts, principally *Wiedergutmachung* (making good again), *Wiederherstellung* (*restoration*), *Entschädigung* (compensation, particularly for an injury), which have made their way into psychoanalysis. They have become, mainly in the Kleinian and object relational psychoanalytic traditions, words for making amends, of recognizing the reality of damaging the good object and of redemption of the ego in the process, akin to a state of grace. They have been translated into English as reparation.

These nuances have been brought out in clinical understanding, based on the idea of an internal world. In the external world, one can pay another person for injury, as in compensation claims. Think of insurance claims, in which specific losses of, for example, body parts, have financial values attached to them. They recognize that an injury has disabled an innocent victim or deprived him or her of a body part—an injury with a financial equivalent. But the payment cannot undo the loss, foster hope or restore the wholeness of the body *or mind*; nor can it restore or create a bond of understanding between agent and object, based on identification or amends, which could bring them into a common tragedy. An aching inadequacy or despair exists in the internal worlds of agent and of object, regardless of compensation paid in the external world. Were a relationship of identification and amends achieved or even adumbrated, it would mirror and contribute to a mending of the victim in his/her internal world. Such a process is never complete—that would be an illusion of 'undoing' the injury. Instead, it remains, in best instance, an area of concern for both agent and victim, ego and object; what Klein called 'depressive anxiety'.

This meaning of reparation gains credibility by triangulation from a wholly different field. In his extensive and detailed study of the origin and function of money, the anthropologist, David Graeber (2011), has concluded that money did not arise from the need for a convenient mode of exchange, but from an adequate way to retire a debt. Debt could never be eliminated: the ultimate debt was for a life, but forms of exchange could allow social relations to continue. One could, for example, stockpile a means of exchange against a possible debt, and it would at least forestall, perhaps indefinitely, an ultimate settlement. In his analysis of the acquiring and settling of debt, Graeber has perhaps unwittingly highlighted the paradox of reparation. On the one hand, we aim—and our vocabulary supports this aim—to compensate the injured object totally, and, so to speak, to tear up the retired contract. On the other hand, there is a fundamental sense of indebtedness for injury that can neither be undone nor compensated by payment. There is no 'in kind', no way to settle it. It is a cause of sadness, remorse and a continuing urge to make the object better. It rests on a new relationship with the object, one based on identification between ego and object, thus, on a recognition of the ego's responsibility for a tragedy that abides in the ego as it does in the object.

It is difficult to define 'reparation' succinctly, because, unlike persecutory anxiety, it is not linked to an action. Persecutory anxiety provokes a move to alleviate an accusation, whether by trying to do good or by defending against it, perhaps aiming to triumph over it: what Melanie Klein called 'manic reparation'. With reparation, we seem to be left with the fact of perpetration and a damaged object. The reparative urge, impelled by guilt, is not necessarily aimed at the damaged external object, but at the internal object, which may or may not be closely linked to it. It is a form of relationship between ego and object, based on a kind of identification called 'introjective identification', in which the ego and object are in a loving relationship of deep involvement, not projective distancing and control. The ego and the object are in the tragedy together, with full recognition of perpetration, and without triumph of either over the other, as happens with the requirement to repair, in manic reparation or in manic hoping.

Dialogue with History

I make a distinction between 'remembering true' and 'remembering false'. 'Remembering true' is a form of reparation and of thinking. It refers not to a final record, taken to correspond to the facts of past, but to a continuing process of finding and excluding distortions. It won't represent a coherent memory, shared by everyone to whom it might apply, but a self-reflective openness. It won't express a unified identity—in this case, of post-war West, or East, or unified Germany—but rather the difficulties in, and obstacles to, remaining in a quest for an identity lodged in memory. It is a quest in democratic society and among historians who aim to converge in a truthful history. Charles Maier (1988) likens this process to psychoanalysis.

> [T]he social sciences and historiography should be able meaningfully to supersede ideological partisanship – not by denying that these scholarly activities are conditioned by politics, but by recognizing their commitment to a shared project of knowledge. Of course, this requires a preliminary effort at self-reflection, of thinking through how the historian's own views of the past are shaped by political or psychological preferences. This is the equivalent of the psychoanalyst's own analysis…At the very least the writer of history requires a reader [a citizen] prepared to be open-minded…The writing and reading of history must rest upon intellectual sociability. (p. 62–3)…What is the quality of identity [that rests on memory and history]?…'Germany is alive in us, we represent it, willy-nilly, in every country to which we go, in each climate. We are rooted in it from the beginning, and we can never emancipate ourselves from it'. Habermas could have written those lines [written by Leopold von Ranke] (p. 65) [For Habermas (1986, pp. 232, 233)] 'the simple fact is that even those born later have grown up in a context of life [*Lebensform*] in which [the Holocaust] was possible…[O]ur identities as individuals and as Germans are indissolubly woven into' (p. 57)

Maier is defining the professional stance of the historian in the face of intensely disturbing historical situations. Like Habermas, he sees a convergence between this stance and an appropriate, moral, perspective—not a moralistic position, but a capacity to hold to a line of analysis that could otherwise be submerged in the 'facts' of history. The tension between a view of historical research as a search for facts, unrestrained by interference by judgements, and a view of all enquiry, which can and should retain a capacity for judgement, but judgement that does not distort the search for truth, drove the German 'Historians' Debate' in the 1980s. The same tension drives a similar debate today.

As Saul Friedländer (2000) puts it,

> To this day, the intertwining between the writing of the history of the Holocaust and the unavoidable use in its interpretation and narration of implicit and explicit moral categories remains a major challenge. It is around these shared moral categories that history and memory encounter one of their central differences. It may well be that the apparent dichotomy between a necessarily 'detached' history of National Socialism and the no less unavoidable presence of a moral dimension in dealing with this epoch may find its resolution only in the sensitivity and creative intuition of the historian.(p. 12)

The problem of remembering in post-war Germany has been researched in detail and often deals with the common expression, *Vergangenheitsbewältigung*. Loosely translated as 'coming to terms with the past', it implies mastering rather than engaging with a clear eye and a willingness to recognize the actuality of what happened, and empathically to join with the victims, rather than find ways to avoid the reality of the perpetration. With remembering as a form of reparation, the defensive avoidance is a form of manic reparation.

The historical dimension of this book, reparation in post-war Germany, is important in its own right. In terms of a dialogue between psychoanalysis and the history of post-war Germany, we have to look at both sides.

The Argument

The Holocaust has come to stand for the atrocity of genocide; that is, for the infliction of a suffering that aims to destroy the physical and psychological existence of a people, but, even more, to annihilate its very identity: for the Jews, even the memory of the people. Genocide was recognized by the United Nations in its definition of 1948, based on the Nazi aim to eliminate the Jews as a people. Unfortunately, the history of the idea of 'Holocaust' has also evoked discontent, as if it were claimed uniquely by the Jews and diverted attention from other genocides: the so-called singularity thesis. I don't accept the premise of this objection. Any comparison between atrocities undermines the idea of erasing a people; there cannot be a measure of 'erased'; no 'more (or less) erased than…'

This history brings out the paradox that reparation cannot be achieved. The contradictions are stark in the disputes not only on political, ideological and representational grounds but also on unconscious grounds. The unresolvable dilemma in which the recovery of national esteem runs aground on the repeated discovery of debased motives points up the fact that reparation cannot take place without manic reparation; that manic reparation is always present as the action-pole of the urge for reparation, as well as a defence against guilt and reparation. Something must be done to heal the damaged victim, yet the doing brings with it the defence against guilt and the reparative impulse.

The Holocaust was an attempt to eliminate a people, to eliminate the idea of there being this people, and to found a Germany established on this total eradication. I aim to sharpen this basis by adding the unconscious dimension in which the identity, Germany, was *equivalent* to the destruction of the Jews, including the very idea of the Jews—Germany was concretely the other face of the elimination of the Jews. The atrocity that I try to understand is not suffering torture itself, but, following Confino (2014), the anguish-to-desolation of there being no future, no present and no past: an erasure of identity through the elimination of a people, now and, therefore, in the foreclosure of a future, and the erasure from German memory as the condition for the future of the German people. There was to be no trace of the Jewish people apart from a possible archaic curiosity, in the minds of the German people, whose existence was predicated on this erasure. I do not aim to adjudicate whether or not there have been other examples of this plan, but I do mean to insist on the whole plan. The atrocity is at the core, but does not on its own define the Holocaust. The genocide is also at the core, but not sufficient to define the Holocaust. The additional element—the founding of a new people in the new German nation—is essential to the definition of the Holocaust.

Hannah Arendt was working towards such an idea (conceivable, though not for her, only within the dimension of the unconscious) with her concept of Radical Evil. Three historians stand out in their attempts to grasp this total dimension of the Holocaust: Alon Confino (the imagination of a world without Jews), Saul Friedländer (redemptive anti-Semitism) and Daniel Goldhagen (eliminative anti-Semitism). Curiously, they don't take much notice of their holding a thesis in common. I will discuss Confino and Freidländer in the appropriate places. I do not take up Goldhagen, because he was more concerned with the willingness of soldiers actively to carry out the extermination of the Jews.

I base my argument heavily on the conclusion reached by these three historians: that, in Nazi ideology, the founding the new Germany was based on the elimination of the Jews as a people. But I pursue a separate line of thinking. I think that post-war Germany has also been seized by the turmoil of reparation. It raises the question, 'How can we attribute such a process to a society that produced the Nazi regime, whose aim was to create a new Germany on the elimination of the Jews in all the forms described above?'

For Langer (1991), one can be drawn to misunderstand and misrepresent the actuality of the Holocaust, by trying to see a positive yield, as something good acquired from the darkness itself. I agree that the anguish of the victims cannot be undone, and that the rupture between their past and their present might often remain unbreachable. At the same time, my emphasis is on reparation by perpetrators: the drive anyway to make better. Reparation is driven by guilt at damage done and not undoable, but which nonetheless persists. I argue two, related points, both of which follow from a psychoanalytic enquiry: first, reparation means recognizing that recovering national esteem has to be based on reckoning with the depths of the darkness of the perpetration in all its dimensions, including the perversity that distorts a redemptive aim; second, this process of reparation continues without end. Such a recognition cannot occur without also understanding the conditions under which the perpetration became possible. To allow ourselves to enquire into this possibility is not the same as diluting the enormity of the crime by saying that anyone could, under the right circumstances, commit the same crime and, therefore, guilt can be exonerated. That line of argument fails to discriminate persecutory anxiety from guilt and presumes that understanding means complicity with exculpation.

Reparation entails the recognition of reality instead of delusion, and implies, as a retrospective recognition, that an introjective identification with the victims of perpetration has taken place. This aim is undermined by a defensive repudiation of reparation—a manic reparation—which is insidious because it looks just like reparation, and, as an action, contributes to a self-serving satisfaction with one's deeds. A pairing of reparation and manic reparation occurs in memorials and commemorations, the ambiguity of which provides occasions for extremist protest next to mourning at the losses caused by the perpetration. The test of reparation as opposed to manic reparation is whether there is pressure to see the end of it, an obligation fulfilled, a debt paid off. Reparation does not operate in that mode. There has been a current of opinion in Germany, from the end of the war into the present, in which German national esteem has suffered from its submission, whether to the Allies or to Germans themselves. In this view, it is time to make an end to making good the victimization of the Jews. The twinning of manic reparation with reparation allows this doubled current to persist.

Quite apart from the atrocities of war and the compensation demanded by military victors, the Holocaust pushed into public awareness the deep meaning of reparation. The very idea of compensation as a payment for the debts accrued though military destruction was both essential and irrelevant to a claim that might redeem the German nation from the guilt of unspeakable crime. The extremity of national sentiment, thinking and behaviour presses us to attend to the meaning of reparation. Historians and philosophers of the Nazi period will meet the same concern among psychoanalysts. Germany has enacted legislation banishing anti-Semitic language; it has paid victims; it has established a huge number of memorials and many commemorative events. It has dedicated itself to reparation. At the same time, from the earliest post-war days, it has also defended itself against knowing what was known and against unreservedly committing itself to the very reparation to which it also has committed itself. With a definition of guilt, not based on persecution and accusation, the question of continuing responsibility for reparation can no longer be dismissed as a burden on innocent succeeding generations.

The capacity for reparation is one face of the capacity to mourn; the defence of manic reparation is one face of melancholia as defined by

Freud, in the manic swing to superiority over the object (see Chaps. 8 and 9). The incapacity to mourn; the way it locks the generations into a prison in which the inability to recognize and mourn the destruction of love objects is coupled to an inability to forgo the idealization of self, identified with the nation as an ideal. This confusion of 'reality' with the ideal must not crack. The psychoanalysts, Alexander and Margarete Mitscherlich, published a deeply insightful book in 1967: *The Inability to Mourn*. Based on clinical work with 4000 patients, they argued that Germans had not been able to face the destruction of their idealized nation. They retreated into a haven of not experiencing the actual loss for their victims or for themselves. In such a state, there was no possibility of facing their perpetration, their reality or that of their victims. There was no possibility of remembering as reparation.

The Inability to Mourn has been controversial on several grounds, including whether it describes an actuality. From that angle, it became part of a controversy over whether the Germans really were locked traumatically into silence and denial. In my view, the debate has been hindered by not taking a full enough view of defence. Silence is not a powerful signifier of defence and talking is not an expression of knowing. The important issue is affect. The capacity to mourn implies a capacity to experience guilt and to recognize suffering caused to the object of perpetration. In my view, guilt is a historical force and historical enquiry must deal with it.

The Mitscherlichs introduce the importance of psychoanalytic concepts and clinical experience to historical enquiry. Historians have repeatedly tried to comprehend the nature of Nazi ideology and the active or passive complicity of the German people. Behind this preoccupation, lies the implication that if one could make any sense of such an assault on life, one would lose the very idea of meaning itself. Saul Friedländer (1984), one of the main contributors to the history of this period, wrote of kitsch and death: the conjunction of horror beyond comprehension with bland, sentimental, everyday life. Together they point to the sheer emptiness of the Nazi dream, about which only silence can speak. I take him to mean that even shame is too engaging an idea, apt to be fascinating about what is nothing. I think that psychoanalysis does open up a way at least to approach the idea of what reparation for such an abnegation of life could mean. In my view, tied to this same possibility is what it means to remember: not just to call to mind or to describe on paper, but to re-member. Interestingly, the German, *sich erinneren*: to bring inside oneself or to internalize—to develop an internal world—captures the essence of remembering as reparation. It leads to the idea of an internal, unconscious, world of an ego with its objects in an introjective relationship.

There is another way in which this issue becomes inherently psychoanalytic. Historians have converged on a particular interpretation of the German evasion of the Holocaust: To themselves, the Germans, not the Jews, were the victims of the Nazi regime and also of the Allies. The Allies, in this account, did not aim to remove the Nazis from power, but to destroy the German nation. As we will see, Andreas Hillgruber's (1986) book, *Zweierlei Untergang: Die Zerschlagung des deutschen Reiches und das Ende des europäischen Judentums* (Two Declines: the smashing of the German Reich and the End of European Judaism) sparked off the *Historikerstreit*—the debate of the historians—by advocating this line of thinking. Of course, any dutiful German soldier, no matter how anti-Nazi, could not tolerate such a war aim. Contemporary historians, he argued, were bound by the integrity and scientific aim of the profession, to identify with the soldiers on the Eastern front, who fought relentlessly against certain defeat.

In prescribing the terms for historical research, Hillgruber removes the object of study from its context and, in effect, suggests an equation between the defeat of the Germans and the elimination of the Jews, itself diluted into 'the end of Judaism'. We will discover another, more unconscious, motive identified by historians who opposed Hillgruber and the generally conservative understanding of German complicity with the Third Reich. It was something closer to enthrallment: what Martin Broszat called the *Führerbinding*, the leader-bond; what Ian Kershaw called 'working towards the leader', a drive to fill in, substantiate, realize the Führer's chiliastic dream of, in Alon Confino's words, a 'world without Jews'.

There has been enough convergence among historians of their accounts of this kind of regime to allow a linking—a dialogue—between history and psychoanalysis. In psychoanalytic thinking, such a state is a delusion, an idealization in an imaginary dimension, for which Hitler was only a representative, but one so tightly bound to it that his death brought the immediate collapse of the delusion. This collapse was a narcissistic catastrophe: it was, in Kershaw's (2011) language, simply 'the end'. In such a state, the object, in psychoanalytic, object relational terms, is not anything other: it is the subject itself; the ego of the individual and the group equivalent, for the society.

In the Kleinian language of this book, this line of thinking leads to the interpretation of the post-war German mentality as paranoid-schizoid; that is, preoccupied with survival against hostile forces: not with concern for the object, the other, the Jews in the case of the Holocaust. 'German society is a society without Jews…The Germans speak about the Jews instead of with them, and they do not listen to them' (Domansky 1993, p. 195). And this paranoid-schizoid mode of thinking allows us to add a distinctly psychoanalytic dimension to another historical actuality. The Allies divided Germany into two states; each absorbed into a power bloc; each now the enemy of the other; each, in its own terms, superior to the other. It was consciously resented by the German people, but in my view, the division acted, unconsciously, as a defence against the memory of, and the guilt for, the Holocaust.

In this way, the division was a defence against the concern for the other, against the 'depressive position', with its need to repair the damaged object. This urge is, psychoanalytically, reparation: not compensation or the restoration of stolen property, but recognizing the reality of the injury, bearing the guilt for it, not blaming anyone else. It also means something like grace, a state of mind in which the ego and the object allow a bond, a bond in which, whatever was expelled into the object, making it into the righteous target of abuse, is now accepted in the ego and rehabilitated. In this process, memory and reparation come together.

Psychoanalysis brings both concepts and methodology to this enquiry. It opens a view of memory as reparation, hedged by an array of defences. But just as important, psychoanalysis brings a non-moralistic approach to the relationship between observer and observed, researcher and object of research. Their emotional closeness and distance are often distressing and can be misleading, but they are also tools of analysis. The debates between historians express differences of evidence and evaluation, but they also reflect this internal tension, projected into the community of researchers. As Maier and Friedländer suggest, the self-reflective analysis of these two relationships, between observer and observed and between observers, is not only unavoidable but essential and fruitful.

Summary

My aim throughout the book is to develop a continuing dialogue between psychoanalysis and history, focusing on reparation as a common theme that emerges through seeing memory as a form of reparation. The plan of the book is, first, to explore the psychoanalysis and the history separately, in order to bring each to a focus and show their convergence. Then, at that point, reparation becomes the theme of a psychoanalytic-historical dialogue.

I pursue this topic through three grounding themes: first, that societies, as well as individuals, remember; second, that remembering as reparation does not expunge or compensate for the past, but recognizes the actuality of perpetration and victimization; third, that a dialogue between psychoanalysis and historical research into remembering the Nazi period is essential to both fields, focusing in this case on the Holocaust. Psychoanalysis, clinical and theoretical, along with recent historical scholarship on memorialization in post-war Germany, forms the spine of the book, which progresses as follows.

Chapter 2: The Internal World

The idea of a world for the psychoanalyst is like that of a geographical map for the geographer. The psychoanalyst's world is the unconscious psyche as a territory with its contents—agencies, internal objects and activities, emotions—as relationships inside the psyche and between psyches. One can, so to speak, move his/her (subjective) world into an other's world (projective identification), or assimilate an other's (introjective identification), or move subjectivity into an external, objective world (delusion), or bring an external, objective world into one's subjective world (reality testing). This chapter begins a psychoanalytic-historical discussion by setting out the psychoanalytic foundation for arguing that an adequate historical, sociological, economic or cultural account of social phenomena must include emotion-driven states and, therefore an internal world.

Chapter 3: Psychoanalysis and the 'Social Subject'

Far from accepting the common rejoinder, that psychoanalysis belongs in the consulting room, limiting its aim to understanding and interpreting the individual psyche, I argue that psychoanalysis can and should extend to the social world. I also propose a methodology for this social analysis, and I argue that we could, and must, speak of a 'social subject'. I do not claim that there is a social mind, but that the social has properties of a subject. We can model the social as if it were a subject and that it is methodologically viable to do so. We can, and should, therefore, introduce psychic reality into historical understanding, including affective states, such as guilt. I provide extensive clinical examples to support this case.

Chapter 4: Delusional Enemies

The concept of psychic reality extends into the creation of enemies. Extremist prejudice and racism are typically attributed to the hatred, exclusion and persecution of others who are different. I argue that, starting from psychic reality, it is sameness that leads to enmity. Some, otherwise insignificant, perceived feature of another group provides stability in the face of a delusional creation of difference, and a channel through which the enmity erupts. It anchors this psychotic core in external reality, protecting it from the dread of collapsing into itself in the identicality of an other, while the other acts as repository into which this dreaded, despised core is projected. Jews, indistinguishable from other Germans, even admired, functioned as a repository for the Nazis.

Chapter 5: Solidarity, Catastrophe and Ambivalence

I argue that the creation of a delusional enemy is a defence against a primal catastrophe in an unstable core of the self or society. I build my case on two of Freud's powerful concepts: the narcissism of small differences, according to which aggressiveness intensifies with closeness; and his *Unbehagen in der Kultur*—an unease or malaise intrinsic to culture, charged with immanent explosive violence. From this model of an elemental state, we can ground the basic processes in psychic development and maintenance, which build up structures of the individual and group or society as forms of management of a psychotic core. These processes and structures need repositories for projection. The Jews as a people provided such a repository for Nazi Germany.

Chapter 6: Conflicts of Remembering—The *Historikerstreit*

Post-war Germany has faced a dilemma of how to remember, when memory underlies social esteem and cohesion and also means integration of an unconscionable period of history. Memory has a moral dimension, but as memory fades into history, so it must be assimilated into reality against the lure of illusion and the temptation of distortion and falsification. This process has been called *Vergangenheitsbewältigung*—coming to terms with the past—and with it the ethical problem of whether it could ever be finished and the political desideratum of forming a state with the capacity to bear its history. It brought the very public debate among intellectuals on the conflict between normalizing German history and questioning this conservative trend as an apologetics for a deeply tarnished history.

Chapter 7: Remembering and Not-Remembering

In ordinary, perceptual reality, remembering means not only recollecting accurately but also the recognition and toleration of others in relationships. In narcissistic reality, it means creating a delusional memory to be annihilated, as in the Nazi 'final solution'. I will speak of 'remembering true' for the former and 'remembering false' for the latter, which occur simultaneously in knowing and not-knowing, as defences not sufficiently encompassed by repression. There is, therefore, an inherent ambivalence in remembering and in reparation as a form of remembering. I will consider three forms of not-remembering, which are relevant to post-war Germany: undoing, disavowal and splitting. Historical research can be advanced by introducing defences of this sort, which are especially relevant to Holocaust studies, including ambivalence in memorialization as reparation.

Chapter 8: The Unconscious Division of Germany

Germany was divided by military and political force, and each Germany was absorbed into a power bloc, each in competition with the other. Two unexpected consequences follow from a psychoanalytic approach. First, these structures of power formed an unconscious defensive organization, based on 'paranoid-schizoid' 'splitting' described by Melanie Klein. Despite the humiliation of defeat, the division of Germany stabilized its identity by breaking up its idealized, illusory omnipotence and sequestering it into the two nations. This conflict embedded a symmetrical set of defences; in effect, an unconscious collusion to marginalize memory of the Holocaust. Second, the reunification of Germany disrupted this collusive defence and brought out again the need to come to terms with the Nazi period in a reality akin to Klein's 'depressive position'.

Chapter 9: Reparation

Reparation is the focal concept of this book and a key concept in understanding memory. This chapter defines the particular quality of reparation, based on 'introjective identification', and distinguishes it from manic reparation, based on 'projective identification'. Reparation is driven by guilt. To remember as reparation is to suffer guilt. It is also to be drawn into falsifying memory and avoiding guilt as manic reparation.

Manic reparation seems the same as reparation, but builds on triumph over the object. Symbols of remembering, such as memorials, become sites of ambivalence, used differently by different groups, at the expense of a convergent memory. They represent both reparative and manic-reparative intentions, as well as intellectual, emotional and political conflict.

Chapter 10: Remembering, Memorialization and Reparation

This chapter focuses on memorials and memorialization, analysed within the framework of reparation and manic reparation. As individuals, we institute sites and occasions for mourning, remembering and reparation. As social groups, we do the same, through memorials, archives, official recognition of special places, such as historic buildings. In both instances, we can speak of a private and a public dimension. Private mourning is more personal, restores memory and is reparative. Public mourning is prone to group pressures, which distort memory and foster manic reparation, which is akin to Freud's concept of melancholia and pathological mourning. Memorials become ambiguous locations for remembering and for the distortion of remembering, for private mourning and for public mourning.

Chapter 11: Conclusion

The themes of this book reduce to pairs of opposites equivalent to remembering true and remembering false: reparation versus manic reparation, guilt versus persecutory anxiety, commemoration versus repetition, thinking versus non-thinking. Each pair tends towards an identity built either on convergence or on divisive triumph. Defence preserves a schism; working through aims to repair it. I close with two areas of research for further development. First is gender relations. The collapse of the Third Reich was also a collapse in masculine authority, which was then reasserted. Second is the counter-memorial movement in Germany, which aims to overcome the tendency in memorialization towards repetitive enactments of static memories, whether evoked by stone monuments or by commemorations. Enactments can undermine the reparative, often mournful, aim of remembering.

References

Britton, R. (2015) *Between Mind and Brain: Models of the Mind and Models in the Mind*. London: Karnac.
Collingwood, R. G. (1946/1993) *The Idea of History*. Oxford/New York: Oxford University Press.
Confino, A. (2014) *A World Without Jews: The Nazi Imagination from Persecution to Genocide*. New Haven/London: Yale University Press.
Domansky, E. (1993) *Die gespaltene Erinnerung*. In Köppen, M. (ed.) *Kunst und Literatur nach Auschwitz*. Berlin: Erich Schmidt Verlag, pp. 178–96.
Evans, R. (2002) *Telling Lies About Hitler: The Holocaust, History and the David Irving Trial*. London/New York: Verso.
Figlio, K. (1998) Historical Imagination/Psychoanalytic Imagination. *History Workshop Journal* 45: 199–221.
Freud, S. (1899) Screen Memories. *The Standard Edition of the Complete Psychological Works of Sigmund Freud* 3: 299–322.
Freud, S. (1918[1914]) *From the History of an Infantile Neurosis. The Standard Edition of the Complete Psychological Works of Sigmund Freud* 12: 1–122.
Friedländer, S. (1984) *Reflections of Nazism: An Essay on Kitsch and Death*. New York: Harper & Row.
Friedländer, S. (2000) History, Memory, and the Historian: Dilemmas and Responsibilities. *New German Critique* 80: 3–15.
Goldhagen, D. (1996) *Htiler's Willing Executioners. Ordinary Germans and the Holocaust*. NY: Alfred A. Knopf/London: Little Brown and Company.
Graeber, D. (2011) *Debt: The First 5000 Years*. New York: Melville House Publishing.
Habermas, J. (1986) On the Public Use of History. Die Zeit, November 7. In Habermas, J. (1989) *The New Conservatism: Cultural Criticism and the Historians' Debate*. London: Polity Press, pp. 229–40.
Hillgruber, A. (1986) *Zweierlei Untergang: Die Zerschlagung des deutschen Reiches und das Ende des europäischen Judentums*. Berlin: Seidler.

Kershaw, I. (2011) *The End: Hitler's Germany, 1944–45*. London: Allen Lane.

Langer, L. (1991) *Holocaust Testimonies: The Ruins of Memory*. New Haven/London: Yale University Press.

Lipstadt, D. (1994) *Denying the Holocaust: The Growing Assault on Truth and Memory*. New York: The Free Press.

Lipstadt, D. (2006) *History on Trial: My Day in Court with David Irving*. New York: Harper Perennial.

Maier, C. (1988) *The Unmasterable Past: History, Holocaust, and German National Identity*. Cambridge, MA/London: Harvard University Press.

Rosenfeld, H. (1987) *Impasse and Interpretation: Therapeutic and Anti-therapeutic Factors in the Psychoanalytic Treatment of Psychotic, Borderline, and Neurotic Patents*. London: Routledge.

Steiner, J. (1993) *Psychic Retreats: Pathological Organizations in Psychotic, Neurotic and Borderline Patients*. London/New York: Routledge.

2

The Internal World

Worlds

The idea of a world for the psychoanalyst is like that of a geographical map for the geographer. With a map, the geographer can visualize a territory with its contents—people, things, activities in locations—as objects and exchanges within the territory and between territories. The psychoanalyst's world is the psyche as a territory with its contents—agencies, internal objects and activities in locations—as relationships inside the psyche and between psyches. The geographer looks objectively at the map from the outside. The psychoanalyst aims to harness his/her subjectivity to seeing the psychic world objectively as a world of subjectivity: of agency, affect, receptivity, belief, illusion. The internal world is inside a boundary, not physical, but one of sensation, emotion and cognition. External means either another's subjectivity or the objective world outside subjectivity. One can, so to speak, move his/her (subjective) world into an other's (projective identification), or assimilate an other's (introjective identification), or move subjectivity into an external, objective world (delusion), or bring an external, objective world into one's subjective world (reality testing). The psychoanalytic geographer-observer occupies a 'third position' outside two subjectivities (Britton 1989).

At the root of this chapter and the book as a whole will be the question, 'Can one give an adequate historical, sociological, economic or cultural account of social phenomena without including emotion-driven states and, therefore an internal world'? I am not alone in answering 'no'. The importance in recent decades of history 'from the bottom up' or of the sociology of intimacy testifies to it. But I am referring to a particular kind of emotion-driven state. I mean the psychoanalytic idea of an internal world of primitive phantasies and guilt, and defences against them. This world infuses the common-sense, apparently rational external world with extremes of emotion and seemingly crazy ways of thinking. It makes living in the world like Freud's theory of a dream, in which a residue of unmetabolized day-thinking is used as a vehicle for expressing an unconscious situation. In the extreme, when conscious thinking cannot master the erupting unconscious, the uncontained dream becomes a nightmare.

Just as we speak of an internal world of the individual, so we must speak of an internal world of a group. The opposition between the individual and the social vanishes the more one approaches the primitive levels of the psyche. At this elemental level, the fundamental distinction to be made is not individual versus group, but primitive versus developed emotional states. It may stretch credibility to say that the overthrow of a leader or a nation is an oedipal enactment of killing the father and possessing the mother, but at a primitive level, it is credible to think of it as a delusional moment of omnipotent incorporation of the power of the father, or of a group acting psychotically, while its members remain 'normal'. It is possible to think of territorial expansionism expressed as the military and political necessity to defend borders against encroachment, and as an omnipotent defence against a psychotic terror of extinction by incorporation. Though seeming to be a self-evident matter of political and military history, it remains an attitude that can only be described in psychological terms, more tellingly, in primitive psychological terms. Whatever the strategic justification and the historian's interpretation of it, expansionism is also a form of narcissistic expansion—a delusion of transcending the boundedness of external, perceived reality.

In later chapters, we will show a social organization acts both to further conscious, rational goals and simultaneously to defend against primitive anxieties. I will make use of the psychoanalytic theory of 'psychic retreats' and the related group theory called 'social defence systems'. In order to draw more generally on this way of thinking, I shall speak of 'psychosocial enclaves'. The basis of this model is that social organization and processes maintain collective defences against primal—psychotic—anxieties and guilt. Group defences transform this crippling, indescribable anxiety and guilt into a realistic fear of identifiable threats. In the process, they confer on the mass of individuals a sense of collective identity and normality in their facing common problems and enemies, and this defensive identity supplements the collective identity of common nationality, culture, religion or political affiliation. I will address this theme methodologically in Chap. 3.

The Psyche as an Internal World

First, let us develop the psychoanalytic concept of an internal world. In Freud's model of the psyche, there was a primal loving—libido—within the infant as a primary narcissism, which then enveloped objects of perception, like protoplasmic extrusions in unicellular organisms.

> [Primary narcissism] lasts until the ego begins to cathect the ideas of objects with libido, to transform narcissistic libido into object libido. Throughout the whole of life the ego remains the great reservoir from which libidinal cathexes are sent out to objects and into which they are also once more withdrawn, just as an amoeba behaves with its pseudopodia. It is only when a person is completely in love that the main quota of libido is transferred on to the object and the object to some extent takes the place of the ego. A characteristic of the libido which is important in life is its *mobility*, the facility with which it passes from one object to another. (1940 [1938]a, pp. 150–1; Freud's emphasis)

From this mobility arises the phenomenon of transference, in which objects can, unconsciously, bear the characteristics of each other. The inclusion of perceived objects as love-objects inside the ego builds up an internal world of enlivened objects.

But a stable internal world can be established only if there is, in addition to this assimilation—introjection—of external objects, also a projection, through which the ego becomes bounded next to the objects it has libidinalized—enlivened—both within an internal psychic space and in relation to the perceived, external world. In the extreme, such projected, internal objects are like an internal agency, separated from the ego and observing it from a great height—a superego. In part, Freud had in mind reports by patients that

> all their thoughts are known and their actions watched and supervised; they are informed of the functioning of this agency by voices which characteristically speak to them in the third person ('Now she's thinking of that again', 'now he's going out'). This complaint is justified; it describes the truth. A power of this kind, watching, discovering and criticizing all our intentions, does really exist. (1914, p. 95)

In part, he also had in mind the idea of a dream censor, which concealed the unconscious, latent content of dreams from consciousness. In part, he also had in mind the gathering of the perfection of a lofty agency called the ego-ideal.

The watching superego and the ego-ideal together account for the experience of conscience. For now, we want to notice that they are inside the psyche, in an internal psychic space. It acts as if it were outside, like a figure of authority, but it gets its power from being inside, where it is privy to the deepest hints of intention and is inescapable. It can be projected into an external object, infusing that object with the stature of the superego. A vivid example is given by a patient who had been trying to express the peculiar, demeaning quality of a voice he associated with his cousin. Then one day, walking down the street and remembering that he had left a document he needed at home, he turned around suddenly and walked straight into her. At this moment, the external world, in which this startling but ordinary experience occurred, dissolved into an internal world as a relationship with the character he was trying to capture and stabilize in conscious thinking.

Freud points out that such an observing internal figure can be intercalated into a scenario in which a neurotic constellation is enacted in the transference, as opposed to being reported as symptoms that beset one in outside life. He gives a vivid example from his analysis of a patient suffering grievously from obsessionality.

> And so it was only along the painful road of transference that he was able to reach a conviction that his relation to his father really necessitated the postulation of [an unconscious parricidal rage]. Things soon reached a point at which, in his dreams, his waking phantasies, and his associations, he began heaping the grossest and filthiest abuse upon me and my family, though in his deliberate actions he never treated me with anything but the greatest respect…[H]e would get up from the sofa and roam about the room,—a habit which he explained at first as being due to delicacy of feeling: he could not bring himself, he said, to utter such horrible things while he was lying there so comfortably. But soon he himself found a more cogent explanation, namely, that he was avoiding my proximity [as his father] for fear of my giving him a beating. (1909, p. 209)

In this case, Freud and his patient could 'see' the repressed memories and phantasies about the patient's father in his behaviour. The scene dramatized by the transference did represent a memory of a scene with the father, and through that memory, a relationship with father, unconscious until this moment.

In the following vignette (Sapisochin 1999), we get closer to the experience of an internal object relationship, projected into an external situation, which was a dramatized scene, but could not have been a memory. The transference represented a phantasy, which could be linked to memories, but was not any of them.

The analyst was a male Argentinean, living and working in Spain. His patient was a woman who was aware of his Argentinian origins. Although Spanish herself, she had used characteristic Argentinian expressions. During the sessions, the analyst noticed a compelling homely feeling, including reminiscences of particular Argentinian foods. It was as if she were unconsciously feeding him an unconscious residue of his childhood self, and conveying to him a belief that he felt known by her as a mother would know her son—a belief with which, in his dreaminess, he concurred.

She remembered that her father, an Italian, 'was "*amazed*" to hear her perfect pronunciation of the dialect of a certain region of Italy'. She also reported a ceremony she used to perform. Every night, she turned down the bedcovers, on which the family initials were embroidered, in a particular way. She remembered that, when she was very young, her father had said, 'When I see you arranging the turndown like that, I see my mother.' She went on to say that her father had lost his mother when he had been very small. He had been close to her emotionally; indeed, she had been more important to him than his wife, the patient's mother.

What we see in the analysis is a vivid enactment of the patient's unconscious compliance with her father's seductive inducement for her to replace his adored his mother. As a child, she was seduced into the *amazing* phantasy that she was her father's mother. Now, with her analyst, she adopted the seductive aim herself and drew the analyst into an unconscious belief that she was his mother.

In this vignette, we 'see' an unconscious, internal object relationship, 'seen' in the experience of the transference. The transference contained information, such as the memory of turning down the bedclothes in a particular way, but also phantasies, which could not be conveyed as facts of memory or experience. The whole scenario, which structured the transference as a piece of organized behaviour, garnered its power from an oedipal illusion of a son with his mother, but also from cultural history. We can identify two unconscious aims: the patient aimed to recreate her own regressive urge to relive her early life as father's love object, and she aimed to fulfil it by drawing on her analyst's regressive urge to relive his early life with his mother in his mother country.

Drawing these vignettes together, we are led to the idea that we can visualize an internal world, in this case, oedipal. We also know of more elemental psychic objects and processes. At the core of the internal world are constellations of unconscious phantasies and associated anxieties: of idealizing or debasing a 'good' object; of the dread of extinction or dissolution; of manic elation and triumph. It is a world of bizarre 'part-objects'—really functions—such as mouth-with-breast. These functions can be benign or destructive, but they are elements of both individual and group psyches. These objects and processes act through a primal communication seeking transformation into consciousness and thinking.

The Psyche as an Internal World

A psychotic patient of Bion's offers an example of such communication. In a session, he became aware that his speech was so mutilated that it obstructed creative work.

> I remained at a loss until one day, in a lucid moment, the patient said… 'that I could not stand it'. I now worked on the assumption that the persecuting object that could not permit any creative relationship was one that 'could not stand it'…[I]t [later] became clear that… what I could not stand was the patient's methods of communication. In this phase my employment of verbal communication was felt by the patient to be a mutilating attack on *his* methods of communication[. H]is relationship with me and his ability to profit by the association lay in the opportunity to split off parts of his psyche and project them into me…[E]motionally rewarding experiences [included] the ability to put bad feelings in me and leave them there long enough for them to be modified by their sojourn in my psyche, and the ability to put good parts of himself into me, thereby feeling that he was dealing with an ideal object as a result. Associated with these experiences was a sense of being in contact with me, which I am inclined to believe is a primitive form of communication that provides a foundation on which, ultimately, verbal communication depends. (1957, pp. 90–1; 92; Bion's emphasis)

What Bion discovered was a fundamental form of receptivity to a basic communicative need, which, together, is experienced as a primitive object relationship: the need to press an internal object into an external object. Melanie Klein (1946) called this communicative imperative 'projective identification'. She called the radical separation of 'good' and 'bad', splitting; and Bion (1970, pp. 72–82) called the transformative receptivity, 'containment'. The projective use of the object to contain its ego states is an elemental form of building an ego in its object world.

Let us turn to another clinical vignette of a psychotic patient by Bion, which gives a glimpse into the primitive, sensorimotor nature of the internal world and the function of the external world in relation to it.

> As [the patient] passes into the room he glances rapidly at me…While I close the door he goes to the foot of the couch, facing the head pillows and my chair, and stands … head inclined to the chair, motionless until I have passed him and am about to sit down. So closely do his movements seem

to be geared with mine that the inception of my movements to sit appears to release a spring in him. As I lower myself into my seat he turns left about, slowly, evenly, as if something would be spilled, or perhaps fractured, were he to be betrayed into a precipitate movement. As I sit the turning movement stops as if we were both parts of the same clockwork toy. The patient, now with his back to me, is arrested at a moment when his gaze is directed to the floor near that corner of the room which would be to his right and facing him if he lay on the couch… When the patient glanced at me he was taking a part of me into him. It was taken into his eyes…, as if his eyes could suck something out of me. This was then removed from me, before I sat down, and expelled, again through his eyes, so that it was deposited in the right-hand corner of the room where he could keep it under observation. [I]f the patient says he sees an object it may mean that an external object has been perceived by him or it may mean that he is ejecting an object through his eyes: if he says he hears something it may mean he is ejecting a sound—this is *not* the same as making a noise: if he says he feels something it may mean tactile sensation is being extruded, thrown off by his skin. (1958, pp. 65–6; 67; Bion's emphasis)

In Bion's analysis, the sensory organs work in both directions: passively, in taking in sensations that form perceptions and ideas; actively, as a psychic motor organ, expelling sensations that must not be sensed or be built into perceptions or ideas, and controlling by precise imitation what has been taken inside (anatomically, sense organs are also innervated by motor neurones). He suggests that the psychotic is beleaguered by a primitive mode of thinking, in which sensing, perceiving and thinking are confused with doing. External objects stand in for internal objects, which can be controlled. The elaboration of thinking into symbolization is constrained by primitive terrors that are released or controlled in this confused internal-external world.

Here is a similar, ordinary phenomenon from an unpublished observation of a normal infant, who seemed to be building these elements of thinking into higher levels of sophistication, by using external objects for symbolization rather than control.

A baby girl of between six months and one year was comfortable in the presence of others in addition to her mother and father. If a small number of familiar people stood in a group, any one of them holding her, the baby would look intently at one for some time, then at another, and another, catching each with her concentrating eyes until she had moved around the whole group. She would then continue to move her gaze from one to the other, often in the same order, as if holding them together by tying the perception of each to the next and, equally, keeping each internal object separate and under control.

The idea that the eye can act as a motor organ seems strange only if we hold to a clear separation between perception, as a recording of the external world, and phantasy, as an imagination withdrawn from that world. A baby's discovery of its foot as its own foot puts paid to such a view. At first its foot or hand seems one of a number of strangers that appear in its visual field, sometimes crashing into it with alarming force. Gradually the baby's capacity to move limbs draws it into its map of the ego. It incorporates its foot, as it incorporates, or identifies with, other external objects. If you think of it, we never lose the magic of being able to move a limb: we just cover the magic with a veneer of common sense. But any challenge to this common sense exposes the magic.

Here is another unpublished observation. This observation, of a boy just under ten months old, shows how imitation is built up into relationships among primal characters on the way to becoming agents. We denote these primal characters in terms of elemental functions and relationships: 'breast-mother' in relation to 'mouth-baby' and 'doing-feeding-father' in relation to the mouth-baby, as a maturation of the breast-mother/mouth-baby relationship.

> Mother has put slices of carrot and several pasta tubes on the highchair tray, leaving it for the baby. Father approaches from a distance with a bowl of food. Baby squeals and smiles broadly, with evident delight. As soon as father is seated and offers baby a spoonful of food, baby turns away and reaches for a pasta tube. This sequence is repeated several times: each time father offers the spoon, baby turns away and reaches for pasta tube or a carrot slice to feed himself. The father draws close, and the baby puts a pasta-tube into the bowl that father is holding. The baby tries to slap the bowl. Mother comes over and tries to feed him, trying to distract him from his game of feeding himself.

Note that the baby prefers mother's—simply available—feeding to father's—active—feeding, and in the process, he excludes father. In rejecting father-food and turning to mother-food, he also actively controls entry into himself. In addition, while feeding from mother, he puts mother-food into father-bowl, thereby structuring a feeding: mother-feeding has been inserted into father-feeding; the magic of mother-feeding has been replaced by the act of father-feeding, with himself as the omnipotent link that moves towards external reality. We have repeated observations of imitation as a way-station towards taking up more advanced behaviour, in identification with an adult. We are, therefore, pretty secure in saying that this baby is imitating mother-feeding as a plentiful resource, but in identification with active father-feeding.

On the way to learning to feed himself, the baby begins to identify with father as a doer, in addition to mother as the magical breast that his need brings into being. He inserts the magic of nourishment into the act of feeding over which he has reality-orientated physical control that is also a vehicle for omnipotent control. He is building an internal world with internal objects that, in their primal form, are elemental phantasies of a mouth, a breast and a feeding object, as a template on which a more organized internal object world of mother, father and child is being built.

The Internal World into the External World

I want to tie the concept of an internal world to an interpretation of memorials, which we will meet later in the book, because memorials are representations of states of mind. They are sites and occasions for introjection and projection, which enliven the object and structure the internal world, a theme we will take up in Chap. 10.

Figure 2.1 is a sculpture in Germany, called *Mother Love*. The inscription reads thus:

In remembrance
Of millions of victims
Especially mothers and children

Fig. 2.1 Memorial to expellees, Pforzheim (From Margalit, p. 217)

In flight and expulsion
After the Second World War

It is one of many memorials to German victims of fleeing and expulsion and specifically to women and children. They are usually interpreted as symbols of German innocence and victimhood. But they are also representations of an internal world, in which the mouth-breast relationship is a psychic element that is split into two extreme forms: good/ideal and bad/persecutory. The memorials of the expulsions of Germans by the Soviet forces or by Poland and Czechoslovakia play a role in German post-war history and memory, but they also evoke a primal idealized breast-mouth in the internal world, split off from a harsh, persecuting breast-mouth.

The baby with mother and others forms the earliest social system: not the baby and mother as we see them, but the elements in relation to each other, making up an internal world. The elaboration of a symbolized world depends on the capacity of this system to manage the concrete primitive anxieties and communicative needs of the infant, helpless in the face of them; that is, to contain them. But this same concrete level remains in the adult and, therefore, in normal society, as in the memorial above. These primitive anxieties and defences take the form of elemental unconscious concrete object relations. At this level, the baby at the breast sucks it, masticates it, scoops it out and poisons it with urine and faeces. We infer these processes from observations, child analysis and adult analysis. Because they are the elements of the earliest social system, we are justified our making use of what we learn of them in the consulting room to understand social structure and function in terms of primitive anxieties and defences against them.

Let us generalize this simple social system to the general case of a leader with the led. Again, it is not the leader as a person or an ideology along with individual followers who comprise a group. Just as the mouth-breast is an element in the make-up of mother, baby and the social system that they take part in, the individuals and the group are, in this model, carriers of internal objects: the elements that make up both group and individual. To start with, let us look at a simple model of social cohesiveness proposed by Freud in 1921. It is an abstraction from his emerging 'structural theory' of the psyche, comprised of an ego and its internal object, the ego-ideal, the lofty observing internal object that we looked at previously.

Each of the horizontal lines represents an individual, each with its own ego and ego-ideal, each projecting its ego-ideal into an object thereby establishing a bond between its internal world and the external world. This sort of thing happens in love relationships, in which the love object is idealized by this projection. Now, suppose the object that each ego

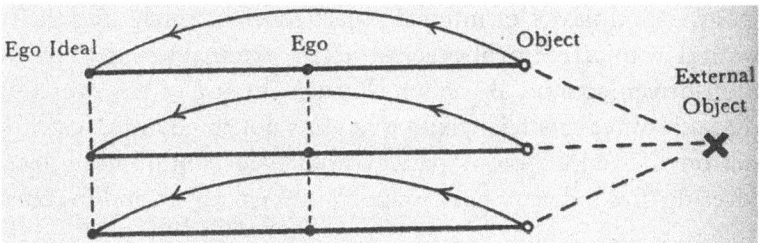

Fig. 2.2 Collectivization under the ego-ideal (Freud 1921, p. 116)

treats as its ego-ideal converges on the same object. It may be a leader, but it could be an ideology, a nation, a flag. In that case, the individual egos identify with each other, collapsing into a single, mass ego, represented by the vertical dashed line. In this way, a homogeneous group forms under the thrall, not the power, of the group ego-ideal that is the convergent projection of individual ego-ideals. Note that two things happen: individuals cohere into a group and the leader's authority becomes absolute, not because of the power to coerce, but because the external, reality-based qualities of the leader are infused with idealization. The group's power grows as its sense of reality becomes delusional.

One feature of this substitution of reality by delusion is a collapse of psychic space; that is, a collapse of the variety of realistic assessments that one makes of an external situation. The relationship with the real world of complexity is compressed into identification with the idealized object or slavish obedience to it or contempt from it. One can see such a polarized world of alternatives in manic depression, which oscillates between a delusional magnificence and an equally delusional self-denigration.

In Freud's model, the slightest departure from the group ego-ideal and the massified ego breaks the identificatory bonds, and that is an *absolute* breach. The deviant ego then becomes a threat to the stability of the massified system. An unexpected conclusion from this line of thinking, which we will develop in Chap. 4, is that actually perceived, non-delusional differences either obscure or normalize hatred of what now appears to be an external enemy, but they do not cause it.

We can study the difference between exacerbation and mitigation of primal relationships in the consulting room. The eclipse of psychic space reduces the complexity of internal object relations, including their projective and introjective involvement with the external world, to primitive, emotion-driven actions. By action, I mean the use of the musculature, but also a form of mental activity that aims not to communicate, but to impact on the object. Bion's patient needed to communicate by commandeering him to become an excluded internal object and to transform it into a tolerable form or to attack it.

In the more primal, elemental internal world, action is an immediate reflex. It is not the outcome of thinking, nor is it constrained by the opposing thoughts that would make up a thinking personality. It is concrete, literal, asymbolic and especially, as Melanie Klein has vividly shown, is clearer in young children.

> The psychoanalysis of young children, which allows a very precise, clear, specific concrete picture of the unconscious conceptions of the mind, led me to use the term 'internal objects' or 'inner objects' and 'good' and 'bad' objects... [T]he term 'inner object'...exactly expresses what the child's unconscious, and for that matter the adult's in deep layers, feels about it. In these layers it is not felt to be part of the mind in the sense, as we have learnt to understand it, of the superego being the parents' voices inside one's mind. This is the concept we find in the higher strata of the unconscious. In the deeper layers, however, it is felt to be a physical being, or rather a multitude of beings, which with all their activities, friendly and hostile, lodge inside one's body, particularly inside the abdomen, a conception to which physiological processes and sensations of all kinds, in the past and in the present, have contributed. (Ms quoted by Hinshelwood 1997, p. 885)

The elemental level of the psyche is an internal world that is concrete, omnipotent and psychotic. Bion's patient with mutilated speech was plagued with overwhelming anxiety at the destructiveness of attacks on his object world. They literally broke up his speech, rendering it disjointed and incoherent. In 1966, the Italian psychoanalyst, Franco Fornari, turned the common-sense understanding of organized, violent aggression on its head. Organized conflict, as in war, was not, in his view, an expression of an instinct of aggression. Instead, he argued, it was based on the management of the psychotic anxiety of the internal world, and the psychotic anxiety was, in turn, a defence against loss expressed in mourning. Far from being an instinctual eruption, it was a *'paranoid elaboration of mourning'* (p. xiv). War, he argued, was a 'social institution the aim of which is to cure the paranoid and depressive anxieties existing…in every man' (pp. xv–xvi). In other words, this viciously aggressive social form of destructiveness—far from being an eruption of an instinct of aggression—protected against individual suffering of the primitive, destructive—basically psychotic—anxieties, identified by Melanie Klein.

War gives full and legitimate expression to sadism and to the vanquishing of enemies. In addition, the group promotes the projection into an external enemy of persecuting internal objects, thereby replacing an internal environment of persecution by an external focal enemy. In war, the enemy nation should also suffer loss; not just the loss of people and property, but the loss of the good object that it fought to protect. To vanquish a nation was to triumph over it, in order to protect itself from loss by projecting it into the core of the enemy; to damage its internal world; to cause the enemy to mourn. Inside the organization engaged in conflict, the individual leads a 'normal' life; not in the sense of peaceful, untroubled or without loss, but in the relief from depressive and paranoid anxieties.

Conclusion

In this chapter, I have discussed a psychoanalytical way of thinking, which is based on the concept of an internal world: one in which internal objects are concrete, omnipotent, idealized, persecutory, and delusional. Figure 2.3 vividly portrays an internal world that is also an external world, and sets us up for Chap. 3, in which we will examine the concept of a social subject. This drawing was made by a ten-year-old English boy, evacuated to Scotland during the Second World War and analysed by Melanie Klein.[1] The jaggedness expresses the conflicted, tense state of his internal world. The West side is occupied mainly by his mother and him; the East side by the men: father, brother, himself, with father as the intruding authority that separates East from West. It is a drawing of his phantasy of his family relationships, all inside mother, but also of the territory in which the war was fought, including the suspect Eastern Soviet ally,

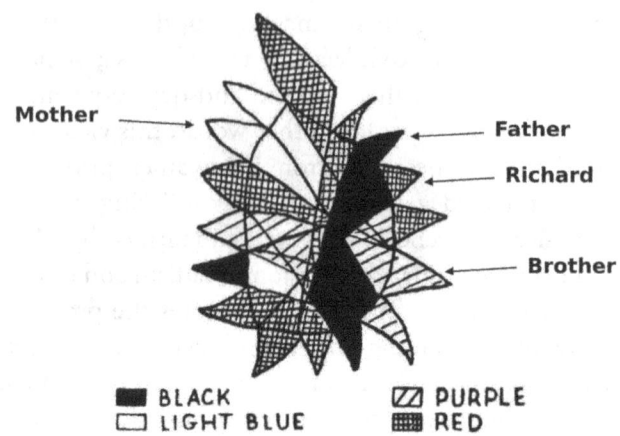

Fig. 2.3 Drawing by Richard (From Klein 1945, p. 379; Melanie Klein Trust)

which was also himself. It is simultaneously a geographer's and a psychoanalyst's map.

Now we will move squarely into the social world. In order to do so, we will consider the methodological prerequisites for a concept of an internal world of a social group. On the basis of a social internal world—that of a social subject'—we will go on to examine the way it remembers but does not remember, knows but does not know, seeks the truth but falsifies it, aims to repair the injury of perpetration but also aims to repudiate it: the problem of reparation and historical memory.

Notes

1. Klein (1961) recorded the whole of this relatively short analysis, including reproductions of the child's prolific drawings.

References

Bion, W. (1957) On Arrogance. *International Journal of Psychoanalysis* 39: 144–6. In *Second Thoughts: Selected Papers on Psycho-Analysis*. London: William Heinemann, 1967; Karnac, 1984, pp. 86–92.

References

Bion, W. R. (1958) On Hallucination. *International Journal of Psychoanalysis* 39: 341–9. In *Second Thoughts: Selected Papers on Psycho-Analysis*. London: William Heinemann, 1967; Karnac, 1984, pp. 65–85.

Bion, W. R. (1970) *Attention and Interpretation: A Scientific Approach to Insight in Psycho-Analysis and Groups*. London: Tavistock.

Britton, R. (1989) The Missing Link: Parental Sexuality and the Oedipus Complex. In Britton, R., Feldman, M. and O'Shaughnessy, E. (eds.) *The Oedipus Complex Today: Clinical Implications*. London: Karnac Books, pp. 83–101.

Freud, S. (1909) Notes upon a Case of Obsessional Neurosis. *The Standard Edition of the Complete Psychological Works of Sigmund Freud* 10: 151–318

Freud, S. (1914) On Narcissism: An Introduction. *The Standard Edition of the Complete Psychological Works of Sigmund Freud* 14: 68–102.

Freud, S. (1921) Group Psychology and the Analysis of the Ego. *The Standard Edition of the Complete Psychological Works of Sigmund Freud* 18: 65–144.

Freud, S. (1940 [1938]) An Outline of Psychoanalysis. *The Standard Edition of the Complete Psychological Works of Sigmund Freud.* 23: 141–208.

Hinshelwood, R. D. (1997) The Elusive Concept of 'Internal Objects' (1934–1943): Its Role in the Formation of the Klein Group. *International Journal of Psychoanalysis* 78: 877–97.

Klein, M. (1945) The Oedipus Complex in the Light of Early Anxieties. In *The Writings of Melanie Klein*, vol. 1. London: Hogarth and the Institute of Psychoanalysis, 1975, pp. 370–419.

Klein, M. (1946) Notes on Some Schizoid Mechanisms. In *The Writings of Melanie Klein*, vol. 3. London: Hogarth and the Institute of Psychoanalysis, 1975, pp. 1–24.

Klein, M. (1961) *Narrative of a Child Analysis: The Conduct of the Psycho-Analysis of Children as Seen in the Treatment of a Ten-Year-Old Boy. The Writings of Melanie Klein*, vol. 4. London: Hogarth and the Institute of Psychoanalysis, 1975.

Sapisochin, G. (1999) 'My Heart Belongs to Daddy': Some Reflections on the Difference Between the Generations as an Organizer of the Triangular Structure of the Mind. *International Journal of Psychoanalysis* 80: 755–67.

3

Psychoanalysis and the 'Social Subject'

Introduction

In this chapter, I make a case for a psychoanalytic understanding of the social world. Such a case has to be made in order to understand memory as reparation in both the individual and society, as a clinical analyst and as a social analyst. I will argue that psychoanalysis legitimately includes the social subject—a legitimacy that is typically ignored in historical work. Psychoanalysts clearly feel drawn to the social world outside the consulting room. Think of topics of current psychoanalytic concern: war, neo-Liberalism, climate change, terrorism, fascism. We find occasional references to psychoanalysis in historical writings, but mainly, historians think that psychoanalysis concerns the individual and mistakenly attributes psychological qualities, such as emotion and personality—everything that psychoanalysts would call an 'internal world'—to the social world, as if it were a subject.[1]

Far from accepting the common rejoinder, that psychoanalysis belongs in the consulting room, limiting its aim to understanding and interpreting the individual psyche, I argue that psychoanalysis can and should extend to the social world. I also propose a methodology for this social analysis, based on how we might think of the social world as a social subject, not tied to the idea, developed from personality theory, that society has, in effect, a group mind. I will show that both clinical and social analysis can share a focus on moments of change. Change brings out features of both for analysis within the same vocabulary and working with similar presentations for analysis.

Just as the analyst works with a subject in the consulting room, in the living relationship of the transference, so too the analyst can work in the social world, if it also is a subject. Both are possible within the technical discipline of psychoanalysis. Both are encompassed by the formulation of the philosopher, Jürgen Habermas, in which analytic work proceeds as a communicative interaction built on, and forwarding, self-reflection, in which communication is a process of enhancing self-reflection by the interlocutors—we don't communicate with machines or computers. The basis of this communicative self-reflection is a common universe of understanding and reference, based on language (Habermas 1988).

Psychoanalysis and history both embody communicative, self-reflective, interaction: analyst and patient; social actors among themselves; historians as social analysts and the social actors with whom they identify. There is a common feature, which methodologically ties both into psychoanalysis. Both inside and outside the consulting room, the psychoanalyst attends to moments of change, when the dynamics of the relationship between analyst and subject are suddenly exposed by the discontinuity and made available to analytic work. These moments of change bring out the superego as an authoritarian and/or protective agency in relation to the ego. This relationship, forced into the open, informs the thinking, feeling and behaviour of the individual subject, and through a social superego, it similarly informs the thinking, feeling and behaviour of the social subject.[2]

The moment of transference interpretation with a social subject, as in the case of an individual subject, is not a sharing of personal stories, whims, illusions or beliefs, but an engagement of reflective agents, and the engagement is not symmetrical. The analyst in both cases aims to understand the other subject on that subject's behalf, on the basis of psychoanalytic theory, whether implicit or explicit at the moment of interpretation, to be reviewed more systematically at a later time.

The mistaken disenfranchisement of psychoanalysis by historians follows from a misunderstanding of the individual. They have in mind something like a self, a personality, an indivisible individual, whereas for psychoanalysis, the individual is an internal relationship, and one that cannot be comprehended without including the unconscious and the irrational authority of the superego and its component ego-ideal. Once this relationship is factored in, the apparent disjunction between the individual, as the province of psychoanalysis, and the social, as decidedly not the province of psychoanalysis, vanishes. Guilt, shame, narcissism, mourning, reparation and defences of the ego become essential to it.

Hannah Segal argues (1995, p. 165) that an incitement to war builds on unassuaged guilt from the destructiveness of a previous war; that guilt be considered a force in history along with politics and economics. The guilt that cannot be assimilated and worked through is beaten away by another round of aggression, in the same way as an individual might stave off guilt and persecution by projecting phantasized aggression into another person and righteously attacking that person. An occasion for mourning turns into a triumphal repudiation of mourning, in which an internal unease is projected into an enemy and quelled. Segal's analysis rests on the legitimacy of attributing guilt and mourning, and defensive evasion of them, to society. In a similar vein, the German psychoanalyst, Helmut Dahmer, expounding the thinking of psychoanalyst and sociologist, Alexander Mitscherlich, argues that, instead of shouldering the memory-work demanded by the Holocaust and the mourning of the terrible losses, post-war Germany has become a weapons arsenal, caught up in mutual aggression between two great power blocs (1982, p. 1072).

There are many examples of denial of social mourning, memory, guilt and reparation. In these cases, one might say that individuals could mourn in a society, but their feelings are vulnerable to distortion, which builds a wall around memory and the mourning that would accompany it. In 1987, 20 years after the Mitscherlichs published, *The Inability to Mourn*, Margarete Mitscherlich reflected on German memory, and restated their diagnosis that German society could not bear the loss of narcissistic esteem, rather than defeat in itself; and was silent on the losses that it had wreaked on others and on itself. There was, instead, an encysting of loss, mourning, guilt and reparation in defensive structures.

3 Psychoanalysis and the 'Social Subject'

One can object that a 'diagnosis' implies a pathology, a concept unwarranted in speaking of a society. It is legitimate, however, to work backwards from behaviours as symptoms, which starkly announce themselves, to the defences that underlie them, to the internal world. Although Germany has been involved in the most persistent, resilient and visible struggle to make better, both in economic support for victims and in the refashioning of German politics and society, it does not give unambiguous evidence of loss, mourning and reparation. Mourning is internal, occurring with no visible signs, while the symptoms and defences against it are loud. This loudness, which comes easily to dominate group relations, not only swamps but also gives evidence of the silent process in the internal world of both the individual and the society. Inside the defence is an internal world, a social subject, which is our focus.

The forces that hold groups together are the same forces that offer relief from bearing an emotional burden and complexity in the individual. Holding together in one mind or in one society the culpable misdeeds and the esteem from libidinal, as opposed to arrogant, pride is hard work. One reason for the difficulty is that groups are built on a narcissistic architecture—nationalism in the case of societies (Wirth 2009). Tolerating truth brings disillusionment and fracturing of narcissism. Pride can seem to be retrieved by arrogance and can seem normal. A group picks out unacceptable features in another group, which invites projection of hurt pride and makes antipathy reasonable. What would seem to be a manic defence in the individual becomes reasonable social comfort or even a belief in superiority in the group.

Thinking of post-war Germany, Jürgen Habermas (1989, pp. 249–67, 1998, pp. 203–36) argues that the growth of civilization depends on communicative self-reflection, by which disparate groups based on unreflective prejudice and obscuring and slanting the recognition of responsibility, could come together in democratic society based on 'constitutional patriotism' rather than on nationalism. He is answering a conservative swing in German politics and culture away from democratic values lodged in the Western liberal democracies, towards an apologetic retrenchment against including the memory of the Nazi period—away from ambivalence and towards arrogant pride. Communicative self-reflection can occur only in a society that can tolerate ambivalence. Here is where a marriage of the outside and the inner worlds, supported by the disciplines of each, is called for. The psychoanalyst says the problem is an inner malaise, finding manic solutions; the historian says it is a political conundrum, the detailed record of which bespeaks the problem.

To make the claim for psychoanalysis as interpretation *in* the social, we have to embrace the idea of a social subject: a social with an inner world, to which the qualities of sentience and emotion apply. I will now turn to this social subject.

The Social Subject

The fact that we cannot attribute subjectivity to society does not lessen the importance of understanding how a social group may nonetheless act as if were a subject—that it thinks, feels and acts as a subject. We have, for example, no trouble attributing nationalist sentiment to a nation, nor what defines it; we speak easily of 'British values' or 'Englishness', without regard to establishing the number of believers. We don't even rely on being able to articulate these values. We accept an affective, not a cognitive, attribution to a social unit, as common sense. We understand the notion of values as a sentiment that garners an affective attraction (or repulsion) by a pull into (or a repulsion from) a protective and coercive umbrella of a leader, a religion, an ideology, or a conviction, such as, 'in a democracy, we live under the rule of law'.

This inclusion within an affectively attracting, overarching presence gives a clue to understanding the subjectivity of groups—one that connects the subjectivities of individuals with the way they coalesce into the subjectivity of the group. As we saw in Chap. 2, Freud provides a model in which 'individual' is the wrong level at which to conceptualize the formation and maintenance of a group. He speaks of the 'dependent relationships of the ego' (1923, pp. 48–59) in delineating an agency that he called either the ego-ideal or the superego. The ego-ideal derives from primary narcissism[3] and is, therefore, a preserve of an enclosed territory within the psyche to which the ego is drawn as to a lost ideal state. The superego is heir to the Oedipus complex, and is, therefore, a preserve of authority, which can be persecutory, as well as the object of love. These kindred agencies hold the aspiration, the admiration, the idealization, the subordinating authority, to which the ego is subject. They can be projected into external objects, thereby endowing those objects with these properties, but they remain the unconscious source of deference of the ego, whether by the thrall or by the domination that they evoke in the ego. They are the source of the affects that are experienced in the individual as the values, patriotism and nationalism, which induce one's sense of belonging in common with all others who share these sentiments.

The consciousness of belonging with others is a property of the ego in its relationship to other egos. In Freud's model, the relationship to the group follows from the depositing of each individual superego in the same leader, religion or ideology, which forms a social ego-ideal: an ego-ideal held in common by the individuals because they have conferred their individual ego-ideals on the same ego-ideal object. It follows from Freud's model of the psyche (the 'structural model') that, if ego-ideals are held in common, the individual egos will be held in common by identification (1921, pp. 105–16). In that sense, the group becomes a large psyche with the properties of a psyche. But note: the unit is not the individual of the historian or social scientist. The unit(s!) are the superego and ego-ideal—we can speak of a superego-ideal, to capture prohibiting and identificatory/idealizing functions (Mancia and Meltzer 1981)—and the ego. The unit of consciousness—the individual of the historian and social scientist—is drawn into an irrational, affective sense of belonging or not belonging by these unconscious forces. This sense of a social being has little to do with a declared, conscious self-experience of a person or of chosen group membership. It is to this affective bond that we can attribute social subjectivity.[4]

Without a bond of inclusion, we have no idea of what makes a group. Without it, the historian and the social scientist are left reporting facts. To say that 90% of a population voted for the same leader cannot be translated into, say, nationalist sentiment, without either relying on the common-sense notion that such a majority implies a nationalist sentiment, or without a theory that speaks directly to the unconscious, affective bond, which underlies the experience of conscious individuality and draws individuals into a social formation without regard to their individual, conscious experience.

Post-war Germany provides a good field for applying these ideas. There has been an extensive literature on Germany as deeply conflicted over the burden of guilt, responsibility, collaboration, resistance, bystanding and repression with respect to national esteem. Critics of this view, however, commonly argue that to speak of psychological attributes of a society illegitimately extends those attributes to all the individuals who are, in whatever way, related to the society. So, for example, a German born after the War would still share German guilt for the Nazis. In this example, guilt is attributed to a society (the society as a subject) and to all the individuals in the society. All individuals, by dint of being part of the society, are tainted with its unjustified psychological attributes. Indeed, aren't we in danger of assuming without warrant that even the wartime generation felt guilty?

The historian who, from external criteria, decides that it is unwarranted to include Germans born after the war avoids looking into how an individual feels complicit with his/her society in the first place, and cannot more broadly understand how he/she remains part of a society. External factors cannot account for identification, with its unconscious motivation to be as one with the society. But if we look more closely, we can see the guilt, the feeling of complicity and the grounding feeling of belonging in intergenerational conflict. Two (in this case generational) groups—the one comprising adults during the Nazi period, the other, adults only after the Nazi period—produce a 'splitting' between them. The 'innocent', post-war group, ushered forth as evidence of inappropriate attribution of guilt, requires the wartime 'guilty' group, in order to maintain its innocence by projecting any trace of guilt into it. The innocent group thereby represses by projection, not just complicity, but also mourning for the loss that they experience, so to speak, in the atmosphere. The guilty group requires the innocent group to consolidate its identity by reinforcing the righteousness of its solidarity, in forms such as the idealization in right-wing triumphalism, nationalism, patriotism. This defensive mechanism can be discerned in the overt self-proclamations of each and in the relationships between them, and it forms part of the justification for attributing guilt to the wartime generation itself. The principal driving force is a defence against guilt, mourning and anxiety, which is passed instantaneously from individual to individual and from individual into the group, to ground either a shared experience of memory- and guilt-work, or a shared defence against it.

However we try to make sense of the social subject, we cannot avoid it. Historians assume it as the very ground of their work: that is what distinguishes history from biography. The question is how best to go about it. Historians interpret their evidence into an argument: archives in which thinking and purposes are recorded, canvasses and surveys, voting records. But what remains is the elusive idea that the group thinks, feels and acts, comprised as it is of individuals who think, feel and act in line with an imagination embedded in their minds of the society in which they do it (Anderson 1983).

The passion of imagination can only be described with words such as recognition, love, hate, shame, guilt, reparation. But they do attach to cognitive content: love or hate of the nation or its leader, its behaviour, their shame, guilt and reparation. Affects remain unformed until they attach to content, without which the subject can fall into an abyss of anxiety. In my historical model, there is a social subject. It is composed of the psychic agencies of individuals (ego, id, superego and the more complex object relational versions contributed by psychoanalysis since Freud). These agencies coalesce into social groupings because they assimilate anxiety, shape it into social processes. They retain their root characters, and one can, therefore, speak of social guilt and reparation—of recognizing and remembering as reparation. We need to put flesh on this conceptual framework, and it must be rooted in psychoanalytic clinical experience. From these roots, we will be able to speak of a social unconscious, a social superego and the mechanism of social defence. I now turn to this psychoanalytic clinical evidence.

Hopper (1996) presents a clinical account of an emerging sociopolitical theme in the small society of group analytic sessions. A woman had left the group. Hopper took a new referral into the group, albeit feeling that it might be premature and might impede the group's mourning the lost member. Intense and heated exchanges followed, with the group divided into 'non-professionals', in whose view the 'professionals' thought they knew it all. After a couple of weeks, the group consolidated around scapegoating the new, professional woman, 'who was perceived as both an unyielding and intrusive foreign object, and as very needy and vulnerable. She ... was regarded as interfering with their perfect communion with the Group as a whole and with me' (p. 143).

Hopper sees in this process an 'encapsulated trauma', capturing individual experiences but holding them in an aggregation. The explicitly socio-political focus emerged from this aggregation through an interpretive question of one of the group members. She wondered whether the others were worried about the National Health Service and about the Maastricht Treaty, from which discussion of helplessness and conflict between blacks and whites, Jews and non-Jews, natives and immigrants, followed (p. 144). Hopper concludes that this shift in focus to the external world was related to their concerns in the group, and that the effects of the Maastricht treaty 'were as unconscious as the effects of various aspects of their experience as infants and children'; that is, of the stuff of here-and-now, transference interpretation (p. 145). The social context was as central to the work of the group as the apparently more immediate clinical process. The group had formed itself as a small society by settling on a socio-political theme in which the members could share their anxiety by being a society with an anxiety, a trauma to process together inside a social bond that was as real as the individual anxieties expressed in the clinical setting. The group formed around unprocessed mourning at loss of one of its members and consolidated around helplessness at a society's loss of control to larger-scale forces—a suffering social subject.

I want to pick up a particular aspect of this process. The group—the society—forms to process anxiety. The society consolidates to protect the individuals and becomes the bearer of their anxieties, as it coalesces into a society, in effect, with an anxiety of its own. The group then has 'real' concerns such as subordination to the Maastricht Treaty. Here is a vignette in which we can look into the fine structure of the formation of social havens or enclaves, which both corral and promote an illusion of protection from anxiety recast as a threat in the external world. In it, the analyst tries to understand German society as a social subject by her living relationship with it.

In a case reported by an East German psychoanalyst living in West Berlin (Kothe-Meyer 2000), a six-year-old boy from the GDR was adopted by parents who had moved to the West just before the fall of the wall. The parents described him as 'wicked, constantly fighting and thieving', which, they feared, would lead to his having to leave school and to their humiliation as a problem family. This sort of severe description of a child by parents from the GDR was a common experience for the analyst, who saw in it the imprint of the severity of GDR authority. But more immediately, her own reactions to the mother, who brought the boy, and to mistakes that followed on from her reactions, could be understood as an unconscious superego interchange between her and the mother.

The severe description of the boy was that of a parent seeking approval from severe—GDR—authority, transferred to the analyst, Irmhild Kohte-Meyer. The analyst was born in the GDR, but had lived in West Berlin for many years. The analyst found herself uncharacteristically judgemental and hostile. When the parents failed to bring the boy to a session, she searched for her clinical notes, but found them missing. She became the mistrustful target of the same mistrusting, severe—GDR—surveillance. The unconscious, disorientating impact of a GDR superego was confirmed when she found her clinical notes and discovered that she had given the parents a different date.

The analyst's social and educational history gave her an insight into the difficulties faced by migrants from one side to the other, specifically the maintenance of prior collectively instilled psychic structures from the GDR; so she was interpreting in the social in both the immediacy of the transference and in the dependence of her ego on the social superego. What she witnessed in the parents' denunciations of their children were 'highly moralistic, judgmental remarks of the GDR superego,' which also 'often held an uneasy, fearful undertone' of anxiety in the face of children who showed an autonomy from authority [an autonomy they also feared in themselves]. The GDR superego, with which they identified and which they feared would say, for example: 'He lies often-nearly always.' 'She never does what she should, only what she wants.' 'She is remarkably malicious.' 'He will not accept any duties or take any responsibilities' (2000, p. 419).

The detection of this cultural incompatibility, produced by the social superego was a clinical finding in psychoanalytic work with migrants. It builds on the anthropological-psychoanalytic tradition based on Mario

Erdheim's concept of the social production of unconsciousness (Erdheim 1984; Kohte-Meyer 1994; also Parin 1977 on social adaptation as a process by which the ego is relieved of conflict unless this harmonious relationship is challenged). The ego of the migrant, challenged by coming into conflict with the social superego of the home culture, retreats, pushed by the persecutory side of the superego and allured by its protective side. This superego can be retained, producing the judgemental parents, or projected into the analyst, who becomes a threatening figure. The analyst experiences anxiety and loss of competence, as his/her ego is crippled by the 'social superego, acquired in the cultural space of the old DDR…In the failed correspondence of the prevailing "inner management plan" the ego-identity of the patient was shattered, [and the] ego, under the superego anxiety that broke out, was unable to function. An irritated feeling of demolished comprehensibility of the situation arose in me' (Kothe-Meyer 1994, p. 255).

This analysis makes sense only with Freud's structural model of the psyche (superego-ideal, ego, id). The parents were identified either with egos subservient to a punitive and all-embracing superego, or with the superego itself. The positioning depended on the interlocutor, who would transferentially enact the complementary agency: ego to superego or superego to ego. This unconscious structure defended against the anxiety of ego consciousness should anyone begin to see what was going on. And this superego was fashioned in social environments that carried the unconscious defence: the GDR formed from resistance to the West Germans and from being unable to depart from a superego intolerance of West German individuality. The persecutory dimension stands out in this vignette, but the analyst also emphasizes the importance of the protective umbrella offered by the GDR state.

At a social level,

> These almost unbearable emotion of rage, grief, depression, and even shame are usually avoided, so that, through the individual denial of emotions on both sides, the dialogue between 'East' and 'West' Germans may quickly become derailed. Consistent misunderstandings and consolidation of the splitting processes result, and dialogue and possible beginning of a sympathetic relationship come to an abrupt end. (2000, p. 427)

She continues

> It is just this derailed dialogue … that should be recognized and understood, and it is the continual switching of roles between 'hunter' and 'hunted,' [transferred into the analytic relationship] induced by persecuting and paranoid fantasies, that should be revealed. I am convinced that development and integration can only begin through this psychoanalytical process. (p. 427)

The social superego of the GDR both protected and persecuted: the GDR did provide welfare and it enforced the socialist ideal through the teaching of children, which had both the persecutory and the protective sides. Introjected, it offered a collectively reinforced stability to the subservient ego, but at the cost of splitting and projecting whatever did not fit its ideology. Next to the GDR-stabilized ego, West German individualism was 'ego-oriented and narcissistic' (2000, p. 426). The outcome was an irrational, accepted, mutual hostility between two societies, the roots of which remained unconscious and persisted into reunited German society. In Kohte-Meyer's words

> With the turning away from the old traditional cultural space and moving towards the cultural space of the new social territory something essential can be lost to the ego: consciousness and capacity for scenic phantasies and role identifications, which concerned the socially allowed drive satisfactions and, as identifications, were part of the old ego-identity [in a] process … comparable intrapsychically to the process … described for whole societies and groups in Mario Erdheim's concept of the 'social production of unconsciousness'. (1994, p. 257)

Kohte-Meyer's model of the social superego fits with Freud on group psychology described in Chap. 2. In this case, the investment of the individual superegos in the same object could be taken, instead of an investment, to be a forced introjection (Hinshelwood 1986, p. 209).

Roger Frie (2011) has shown how language, expressing cultural similarity and difference, can embed a safe enclave in an analysis, in which important issues are addressed but from the vantage of a socially rooted haven. Frie is a Canadian, second-generation German, fluent in English and German. His patient, Daniel, was an Austrian Jew, whose father, whom he feared, was a concentration camp and holocaust survivor of very stern disposition; and whose mother survived the war but died when he was 10 years old.

Frie and Daniel studied at the same English university at the same time. Their similarities 'masked a central difference between us…: Daniel was the son of Holocaust survivors, and I was the son of Germans' (p. 141). Frie entered the work 'with the weight of historical guilt and shame connected to my cultural background' (p. 140). In the early days, the analysis was conducted in German, and 'Daniel seemed pleased, and actually relieved, to be able to speak German. His emotional and dream life was very much rooted in his mother tongue, and he missed not speaking German, although his English was also excellent' (p. 143). They did switch language, and Frie came to think that responding in English maintained an emotional distance, while German opened affective spaces. But there came a moment when the meanings of German and English brought a potential crisis to a head. (p. 149).

The turning came when Daniel, wanting to know more about the father he dared not question, and fearing it, wanted to know how it was that Frie spoke such good German. What did his parents do in the war? His analyst's neutrality had become suspect, while Frie's 'ability to withstand Daniel's scrutiny…seemed very important to our work together' (p. 149). But this exploration of Frie's past and identity took place entirely in English, in which they also shared an education in philosophy. Frie said their use of English, 'felt like we were conducting a unilingual therapy in which the question of German and Germanness, be it linguistic or cultural, personal or social, was entirely absent. It was as though we were … two English-speaking, English-educated, New York immigrants' (p. 149).

Here was a linguistically embedded social organization, built around the patient's family and his Austrian Jewish heritage, and embedded in the analysis through the shared construction of a terrain from which to view the impact of Nazism on his Jewish life and culture; first from within a haven, then, through the suspiciousness of a false neutrality on the part of Germans—with his analyst as the possibly deceitfully neutral, helpful professional. Just this core impasse in his psychic development could come to the fore in the intensity of the analytic setting. Frie says that his work with Daniel 'revealed…the extent to which the negotiating of cultures and identities defines who I am and how I experience and view life', including a willingness to 'confront and live with shame and anxiety in the presence of others' (p. 155). 'On the face of it, I do not appear German. I have no accent, carry a Canadian passport, and am second generation. Yet, language and identity do not simply melt away' (p. 142), nor does the social superego, which 'knows' the interior of the German mind.

Fakhry Davids (2011) has identified a similar socially framed and reinforced defensive structure, which he calls the 'internal racist' in both the internal and the external worlds. In the following vignette from an analysis with an ordinary patient, an internal, defensive, racist structure suddenly erupts, precipitating a crisis, serious enough to provoke an attempted suicide. Together with the vignette from Kohte-Meyer, it exemplifies the methodological theme held in common by clinical and social analysis: a moment of change, when the (social) superego stridently comes forward to threaten and to protect the (social) ego.

Davids' patient, Mr A., was an intelligent, white Englishman, of whom much was expected. His analyst was a foreigner with brown skin. Mr A came into analysis as 'the most rigorous and demanding form of treatment available', because he wanted to avoid a repetitive cycle of abandoning treatment when 'the pattern of his life – of going along with others in the hope of salvation and triumph over adversity – was repeating itself. It was then that he would break off, determined to find his own way, only to return when he realised he was getting nowhere' (p. 20). Davids understood the patient's worry, and his patient's relief in the analysis confirmed the trust between them. Davids' countertransference, however, suggested being kept at an arm's length. Reminiscent of Frie's experience before the crisis, analyst and patient seemed to be 'two rather sensible chaps able to discuss all manner of difficult things that were either *in the past* or *elsewhere*; between us, in the here and now, there was no fear, no anxiety, no danger, and no problem' (p. 21; author's emphasis).

The sudden, explosive turning came when Mr A described defying his father, with the consequence that father then held him to account for charges to repair damage to the family car. The conflict arose when 'he heard a strange noise coming from the engine of his new, and hence unfamiliar, car. He became convinced the engine was about to explode and, fearing for his life, he stopped, got out and locked the door behind him' (p. 21). He panicked, unsure of the reality of the situation, and to stop his vacillation as to whether or not to go back, he dropped the keys down a drain.

Davids took the new car to stand for the new therapy, in which Mr A's own impulses could precipitate an explosion. To open up analytic territory, he 'thought [Mr A] wanted me to know he had *enormous* rage inside, and he feared that were this touched in his therapy I would not be able to cope with it' (p. 22; my emphasis). Now, this interpretation seems entirely in line with the development of the analysis and aimed at gently directing Mr A's attention to what he was anxious about: that he would have once again to comply with keeping a lid on his emotion and would have once again to leave treatment.

> For some moments he seemed, silently, to be mulling over what I had said. Eventually, through gritted teeth, he muttered that it was always the same: his rage was always *so enormous*. His voice became strained and choked, its reasonable tone giving way to a furious onslaught against my use of the term *enormous*. He heard this as a complaint at the extent of the rage I saw in him. [H]e believed I was simultaneously warning him that I was aware of it and pressurizing him to suppress it…. In a fit of uncontrollable rage, he flung out an unending string of accusations [against parents, teachers, therapists]…every time, he was taken in by their empty promises! Yet, no one ever wanted to know about the *enormous*, ugly, horrible rage that was *in* him. By now he was yelling uncontrollably at me…Never again. He knows that fitting in with others is part of the problem, and never ever would he allow anyone to bully him into believing this is a solution. (p. 22; author's emphasis)

The rant left Davids feeling 'well and truly done over. His ferocious attack got through and left me reeling' (p. 23). Subsequently, Mr A said he had no reason to doubt his analyst's credentials, but 'who was I really? Where was I from?' (p. 26). The referring analyst was decidedly English, which had comforted him, whereas Davids was a foreigner, clearly racially different. 'In truth, he feared that his attack had got through to me and, in revenge, I would retaliate by exploiting his dependency to take him over and do with him what I liked' (p. 26). Later, Mr A confirmed his noticing his discomfort at David's foreign, racial difference, and in response to interpreting it as a possible basis of Mr A's attack, he asked, 'Are you accusing me of making a racist attack on you?' (p. 27).

Here we get to the nub. Mr A transformed his own horror of dependency into a conviction that his analyst was sensitive to his minority and denigrated position as a racial outsider seeking acceptance by the British psychoanalytical establishment.

> Through projection I was transformed, in his perception, from an individual who happened to have a brown skin (and a strange accent) to a foreigner struggling to find acceptance in a hostile (xenophobic) Britain. *His problem with finding acceptance was therefore relocated in me*... [T]his problem – now mine – was to be faced on the street outside, where nameless xenophobes would threaten me. This enabled the consulting room to become, from the outset, the cosy meeting place of the [previous] sessions. (p. 29; author's emphasis) [, but] everything I said had to be consistent with the picture of me as an immigrant with a problem. (p. 30)

The patient's unconscious aim was to limit the analysis to a shared and sympathetic recognition of the problems faced by immigrants, especially racially different and denigrated immigrants. At this level, they could agree—Mr A was an ordinary, liberal man: not, by any reasonable standards, a racist. But the moment his own ego-directed individuality came to the surface, it came as defiance (to father, in his case), to be suppressed by humiliation and by his joining forces with a socially maintained superiority to an outsider race. The salient feature was the acquiescence with a *normal*—even laudable—liberal social convention. These normal conventions enact a social defence, which operates through the superego, not through the individual known by the historian or social scientist: the psychoanalytic individual is not the cognitive, rational—if at times unreasonable—person, but a cauldron of ego-superego-id relationships.

So it is with cultural heritage, which is not the individual inheritance known by the social investigator, but as Freud says

[A] child's super-ego is in fact constructed on the model not of its parents but of its parents' super-ego; the contents which fill it are the same and it becomes the vehicle of tradition and of all the time-resisting judgements of value which have propagated themselves in this manner from generation to generation... The past, the tradition of the race and of the people, lives on in the ideologies of the super-ego, and yields only slowly to the influences of the present and to new changes; and so long as it operates through the super-ego it plays a powerful part in human life. (1933[1932], p. 67)

While the specificity of the social world requires historical and social analysis, the nature and intensity of emotional force speaks of social order as a defensive structure that garners and appeases catastrophic anxiety. The social superego blends into normal life, rendering it invisible. To question it is, therefore, rejected as irrational and dangerous to social life. But beneath the social order lies the catastrophe of psychotic anxiety (Davids, p. 161). Mr A's response was paranoid. He felt nailed by an accusation dressed up as an interpretation that concealed a retaliatory attack. As such, it could not be tolerated for an instant, and had immediately to be ejected.

The same thing happens in the social world, in which groups amplify paranoid phantasies by the ease with which they split into sectors. The need to disperse anxiety by projection makes use of the ready supply of repositories into which the attack can be instantaneously eliminated. In the process, this mechanism also consolidates a society by handing around projections that capture anxiety and, in so doing, create havens.

The divided psyche spreads parts of itself around a group instantaneously, setting up a series of projective systems that consolidate social units and the individuals in it. Their relationships defend against the irruption of intolerable emotion. One can see how this process informs extremist ideology and an extremist current in ordinary society. The simplicity of an object homogenized to remove internal complexity is met by a subject similarly homogenized and simplified to remove internal complexity. They are connected through projective identification, in which the extremist subject is idealized and triumphant, full of rectitude in its denigrating and defeating the object. The projective bond can be further simplified and strengthened by physical action in violently suppressing the object, not just as behaviour, but as projective identification. Both are actions that push out emotion to pacify the internal world.

I want to give a brief example of the need of psychoanalytic interpretation in a specific historical situation reaching for a psychoanalytic formulation. Jürgen Habermas approached the way the individual lives as part of a social subject. He precipitated what was called the historians' debate in a newspaper article published in 1986 (1986a; to be discussed in Chap. 6). The background to this debate had been forming over a period of years into a conservative swing in support of a normal post-war German identity, no longer laden with memory of a past belaboured with Nazism. Habermas aimed to identify and oppose what he saw as a dampening of responsibility for the Holocaust within the scholarship of highly respected, established historians. He argued that Germany—German citizens, even those born since the War—must continue the work of memory. By memory, he meant, not the third-person scholarly knowledge of the past, but the first-person understanding of individuals who were, for themselves, German. 'This arena, in which none of us can be nonparticipants, should not be confused with discussion among scientists and scholars who have to take the observational perspective of a third person in their work' (1986b, p. 237). Memory work for Habermas refers to a

> context with which one's own existence is historically interwoven…through remembrance, practiced in solidarity, of what cannot be made good, other than through a reflexive, scrutinizing attitude toward one's own identity-forming traditions[. T]he less internal communality a collective context of life has preserved [and] the more it has maintained itself externally, through the usurpation and destruction of life that is alien to it, the greater is the burden of reconciliation imposed on the grief work and the critical self-examination of subsequent generations[.] (1986b, p. 236)

What a society cannot assimilate—*internally*—in ambivalent, regretful, self-reflectiveness will be projected and repeated externally. In 1980s Germany, there was a gathering polarization between two pathways of remembering: one committed to self-reflection, responsibility, bearing the reality of the Nazi period as a German perpetration; the other tending to draw a line under remembering, to normalize German national identity within European history. Habermas argued that, through a reflexive, historical recognition of—and working with—reality, societies can face their past, including all its ambiguities and ambivalences in a state of what, in the Kleinian tradition, one would call depressive reparation. But the closer they get to it, the more they will feel driven by the social superego of tradition to evade it with mitigating memories. Along both pathways, individuals form groups with first-person relationships confronting social superegos that either tolerate ambivalence and self-reflection or severely dismiss them.

The historians' debate also repeated, in a more self-reflective form and environment, the unresolved, catastrophic impact of the end of the war. For Ian Kershaw, the absolute defeat of the German Army and surrender of the German Reich brought the collapse of the charismatic structure of the regime.

> All the other factors [including] the ferocious terror apparatus [and] the fear of Bolshevik occupation,… were ultimately subordinate to the way the charismatic Führer regime was structured [and] functioned, in its dying phase. Paradoxically, it was by this time charismatic rule without charisma. Hitler's mass charismatic appeal had long since dissolved, but the structures and mentalities of his charismatic rule lasted until his death in the bunker. (2011, p. 400)

'Correspondingly, once he had gone, the whole edifice crumbled into dust' (Evans (2015), p. 351). Here the historian diverges from the psychoanalyst. For the historian, the crumbing of the edifice is simply 'the end'. But just this collapse, which seems obvious, needs to be explained. For the psychoanalyst, the collapse is the loss of the ego-ideal, which forced post-war Germany out of narcissistic illusion and into a defence against mourning in submission to tradition embodied in a social superego. This submission took the form of a narcissistic re-creation in nationalism, economic success, reconstruction, and the repression of mourning as memory-work.

For Martin Broszat (1970), one of the leading historians of the Nazi period, a new order seemed continually to be possible. National regeneration, mobilized by anti-Semitism and anti-Bolshevism, would overcome conspiracy and exploitation and social-cultural proletarianization; and the 'Lebensraum-Utopie' would prefigure the 'social regeneration of the people', as a 'projection into the future of a fully independent, autarkic territorial big power' (p. 403). The key phrase is 'projection into the future': the continuous re-creation of possibility as the fuel and the form of illusory fulfilment, in a positive and negative sense: positive as the ideal always projected ahead of realization; negative in the absolute denunciation to the point of extinction of any deviation from participation in this projected ideal, including the 'final solution' (p. 406).

When Broszat speaks of the projection of possibility into the future, the cogency of his analysis needs the theory of the ego-ideal, from which the character of the regime, in its fostering its vague, but positive, and its determined, negative, measures against the people who must not survive, can be understood. Built on narcissism, the ego-ideal remains beyond reach but beckons towards omnipotent phantasy, leading to a euphoria unlimited by external reality (Chasseguet-Smirgel 1985a, pp. 10–25, 1985b, pp. 1–12, 24–34). The historian's account, rich in necessary detail, cannot capture this alluring promise of fulfilment in illusion. The illusion energizes external material and social interests with thrall, and psychoanalytic clinical observation is essential to understanding it. One could also say that the historian's work is essential to reinforcing a manifest reality sense. Then the infusion of phantasy into manifest reality, which creates the full reality, based heavily on unconscious defences, can be investigated (on the recognition of the need to explore both realities among the children of Holocaust survivors, see Grubrich-Simitis 1984).

Narcissistic re-creation in nationalism, economic success and reconstruction, characterized immediate post-war Germany. But it left the tough, internal work of memory, mourning, guilt and reparation within an ambivalent, self-reflective history, in a repressed, schismatic state (Mitscherlich 1987). Habermas caught the swing back to a nationalistic mood of recasting Germany as a normal society as it surfaced in the political and academic scene. Beneath the swing was not just the reconstruction of a defeated nation, but a resurgent narcissistic defence against lost illusion. Here is one of those moments of change, the analysis of which is the stuff of psychoanalysis.

Interpreting in the Social

The social equivalent of interpreting in the transference is interpreting *in* the social. The social of this interpretation is not an object, but a subject. The interpreter lives in the milieu of the subject of interpretation and can detect its significant moments in the same way as in the consulting room. The common theme that ties the above examples together is the moment of change. Reviewing the examples above, Hopper saw a shift in the sudden intrusion of external forces into a small group. Kohte-Meyer detected an interfering domination by a GDR superego. Frie suddenly found himself the object of suspicion; Davids was abruptly stunned by a racist attack; the historians' debate was a growing reaction to nationalist repudiation of responsibility for the Nazi period. They cover the spectrum from inside the consulting room, to the small group, to society, and they share the recognition of a shift in dynamics, which was detectable both outside and inside the consulting room, which opens it to analysis.

These shifts are characterized by the noisy resurgence of a superego, both individual and social, with its authority to corral and subdue an ego and offer protection at the same time. In the normal run of events, this social superego is invisibly aligned with everyday life; only with some dislocation does it stridently irrupt into visibility, inside and outside the consulting room when 'normality' is challenged. In this enclosed space, the analyst becomes the subdued ego or the authoritarian and protective superego. Social groups expose and exaggerate the authority of the social superego by facilitating projection among sectors. The shift brings the superego forward for analysis or for enactment of its relationship to the ego. The analytic confrontation with this strident superego underlies Strachey's classic paper on 'The Nature of Therapeutic Action' (1934), which remains the foundation of clinical practice today.

Here are some entry points into the shifts in the social world, which can engage the psychoanalyst in an interpretive dialogue with historians. They include:

1. Conflict among historical actors, as in the case of German conservative and social-democratic politicians;

2. Conflict among intellectuals and other observers at the time, as in the historians' debate;
3. Conflict and partisanship among current scholars, whose transferential relationships to different historical actors and their social superegos drive them into dispute with each other, producing shifts in position like those described in this chapter;
4. Conflict between politicians and the press, for example, in interviews;
5. Irruptions of indignancy, as in the self-righteous attack on a paediatrician, whose house was attacked because she was a paedo… (Allison 2000)

Whether as historians or psychoanalysts, we are necessarily drawn into a first-person living relationship with our material, including the same factional identifications with egos and with superego traditions, with the same shifts as described in this chapter.

So far, I have aimed to establish the psychoanalytic concept of an internal world in both the individual and in society. The internal world, as opposed to the perceptual, external world, lives in a dynamic system of unconscious phantasy. It pervades the external world, infusing and animating perception with phantasy. In the typical case, external reality reciprocally moderates phantasy. We normally wake up from a dream or see how we made a mistake based on an unconscious belief or assumption. In the extreme, phantasy imbues the external world with delusion, in the sense that 'reality' no longer moderates, but conveys, phantasy as reality with the conviction of rational authority based on 'evidence' and common sense. I have also argued that, methodologically, moments of change throw unconscious dynamics into relief, opening them to analysis, both in the individual and the society. In the next chapter, we will look at such an extreme in the rapid delusional creation of Jews as enemies in the Nazi period, as a shift in background anti-Semitism. The Nazi mind could then think anew, of a reborn Germany as a 'world without Jews' (Confino 2014).

Notes

1. I want to emphasize that I am referring to the work of historians, rather than studies in psychobiography or more generally in social sciences. Exceptions include Saul Friedländer (1978), who explores the possibilities of a theoretically and methodologically grounded contribution to history, which he thinks essential for historical research. Joan Scott (2012) has given a thorough review of historians' and psychoanalysts' views of psychoanalysis as part of historical enquiry. She argues for the fruitfulness of the disruptive impact of the 'unruly unconscious' of psychoanalysis on the flattening character of normative historical narrative. Daniel Pick, historian and psychoanalyst, has written on a number of historical topics, including *The Pursuit of the Nazi Mind* (2012). Lyndal Roper (1994), a historian of early modern Europe, has written a psychoanalytically informed study of masculinity in the sixteenth and seventeenth centuries. Thomas Kohut (2012), also a historian and psychoanalyst, has explored the history of National Socialism as an experiential history, based on interviews with members of the New German Circle, a post-war gathering of the pre-war German youth movement. Roger Frie (2017) combines clinical and historical methods. Stephen Frosh has written in a number of areas in which psychoanalysis can contribute to the understanding of social, cultural and political situations. For an overview, see his *Psychoanalysis outside the Clinic* (2010); also, Rustin (1991). Overall, however, I think that historians rarely turn to psychoanalysis as part of detailed historical research.
2. This attention to change as a moment of discontinuity, which pushes underlying dynamics into the open, accessible to observation and interpretation, is akin to Lorenzer's 'scenic understanding'. Rothe (2009, 2012) has used it to explore forms of not-remembering in a group of Germans who, in childhood, observed the deportation of Jews (see Chap. 7).
3. I am following Freud's theory of narcissism here, which also links with his theory of groups and therefore with my thesis on what makes a society out of individuals. There are two main currents of the theory of narcissism, roughly ctaegorized as 'normal narcissism', associated with ego psychology and self-psychology (Federn 1936; Kohut 1971), and 'pathological narcissism', associated with the Kleinian and broadly 'British School'. The former stresses the idea that ego strength, ego esteem and ordinary psychological development, build on an appropriate infusion of an unquestioned support, which is carried forward from the earliest feelings of satisfaction

in which the ego first experienced itself as a reservoir of libido—primary narcissism. Freud was in no doubt that it was an illusion of autonomy, based on the mother's original provision of a libidinal object, which later allowed the child to experience itself as the source of its independence as an autoerotism (1922, p. 245), a fortunate illusion that buttressed the experience of being oneself. Too much narcissism became an omnipotent defence against the disillusionment at the hands of reality; but insufficient narcissism left the ego in a state of weak deficit in libidinalized esteem and strength.

Pathological narcissism in the British School stresses the defensive side of all narcissism. In 1922, Karl Abraham wrote a brief letter to Freud, which showed his direction of thinking about the relationship between mourning and melancholia, the former engaged in the tough work of accommodating reality; the latter defensively ignoring reality in a manic, narcissistic preservation of the ego's independence from reality. Inherent in this narcissism is the triumph over the object. He was seeing a necessary relationship between what would later be called normal and pathological narcissism. Melanie Klein makes the link between mourning and a manic defence against it explicit (Klein 1940); and Rosenfeld (1964) highlights a perverse attraction to a protective and exciting cover offered by an internal gang of shady customers, whose promise includes the trashing of the object. In this way, he makes a link between the 'normal' but defensive manic—melancholic—phase of mourning and the perverse excitement of an ego overriding any dependence on the (lost, any) object and the reality that it represents. So, in fact, the two current do converge, albeit leaving areas unclear.

On the normal narcissism side, it is clear that triumph over the object can occur if the narcissistic component of an ego suffering loss is too great, but it is left to detailed clinical accounts to demonstrate such a surfeit as if it were also a theory of the ego. On the pathological narcissism side, it is clear that there is a 'normal' ego that can triumph, but is weakened and drawn to the perversity of the promised protection. In this case, detailed clinical description again demonstrates this attraction and the denegation of the object that follows from it, as if it were a theory of the ego.

In both traditions, there is a theory of a normal ego energized, supported, experienced as the source of itself as an independent agency, and a theory of the ego sourced from an object, and a theory of an ego that cannot tolerate dependence and overrides it in an illusion of autonomy. That surmounting of dependence on an object by narcissism can be more

or less triumphal, denigrating and annihilating to the object, and more or less drawn into a perverse relationship with exciting internal objects who substitute excitement for the experience of degrading dependence.
4. Anzieu (1975) has elaborated on this model, proposing that the groups as a whole can become the group ego-ideal, akin to the leader in Freud's analysis of the mechanism of group cohesion. Chasseguet-Smirgel (1985a) considers the same system from a different angle. Individuals acting in concert produce the same group cohesion, in that their synchronized movement constitutes an identification in their egos and posits a leader-ego-ideal in the group as a whole. Interestingly for a dialogue between history and psychoanalysis, the historian, William McNeill (1995), has extensively documented the binding force of co-ordinated activity—a 'muscular bonding'—in religious and military groups.

References

Abraham, K. (1922) Letter from Karl Abraham to Sigmund Freud, March 13, 1922. *The Complete Correspondence of Sigmund Freud and Karl Abraham 1907–1925*. London: Karnac, 2002, pp. 452–4.

Allison, R. (2000) Doctor Driven Out of Home by Vigilantes. *The Guardian*, August 29.

Anderson, B. R. O'G. (1983) *Imagined Communities: Reflections on the Origin and Spread of Nationalism*. London: Verso; revised edition 2006.

Anzieu, D. (1975) *The Group and the Unconscious*. London: Routledge & Kegan, 1984.

Broszat, M. (1970) Soziale Motivation und Führer-Bindung des Nationalsozialismus. *Vierteljahrshefte für Zeitgeschichte* 18(4): 392–409

Chasseguet-Smirgel, J. (1985a) *The Ego Ideal: A Psychoanalytic Essay on the Malady of the Ideal*. London: Free Association Books.

Chasseguet-Smirgel, J. (1985b) *Creativity and Perversion*. London: Free Association Books.

Confino, A. (2014) *A World Without Jews: The Nazi Imagination from Persecution to Genocide*. New Haven/London: Yale University Press.

Dahmer, H. (1982) In Memoriam Alexander Mitscherlich. *Psyche – Zeitschrift für Psychoanalyse* 36: 1071–2.

Davids, M. Fakhry (2011) *Internal Racism: A Psychoanalytic Approach to Race and Difference*. Houndmills: Palgrave Macmillan.

Erdheim, M. (1984) *Die gesellschaftliche Produktion von Unbewusstheit: Eine Einführung in den ethnopsychonalytischen Prozess.* Frankfurt aM: Suhrkamp.

Evans, R. (2015) *The Third Reich in History and Memory.* London: Little, Brown.

Federn, P. (1936) On the Distinction Between Healthy and Normal Narcissism. *Imago* 22: 5–39. In Weiss, E. (ed.) *Ego Psychology and the Psychoses.* Karnac, 1977, pp. 323–64.

Freud, S. (1921) *Group Psychology and the Analysis of the Ego. The Standard Edition of the Complete Psychological Works of Sigmund Freud* 18: 65–143.

Freud, S. (1923[1922]) Two Encyclopaedia Articles: (A) Psycho-Analysis. *The Standard Edition of the Complete Psychological Works of Sigmund Freud* 18: 235–54.

Freud, S. (1923) *The Ego and the Id. The Standard Edition of the Complete Psychological Works of Sigmund Freud* 19: 1–66.

Freud, S. (1933[1932]) *New Introductory Lectures on Psycho-Analysis. The Standard Edition of the Complete Psychological Works of Sigmund Freud* 22: 1–182.

Frie, R. (2011) Irreducible Cultural Contexts: German-Jewish Experience, Identity, and Trauma in a Bilingual Analysis. *International Journal of Psychoanalytic Self Psychology* 6: 136–58.

Friedländer, S. (1978) *History and Psychoanalysis: an Inquiry into the Possibilities and Limits of Psychohistory.* New York/London: Holmes & Meier Publishers.

Frosh, S. (2010) *Psychoanalysis Outside the Clinic: Interventions in Psychosocial Studies.* Houndmills: Palgrave Macmillan.

Grubrich-Simitis, I. (1984) From Concretism to Metaphor – Thoughts on Some Theoretical and Technical Aspects of the Psychoanalytic Work with Children of Holocaust Survivors. *The Psychoanalytic Study of the Child* 39: 301–19.

Habermas, J. (1986a) A Kind of Settlement of Damages: The Apologetic Tendencies in German Historical Writing. *Die Zeit*, July 11; English translation in Knowlton, J. and Gates, T. (eds. and translators) *Forever in the Shadow of Hitler? Original Documents of the Historikerstreit, the Controversy Concerning the Singularity of the Holocaust.* Atlantic Highlands, New Jersey: Humanities Press, 1993, pp. 34–44; extended version in Habermas, J. One Sort of Compensation: Apologetic Tendencies in German Historiography. In *The New Conservatism: Cultural Criticism and the Historians' Debate.* London: Polity Press, 1989 pp. 212–28.

Habermas, J. (1986b) On the Public Use of History. *Die Zeit*, November 7. In Habermas, J. *The New Conservatism: Cultural Criticism and the Historians' Debate.* London: Polity Press, 1989, pp. 229–40.

Habermas, J. (1988) *On the Logic of the Social Sciences*. London: Polity Press, 1990.
Habermas, J. (1989) *The New Conservatism: Cultural Criticism and the Historians' Debate*. London: Polity Press.
Habermas, J. (1998) *The Inclusion of the Other: Studies in Political Theory*. Cambridge, MA: Massachusetts Institute of Technology; Cambridge: Polity Press, 1999.
Hinshelwood, R. D. (1986) The Psychotherapist's Role in a Large Psychiatric Institution. *Psychoanalytic Psychotherapy* 2: 207–215
Hopper, E. (1996) The Social Unconscious in Clinical Work. In *The Social Unconscious: Selected Papers*. London: Jessica Kingsley, 2003, pp. 126–61.
Kershaw, I. (2011) *The End: Hitler's Germany, 1944–45*. London: Allen Lane.
Klein, M. (1940) Mourning and Its Relation to Manic-Depressive States. In *The Writings of Melanie Klein*, vol. 1. London: Hogarth and the Institute of Psychoanalysis, 1975, pp. 344–69.
Kohte-Meyer, I. (1994) 'Ich bin fremd, so wie ich bin.' – Migrationserleben, Ich-Identität und Neurose. *Praxis der Kinderpsychologie und Kinderpsychiatrie* 43: 253–9.
Kohte-Meyer, I. (2000) A Derailed Dialogue: Unexpected Difficulties in the Psychoanalytic Work with Patients from East Germany. *Psychoanalytic Review* 87:417–28.
Kohut, H. (1971) *The Analysis of the Self: A Systematic Approach to the Psychoanalytic Treatment of Narcissistic Personality Disorders*. New York: International Universities Press.
Kohut, T. A. (2012) *A German Generation: An Experiential History of the Twentieth Century*. New Haven/London: Yale University Press.
Mancia, M. and Meltzer, D. (1981) Ego Ideal Functions and the Psychoanalytical Process. *International Journal of Psychoanalysis* 62: 243–9.
McNeill, W. (1995) *Keeping Together in Time: Dance and Drill in Human History*. Cambridge, MA: Harvard University Press.
Mitscherlich, M. (1987) *Errinerungsarbeit zur Psychoanalyse der Unfähigkeit zu trauern*. Frankfurt aM: Fischer.
Parin, P. (1977) Das Ich und die Anpassungs-Mechanismen. *Psyche – Zeitschrift für Psychoanalyse* 31(6):481–515.
Pick, D. (2012) *The Pursuit of the Nazi Mind: Hitler, Hess and the Analysts*. Oxford: Oxford University Press.
Roper, L. (1994) *Oedipus and the Devil: Witchcraft, Religion and Sexuality in Early Modern Europe: Witchcraft, Sexuality and Religion, 1500–1700*. London/New York: Routledge.

Rosenfeld, H. (1964) On the Psychopathology of Narcissism a Clinical Approach. *International Journal of Psychoanalysis* 45: 332–7.

Rothe, K. (2009) *Das (Nicht-)Sprechen über die Judenvernichtung: Psychische Weiterwirkingen des Holocaust in mehreren Generationen nicht-jüdischer Deutscher.* Giessen: Psychozial Verlag.

Rothe, K. (2012) Anti-semitism in Germany Today and the Intergenerational Transmission of Guilt and Shame. *Psychoanalysis, Culture, and Society* 17(1): 16–34.

Rustin, M. (1991) *The Good Society and the Inner World: Psychoanalysis, Politics and Culture.* London/New York: Verso.

Scott, J. (2012) The Incommensurability of Psychoanalysis and History. *History and Theory* 51: 63–83.

Segal, H. (1995) From Hiroshima to the Gulf War and After: Socio-Political Expressions of Ambivalence. In *Psychoanalysis, Literature and War: Papers 1972–1995.* London/New York: Routledge, 1997, pp. 157–68.

Strachey, J. (1934) The Nature of the Therapeutic Action of Psycho-Analysis. *International Journal of PsychoAnalysis* 15: 127–59.

Wirth, H.-J. (2009) *Narcissism and Power: Psychoanalysis of Mental Disorders in Politics.* Giessen: Psychosozial-Verlag.

4

Delusional Enemies

In his book on Nazi anti-Semitism, Philippe Burrin (2005) makes the point that the Nazis progressively, then violently, excluded the Jews from German citizenship, the German nation, German culture and the German people, ultimately aiming to extinguish them as a people. The driver of this finally total exclusion, he argues, was the perceived difference between Jews and Germans. Difference was increasingly exploited, and the Nazis used it to incite anxiousness among the German people of a difference that could spread and contaminate them with its foreign qualities.

> For modern anti-Semitism, particularly in its national level and, above all, its racist variants, constructed an image of the Jews as the absolute opposite and total negative of the identity that it was itself defending and championing. Their physical, moral, and cultural characteristics were represented by a dualist system that placed them, term for term, in opposition to the characteristics of the anti-Semites: nomads vs those with a fixed seat of habitation, gold versus blood, lies versus truth, cowardice versus heroism...Religion was declared too noble for the Jews and was denied them. (p. 25)

Similarly, Alon Confino (2014) argues that 'For Nazis and other Germans, "the Jew" represented different and often contradictory things' (p. 30): rich capitalists, greedy bankers, communism, conspiracy, the devil, enemies of truth, un-German blood. There was, however, an 'internal unity', in 'the idea that the Jews were the creators of an evil modernity that soiled present-day Germany' (p. 31; see also Zimmermann 2008 for a thorough documentation of the process of exclusion).

But what goes unexamined is the origin of this difference. For Burrin, the Nazis exploited Jewish characteristics, turning them into the opposite of German characteristics, in order to intensify and idealize the latter. The contrivance of these manoeuvres seems obvious in the absurd measures taken against the Jews, some local, some national, such as Jews could not be employed in public administration, be jockeys, use Jewish names in telegrams, display Christian symbols at Christmas (see extensive list in Confino, pp. 51, 101–8). The contrivance was built on putatively observable, demonstrable features of Jewishness, no matter how exaggerated, caricatured and misused. One could know a Jew was a Jew and then treat him or her appallingly.

In contrast to this line of thinking, I argue that the claim that the features of Jews were manifestly different from Germans was created as a defence against the unconscious significance of the Jew as identical to other Germans. The Jew was created in the German mind in order to function as a repository of a dread of sameness. In order to act as a repository for projection, the Jew had to be the same as any other German, recreated as different. In this respect, the Jew was different from other persecuted groups. Groups subjected to sterilization and euthanasia were consciously to be cleansed from the German 'race' because they were deemed inferior. By contrast, in an unconscious process, the Jewish people were an ideal recast as an alter-ideal that contradicted the German ideal. It had to be expunged: its identity humiliated and erased, its inclusion in the history of the Germans eliminated. The ideal Germany was to be restored by removing the ideal of the Jew (Arlow 1992; Confino 2014, p. 80).

In its detachment from reality, the relationship of German to Jew was psychotic. The psychosis included a confusion of (internal) phantasy and (external) reality, with a loss of secure empirical footing for individual and social mentalities; a fragmentation of the object (the Jew), who lost personhood and the capacity for relationship; a dread of a menace from everywhere—inner, outer and outside the time and space of reassuring empirical reality—and a paranoid need of an external (externalized) object as a repository against which the German subject could defend itself, as if against an external threat.

Historians have recognized that there was something peculiar about difference in Nazi anti-Semitism. Burrin speaks of an apocalyptic relationship between German and Jew, suggesting that a mystical rebirth of the German people and nation hung on bringing it to a final conclusion (pp. 47–50, 74). Confino argues that, to understand the Holocaust, we have to understand the Nazi imagination, in which a new Germany would arise as a 'world without Jews'. Historians of an earlier generation, dedicated to a scientific history based on detailed empirical study, such as Martin Broszat (1970) and Hans Mommsen (1983), speak of a Nazi social organization built in an atmosphere that one might call a thrall. But as a psychotic delusion, German rebirth was equated—concretely—to the extinction of a phantasized menace. The extinction of the Jews guaranteed the recovery and possession of a lost ideal. It was the sameness—the identicality of the Jews as a people to the Germans, not their difference—which grounded the extreme anti-Semitism of the Nazi imagination.

I want to survey the history of this peculiar relationship in the work of Martin Broszat, Hans Mommsen, Saul Friedländer, Ian Kershaw and Alon Confino. They provide the historical background for understanding the peculiarly Nazi environment and its fascination for the German people. The Final Solution developed in this atmosphere of the Nazi period, created by Hitler as a chiliastic, charismatic leader, and permeated by a thrall in which the future would concretely bring the rebirth of the German people and the German nation.

The Historical Realization of the Nazi Dream

Martin Broszat (1970) makes a case for a peculiar bond between Hitler as leader of the Nazi Party and the people who, in the mass, supported a personal devotion to him: not as the leader whose diktats coerced the people, rather as the embodiment in his person of a 'thrall'—something akin to Ian Kershaw's 'working towards the Führer', in which underlings and the people were drawn into acting as if with Hitler's approval and empowerment (Kershaw 1999). Broszat says that Hitler was not the speaker who articulated an ideology, but the first and only realization of a utopian National Socialist (NS) world view.

> In distinguishing the Hitler movement from other ideologies, it is well-founded to emphasize that National Socialism was not primarily an ideological and programmatic, but a charismatic, movement, the world view of which was embodied through the leader Hitler and would have lost all power of integration without him. Hitler was ... not the speaker of an idea ... ; rather, the utopian NS-world view overall gained reality and specificity first through Hitler's person. (p. 399)

For Broszat, Hitler's authority—the authority of the NS state—took effect through a confusion between responsiveness to the material and social conditions of a middle class, which felt exploited and proletarianized, and a utopian illusion of a future that seemed to realize these material and social interests, but was actually, in its vagueness and pandering, pure illusion. National regeneration, mobilized by anti-Semitism identified with anti-Bolshevism, would overcome conspiracy, exploitation and social-cultural proletarianization; and a '*Lebensraum-Utopie*' would prefigure a 'peoples' social regeneration', as a 'projection into the future of a fully independent, autarkic territorial big power' (p. 403). The key phrase is 'projection into the future': the continuous re-creation of possibility as the fuel and the form of illusory fulfilment, in both positive and negative forms: positive as the ideal always projected ahead of realization; negative in the absolute denunciation to the point of extinction of any deviation from participation in this projected ideal. (p. 406)

Broszat aims to historicize the Nazi period, bringing it into ordinary historical discourse based on historical methodology and evidence, but his view needs to be supplemented. He groups together measures against 'Jews, the mentally ill, the asocial, etc.' (p. 405). In doing so, he skirts around the specificity of the 'final solution' (though he does refer to 'singularity'; Broszat and Friedländer 1988, pp. 101, 102, 103). The people who must be erased were—had to be—also an ideal, not in any common-sense meaning, but as perfection. 'The obsession with the Jews was a result not of a belief in the Jews as weak and insignificant [as it was, say, for the disabled and sick] but, on the contrary, of the belief in their awesome powers' (Confino, p. 80) and of an underlying intimacy and entwining between Germans and Jews, which had to be broken by violence characterized by mockery and humiliation (110, 124). Psychoanalytically, the ideal refers to the ego-ideal, an internal object or agency arising from narcissism, garnering indisputable authority, eliciting an unending yearning and evoking a desire to merge with it or eliminate it (Chasseguet-Smirgel 1985a, b). Eliminating a non-ideal object, as in the euthanasia programme directed at groups deemed inferior, aimed to cleanse the blood-stock, but could not redeem a threatened ideal. Only erasing an alter-ideal—the Jews—could regenerate the Nazi perpetrators.

Broszat (Broszat and Friedländer 1988) posits a scientific history based on historical facticity, aiming to establish what counts as a historical moment and to put anything else aside as a constraint on scientific enquiry. In the project of historicization, the Nazi period must be included within historical understanding based on a 'principle of critical, enlightening historical understanding (*Verstehen*)' (p. 87), by which he means finding an objectifying distance and a subjective closeness, leading to insight in a 'rational comprehension of this period' (pp. 89, 101). One could then explain, for example, racism, as if historical continuity could replace interpretation. Such historical understanding, he argues, must be able to include a 'mythical form of…remembrance', driven by pain and mourning of the Jews as victims, claimed by them as a prerogative (p. 89), but the historian must guard against 'a form of memory which acts to coarsen historical recollection' (p. 94). Historiography is, in Broszat's view, constrained by a blockade (p. 92), and '[h]istoricization is an attempt to break up and dissolve [moral, philosophical and political]… stereotypes, embarrassment, constraints and over-generalizations' (p. 98).

Among these obstructions to historicization is the tendency to reveal backwards the history that led up to the Holocaust, rather than forwards without preconceptions, in line with historical methodology.

The German historian too will certainly accept that Auschwitz – due to its singular significance – functions in retrospect as the central event of the Nazi period. Yet *qua* scientist and scholar, he cannot readily accept that Auschwitz also be made, after the fact, into the cardinal point, the hinge on which the entire factual complex of historical events of the Nazi period turns. (p. 103)

Thus, for example, the extinction of the Jews could take place because it was a side issue, not because people actively suppressed their knowledge (p. 102). Friedänder presses Broszat to state unambiguously his 'plea' for historicization, which his generation of historians claimed was legitimate scientific historical methodology, now constrained by a moralistic scepticism among a younger generation of post-war historians towards what they saw as relativizing Nazism, or even a 'shift of focus' (p. 104). Broszat relies on the idea of a self-evident scientific facticity, while Friedländer suspects the idea of scientific facticity of masking a pre-selection of the areas for just such a scientific enquiry. He suspects further that, over time, the 'normal aspects of the picture of the Nazi epoch will, of necessity, grow in dimension and importance [retaining] just enough elements of the nature of the regime to make them plausible' (p. 126).[1]

Hans Mommsen, like Broszat, advocated a scientific history in which the historical picture would arise from detailed scholarship. For Mommsen, the final solution arose from the un-co-ordinated structure of the system, loss of authority, corruption of resistance, no focus of grievance, brutal and cynical terror, which undermined civilized norms that resist Darwinian struggle (Mommsen 1981, pp. 186, 187). Like Broszat, Mommsen also saw Hitler's 'chiliastic' leadership with respect to the final solution to be the 'ideological and political author', whose 'utopian programme' was 'translated…into a concrete strategy' (1983, pp. 237, 239). Hitler 'avoided any attempt to confront his ideological dream-world with political and social reality' (p. 238); he attempted 'not to be aware of the facts or [supressed] his knowledge [Verdrängen - repression in the German text] as part of a 'collective repression' (p. 238); 'he was the slave of his own public prophecies…At its root was his manic idea that, as bearer of the "National Socialist Idea", he must not allow himself to contradict his own statements' (p. 239). He speaks of a 'near psychotic political sensitivity' (1981, p. 185); of 'psychological mechanisms [that] prevented the national socialist elite from facing up to the escalation of criminality [and if so for them, how much more so for ordinary Germans]' (1983, p. 252). He attributes to Himmler the determination to encompass a delusion within historical actuality by realizing Hitler's prophecy, embodied in his 'timeless programme' of the extinction of the Jews within Hitler's lifetime (pp. 251–2).

Despite the appeal for a scientific, empirical historiography, with its scepticism towards any suggestion of a focus that is revealed in the historical record, rather than caused by it, Broszat and Mommsen do suggest an overarching ideological and psychological dimension. At the pole of such thinking is Friedländer's 'redemptive anti-Semitism' (1997, pp. 73–112). Here is an ideology that informs the Nazi project, even if it occurred step-by-step to the final solution. In an 'imagination of a world without Jews', the German people lived in a world moving towards its ideal (Confino, Friedländer). Even Broszat bases his argument on the illusion of the ever-future and the chiliastic character of Hitler rule, a view that calls out, not only for the empathic understanding that he advocates but also for a grounding in a science of interpretation.

When Mommsen speaks to the projection of possibility into the future, the cogency of his analysis needs the theory of the ego-ideal. The Nazi regime infused the German people with an enthralling sense of belonging to an idealized future—a future that must always remain a future, an illusion of ideality and a delusion of magnificence: a psychotic world in which reality conveyed the delusion as if it were a reality. From such a grounding, one can begin to understand the character of a regime that fostered a vague, but positive future, and determined, but negative, measures against the people who must not survive, if Germany was to arise anew. In this psychotic world, the Jews as a people provided the necessary identicality to the idealized German people to promote irreversibly the necessity to eliminate them. Reality in this world was created as if it were a perception, despite its not being received through the senses.

The Dread of Sameness

I am claiming that, while we normally think that we stick together with others like us and that we exclude others whose difference provokes antipathy towards them, antipathy is rooted in sameness rather than in difference. Consciously, we exclude others who are different, but unconsciously, we dread sameness, and avoid it by creating delusional differences (Figlio 2012). Hatred drives the projection of these delusional differences into the other that it creates, there to be exterminated. Overt differences, to which the delusional differences can be attached, mask the delusional projection and the source of hatred in sameness.

The fear of difference in the Jew as a foreign body covered a dread of an indwelling alien presence, ultimately a primal unease (to be explored in the next chapter), which tarnished the idea of the people as a unity, complete, homogeneous and perfect in itself. For Ernst Rudolf Huber, the leading legislative and political theorist of National Socialism, writing in 1937,

> 'The political Volk ... is determined as a historical phenomenon by the principles of unity and totality. Only as unity and totality is the people a political actuality... The freedom and self-rule of the individual, which followed from the political thinking [in the 'liberalistic' era; P.L.], destroyed the inner unity of the community and broke up every integral order ...'
> The principles of unity and totality presuppose ... that inside the 'unity of the people' only 'organic limbs' can exist, not however 'enemy groups and classes ...' The political behaviour of the people is nothing other than the expression of the inherent striving 'for self-formation and self-presentation, for the deepening and renewal of its type'. (Quoted by Longerich 2007, p. 46, with his insertion, P.L.)

The Nazi regime fed on, and developed, the idea of a *Volksgemeinschaft*, a homogeneous people, which transcended the differences of ordinary reality (Bajohr and Wildt 2009), and sought to create a public space that incorporated all opinion while suppressing all individual expression or debate (Longerich 2007, pp. 23–54). The unity and totality of the people meant absolute submissiveness to the leadership in a homogeneous, collective culture with a collective mind, a *Volksmeinung*; and this fundamental character applied to the 'Jewish Question' (p. 47). The 'public' view of the Jew in the *Volksgemeinschaft* is a version of the imagination of a world without Jews (Confino). In my argument, the *Volksgemeinschaft* also stoked an idealization of a people 'working towards the Führer', drawn towards merger with the group ego-ideal in a delusional phantasy of oneness. It should be understood, along with its historical embeddedness, as psychotic: not marginalized as a psychopathy with no relevance to historical scholarship, but as a mechanism of social and individual existence in a created alternative to external, perceptual reality: a factitious reality in which 'empirical' data, such as small differences, are delusionally fabricated in order to annihilate them in a continuous renovation of the *Volksgemeinschaft*.

In his detailed analysis of the German public, Longerich (2007) speaks of the decisive intention of the Nazis to transcend 'fine distinctions' of habitus by a *Volksgemeinschaft*. The 'reports' of observations on the German population, generated by the regime, 'confirmed' the existence of the 'Jewish Question' with its anti-Semitic stereotypes in the thinking of the Regime (p. 47). These 'fine distinctions' suggest Freud's 'narcissism of small differences', in which neighbours harboured the most persistent grievances against each other. '[P]recisely communities with adjoining territories, and related to each other in other ways as well … are engaged in constant feuds and in ridiculing each other' (Freud 1930, p. 114). Freud went on to say that

> the Jewish people, scattered everywhere, have rendered the most useful services to the civilisations of the countries that have been their hosts; but unfortunately all the massacres of the Jews in the Middle Ages did not suffice to make that period more peaceful and secure for their Christian fellows. When once the Apostle Paul had posited universal love between men as the foundation of his Christian community, extreme intolerance on the part of Christendom towards those who remained outside it became the inevitable consequence. (p. 114)

The clear implication was that Jews provided the 'neighbour' that the host community could vilify, exclude and annihilate on behalf of its own coherence; and they provided it for any community. Without such a contribution, new neighbours would erupt from imminent rifts inside the host community. As universal and eternal neighbours, Jews might be different from their hosts, but as Freud says, 'often in an indefinable way' (1939, p. 91). I think it is reasonable to extrapolate 'indefinable': Freud implies that the antipathy of the narcissism of small differences does not arise as a consequence of difference, but in the creation of difference. The problem is not managing difference, but managing an endogenous unease in human society through creating repositories for delusional hatred.

I will limit my analysis of small differences to German anti-Semitism, and begin with the transformations and outcomes of narcissism, specifically the implication that narcissism intensifies as the overt differences between people decrease, producing a 'narcissism of small differences'. At the heart of it lies an unease that must be projected. It is not that objects—ethnic identities—pre-exist, but that they are created in the process of projection. The differences that spark violence are delusions, fostered by projection: that is implicit in the idea that the group is an ego-ideal for its members (Anzieu 1975; Chasseguet-Smirgel 1985a, pp. 76–93), whose demands are most immediately satisfied by violence against the non-ideal, demeaned other. It seems that to be left with oneself, whether as an individual or as a group, is hateful; to be left with an other very like oneself is nearly as hateful, but it offers a target for a ballistic, projective attack as a way out. To *create* such an other most effectively eliminates inner hatred, because it can be done anytime, anywhere, as an omnipotent phantasy. To retreat into an enclave in which, externally, one appears to act rationally, while maintaining, internally, a delusional world, creates an imaginary but stable structure.

In my view, this kind of psychic structure, stabilized in pieces of perceptual reality, underlies Confino's thesis, in which a world without Jews is imagined and linked into a perceptual world of apparently rational, progressive exclusion of Jews from German society. It was enacted in an immense profusion of legislation and 'informational' propaganda, including news sheets and wall posters that pervaded everyday life (Kaplan 2009). They shaped an experience in an atmosphere of a world without Jews. A letter from a soldier brings out the sense of the unexceptional experience of anticipating such a world. 'Hitler's words are becoming true, when he said at the beginning of the war: if Judaism thinks to instigate another war in Europe, then this war will be not its victory but the end of Judaism in Europe' (quoted by Confino, p. 186).

The Instability of the Narcissistic Ego

Beneath the imagination of a world without Jews lies the illusory state of mind that accompanies narcissism. The more difference diminishes, the more primitive states of mind erupt, including the twinned illusion of omnipotence and helplessness. The immediate corollary of narcissistic eruption is violence, which, in a moment of omnipotence, projects an illusion of difference and helplessness, consolidates them in the targeted enemy and vanquishes them, thereby achieving a stabilization, albeit transiently. Confino makes the point, also psychoanalytically valid, that violence is itself a form of unconscious, publicly enacted, hatred, which has to be repeated in order continually to avoid the guilt that consciousness would bring with it (pp. 134, 136, 139, 140, 168; also, see Freud 1914b). Perhaps the best example, in Freudian terms, of the disjunction between conscious perception of difference, and the unconscious phantasy of sameness that provokes hatred, is that between male and female. It was on this difference, as a sign of castration and the consequent 'taboo of virginity', that Freud (1918[1917]) based the concept of the narcissism of small differences.

In my extension of Freud's account, male and female differ in many aspects, but only the phallic aspect tranches upon the narcissistic core of identity. The penis has attracted impassioned attention because it is a visible male possession, while the invisible, illusory phallus, hidden inside, is the unrecognized source of the passion. Like the delusional enemy, the perceived difference between male and female is also a creation of a difference between the idealization of self (male, nation, *Volksgemeinschaft*) and the denigration of the other (female) as the repository of projection.

The explicit taboo of virginity in some cultures and the implicit taboo in others enact a hatred between the sexes as an avoidance of two, paired, anxieties: that of the female's phallic deficiency and that of the male's phallic insecurity, exacerbated by fear of her castrating retaliation. But, for Freud, a taboo is a defence against a wish (Freud 1912–1913, pp. 69–70). So the horror of castration opposes a wish to be castrated in order to merge with the mother (Anon [Ferenczi] 1933, p. 389). The Oedipal wish to replace father's union with mother—countered by the castration threat—is the wish, not just to enter mother, not just to possess her, but to be at the origination of himself—to be the mother in whom he emerged. Castration horror at the sight of the female would then act as a defence, aiming to maintain the difference between male and female, adult and foetus, against the wish to undo their difference (cf. Gabbard 1993). In fact, difference reassures the male, because the threat now appears to emanate from external object, not as a wish from inside, and can be met by the enacted taboo of virginity or by the overt or covert denigration of the female. Difference undergirds existence itself. The shock of the female-as-castrated-male is a repudiation of the drive to move right through the female to the grandiose, omnipotent phantasy of self-creation.

The drive to be the same is a feature of narcissism, which forces its way into all human relationships because it is there from the outset of psychic life, and remains as a pole of psychic life opposite to external reality. For Freud, the first object for the ego is itself, and from this standpoint, narcissism is an achievement in which the ego comes into being for itself and in itself (Freud 1914a). But it comes into being in a tension between being an object for itself and being replaced by an external object. There is, therefore, a rift in the psyche from the moment one can speak of there being a psyche. In relating to an object, the ego suffers the violation of its narcissism by the external world. The virulent hatred that erupts from narcissism would be quenched only by the extermination of the object that unsettles this narcissism, and even that could not wholly satisfy, because the needed object, into which imperfection had been projected, would then have vanished. In other words, narcissism lives in a world of phantasy, which contact with reality can only contaminate, but which remains necessary.

Thus, there is conflict in narcissism. Difference reassures because it fixes what would be a deeper foreboding of depletion even to extinction. In the world of narcissism, objects are replicas that steal the essence of the self. I offer a clinical vignette that shows this conflict between ego and object in males.

> A man reported a dream, in which he was watching a little boy playing in a fenced children's playground in a park. As he watched the child play, he realised that the child was himself as a child. Since he was both the child and the man who was watching, there could be only one penis [one, concentrated, narcissistic self]. To whom did it belong? Father and son were reduced to the single penis that joined them: a narcissistic emblem that was the marker of both their sameness and their difference.

In this one-penis phantasy, father and son are separated by the difference between the generations, but the difference is eroded because they share the organ on which castration anxiety focuses (also see Isaacs 1940, p. 288, for a case with brothers). To the narcissistic ego, the object is a replica of itself, and, to the extent that the object continues to exist in its own right, it can only signify extinction of the ego. Freud says that the phallic woman reassures the male that there is no castration, because she is the same as he; but as a woman, she also represents an unstable delusion of difference along with the wish to be the same. At a primitive level, it refers to the anxiety of extinction in assimilating to, and differentiating from, an object (Figlio 2000, pp. 61–72, 78–82; Figlio 2010; Freud 1915).

Jokl (1997, pp. 25–48) presents a clinical vignette that portrays self-creation reinforced by the drive to extinguish the usurping object.

> Volker is the son of fanatical NS intellectuals, father having the rank of SS-*Sturmbannführer*. Volker attended an officer-training boarding school for sons of higher party members. Upon release at age 15, as the front collapsed, he volunteered for a machine gun unit to defend Berlin against the Red Army. He later found work in West Germany, and eventually found himself in a circle of anti-Nazis, where he began a new life without any conscious connection to his past. In analysis, in a dream-like state, he reported seeing a severely injured man left to die. Another man comes, shoots him repeatedly, but then returns and hefts the dead man onto his shoulder and walks towards the horizon, the two now bound together. Volker recognizes both men as himself. (pp. 33–4)

In a later scenario, he has become an evil, roaming animal, part of a murderous forest; then, later [there is] a monstrous animal in a round, dark hole, with light at the end. The animal is totally isolated…life is outside. Several times he creeps to the exit and catches a woman to stroke him. Then he kills her. Her anxiety is his satisfaction. That brings him alive, but he must kill her again and again; otherwise she would seem to be a mirror in which he saw himself. (pp. 40–1)

Here is the Nazi mind trying to get free of an internal catastrophe of narcissistic collapse by creating an other in which to carry it away and in which to extinguish it by murder. The murderer and the murdered are parts of the self, and the murder must be repeated because the other must continue to live in order to be the repository for projection of the delusional enemy. It is a peculiar projection, called 'projective identification' (Figlio 2013; Hinshelwood 1991; Klein 1946; Spillius and O'Shaughnessy 2012) because it includes part of the ego: in this case, a concretized, objectified part of the Nazi identity.

In a case reported by Rhode (1994), a patient spoke about

someone he knows who is in prison—and who suffers from an unusual bone disease. The man … appears to have two skeletons—or, rather, one full skeleton and another adjacent one that seems to shadow the first skeleton and to exist only in bits. The fragments of the second incomplete skeleton keep growing … He believes that … at the time he was conceived … [a]n inseminated ovum in part began to split; a pair of twins should have been formed; but the process was somehow arrested. The other twin never reached life, but its residue, the growing bits of bone, continue to exist as a disabling physical reproach within the twin who lives – or partially lives … He now finds himself in a prison, both actual and symbolic. (p. 42)

This image captures well his patient's view of himself. For Rhode, there is a 'foetal consciousness that is vulnerable to binary division' (1994, p. 37) at birth, in the separation of the baby from a mother who, even in the separated infant's imagination, will replace it with another. But the binary division is more powerful at the threshold between what Melanie Klein called the 'paranoid-schizoid position' and the 'depressive position'

(Hinshelwood 1991). Here, the ego in relation to an object sets off a catastrophic change. In the primitive paranoid-schizoid world, the psyche lives in an omnipotent illusion of fantastic good and bad 'part-objects', split from each other and projected into the object world, which then becomes idealized or retaliatory and threatening (Rhode 1994, p. 37).

Twins and Doubles

In Kleinian theory, there are two modes of thought—the paranoid-schizoid, in which the ego is threatened with extinction by the replica other; the depressive, in which the ego gives itself over to protect the other. 'To be a finite human, as opposed to being a psychopathic god' (Rhode 1994, p. 37) is to be able to recognize the urge to project a psychotic part of the psyche. The patient who thought of the prisoner with the double skeleton is reporting a paranoid-schizoid experience of being inhabited by a twin who was not born, and who, as a paranoid projection, has been killed so that he could live. The depressive version, in which he would live because his mother gave birth to him and cared for him, despite the risk to her life, has been invaded by a paranoid phantasy, in which he is haunted by a twin who wants his life back, or threatens to invade him with chaotic fragments.

The full skeleton as a scaffold for a full self is threatened by an undeveloped skeleton, as a scaffold-self that was expelled by the full self. The violence of this process, provoked by an absolute intolerance of thought, would produce a psychotic world, with an ominous cloud of either 'bad objects', or 'bizarre objects', composed of bits of ego encasing bits of delusion, surrounded the non-psychotic ego. These objects cannot be quelled by including them in rational, historical processes (Bion 1957, 1962).

Siblings are similar. Juliet Mitchell (2003) explores the theme of the sibling as an alternative self. She draws a distinction between lateral and vertical relationships; that is, sibling versus parent-child relationships. She follows Freud in seeing early object love as an overflow of narcissism. In the narcissism of the child's love, its sibling depletes its narcissism, and thereby becomes a threat to its existence. A sibling, like a double for Otto

Rank, or a twin in Rhode's analysis, is a preserve of narcissism stolen from the ego by a hated object that has to be eliminated for the self to survive. For Mitchell, the sameness between siblings constitutes an essential ambivalence, in which a threat to existence shadows sibling love. One sibling is born because the other dies. In this concrete, unsymbolized world, a sibling is a twin, a twin is a double, a double is oneself extracted from oneself. Uncannily, a sibling is both a comforting reassurance and at the same moment the thief of one's being. Twins are the objects of ritual, in order to neutralize their power (Blok 2001, pp. 50, 122–3, 264n; Firth 1966; Freud 1919; Girard 1988, pp. 54–59, 61–63, 75, 252; Rank 1914).

Ambivalence lurks inside narcissism. The sibling, and, more specifically, the twin, brings out the relationship between decreasing psychosocial distance and increasing narcissistic intensity. Now we can move directly to the relationship between violence and sameness. This relationship has been addressed most directly from mythological and anthropological angles by Anton Blok (2001) and René Girard (1988), and historically by Jacoby (2011). Girard, like Mitchell, argues that Freud privileged the parent-child relationship and as a result, only dimly recognized the primitive layer of what he calls 'reciprocal relationships' (what Mitchell calls 'lateral relationships'; fraternal for Jacoby). Girard and Jacoby are concerned with a theory of social organization, while Mitchell deals with the psyche, but their thinking heads in a similar direction: the parents and the Oedipus complex are secondary formations to a primal level at which existence itself is at stake.[2]

In this primal narcissistic state, the subject is always threatened by the very existence of an object, because that object is its replica—the self, itself, stolen and displaced into the other. Such a state is psychotic, in that the object world as normal, perceived reality vanishes. In classical psychoanalytic terms, it would be a merger of ego and ego-ideal, with a collapse of the differences of gender and generations, as in the single penis phantasy. The ego-ideal is not attached to reality: it is a narcissistic agency, a preserve of primary narcissism. An identification of the ego with the ego-ideal would be manic, an illusory world of omnipotence (Chasseguet-Smirgel 1985a). In Kleinian and Bionic thinking, one could also see it in terms of massive projective identification, in which the object is appropriated by the subject, creating a confusional world divorced from the reality that relating to the object world would normally produce.

Narcissism and Hatred

If the nuclear core is narcissism with its associated hatred, then the difference between subject and object, which we usually associate with hatred, would in fact conceal the narcissistic urge to assimilate the object, and the dread of sameness that follows. That dread would be fastened to an external object by projection. What is difficult to accept is that the projection aims to dispel, not just the sameness, but the *wish* for it—that, underlying the projection, is the wish to have the qualities of the other, to be like it, to be the *same* as it; to *be* it. Projection not only expels what is already present in the self and unwanted: it creates a confusion between created unwanted parts of the self and external reality in the process of projection itself. Although Freud speaks of an external reality, he adds, that 'the original "reality ego" ... separate[s] off a part of its own self, which it projects into the external world and feels as hostile. After this new arrangement, the ... ego-subject coincides with pleasure, and the external world with unpleasure' (Freud 1915, p. 136). In the limit, the differences are not already there, as fixed points, but are products of phantasy. Far from evoking hatred, the overt differences are reassuring obstructions to undifferentiation.

My point is that difference has to be established. There is no preexistent ego and object. They are mutually created in projection and introjection. In this respect, my thesis seems to depart from the Kleinian roots of my thinking. I don't see it that way. I think there is, in the limit, a primal psychic 'position' (Klein) in which one cannot distinguish defence of the ego from a primordial phase in the development of the ego. I believe I am following José Bleger's (1967/2013, 1974) theory of a primal undifferentiation of ego and object, good and bad, which is condensed into an 'agglutinated nucleus'. There is some similarity between the agglutinated nucleus and what Bion (1957, p. 62) calls an 'agglomeration', which is composed of minute fragments of ego and the object it has invaded by massive projective identification, producing a torrent of 'β elements'. These elements are compressed into a semblance of reality to form the basis of apparent ideas and speech, which lack inner coherence and are, therefore, essentially inarticulate. Bleger's agglutinated nucleus, however, also refers to an earlier undifferentiated core (what he calls the glischro-caryic position; 1974, p. 22), in which parts of ego and object, good and bad, are mixed in an ambiguous state, not a confusion caused by extreme projective identification. Such a nuclear agglomerated state, normally consolidated into good and bad ego/objects in the paranoid-schizoid position, threatens to invade and internally decimate the ego.

Projection of the agglutinated nucleus can replace the dread of internal occupation by psychotic forces with persecution by an external enemy, and a semblance of normality can be maintained by stabilizing this irrational 'organization' in a social structure. The difference that justifies hatred and conflict is such a stabilizing structure. The parties to this hatred sign up to an unconscious contract to maintain this difference as a defensive system organized around paranoid-schizoid splitting and projection, rather than risk a descent into catastrophic undifferentiation. It is a stabilized complex structure that harmonizes with external situations, and achieves a degree of conscious, rational status, but it remains unstable and needing reinforcement through recreating difference, followed by denigration and attack.

Religious and Ethnic Hatred

I have argued that we don't detect differences in the other, and then hate that other for these differences. Instead, we create the other as a psychic reality. The manifest differences between male and female are a matter of indifference; the virtual differences are immensely important. The sight of the female genital confirms the reality of castration only within a phantasy of castration. In this psychic reality, the issue is not the observation that a woman has no penis, but the phantasy that she has been castrated, and is, therefore, vengeful. The castration anxiety of the male is intensified by the feared retaliation for the hatred that castrated her. The phallic woman, for Freud, is a delusional annulment of the phantasy of the castrated woman and of her retaliation. Sometimes this psychic reality can be projected into and held in perceived reality, in which difference is reassuring; sometimes it is imposed on perceived reality, more in the order of a hallucination. Hatred aims to seal this psychic reality in the other, and to destroy it there. Similarly, in Jacoby's thesis, fratricide stabilizes the more fundamental dread of women by holding it in a phallic, oedipal phantasy. The fight for the woman and for the masculine penis with which to possess her externalizes the dread, which is a more internal state, and includes the oedipal father as a moderator. I have added that these processes defend against the wish to be castrated as a phantasy of merging with the mother and, ultimately, of omnipotent self-creation. The fundamental conflict is an immanent primal ambivalence or elemental unease.

Freud (1930) points to an indefinable, uneasy, internal state: an *Unbehagen in der Kultur*, and I have suggested that his characterization of the Jews, as 'often in an indefinable way different' (1939, p. 91), points to the same state. We might add religious differences, which are as internal as the unease in culture, but are treated as external, solid, evident targets of hatred. Jacoby (2011) documents the internecine violence within Christianity, not just between Christianity and Judaism (see also Andrade 2007).

Although I am concerned with the place of the Jews in Nazi phantasy, enquiry into ethnic violence more broadly supports this case. There is substantial documentation of intense, tribal, ethnic hostility between neighbours, including nations and Christian sects (Blok 1998, 2001; Ignatieff 1998; Jacoby 2011; McMahon and Western 2009; Murer 2010; Schulze 2006; Volkan 1986, 2006). Jacoby, Murer and Volkan have studied the intensification of aggression in relation to the similarity between groups, even into the realm in which the differences are 'all-but-invisible' (Jacoby 2011, pp. 55, 56). Nonetheless, the idea that we hate difference and welcome sameness is so deeply engrained that it might be difficult to consider the thesis that it is sameness that we hate. Each case of virulent aggression between ethnic groups strengthens the belief that we hate difference.

4 Delusional Enemies

There have been countless expulsions and relocations of populations following wars, in which national boundaries have been redrawn, and people are suddenly reclassified as foreign. In Yugoslavia, for example, nationalist sentiment among common people was a secondary consequence of political disintegration, a response to the collapse of state order and interethnic accommodation that made it possible. It created communities of fear, groups held together by the conviction that their security depended on sticking together, in opposition to different ethnic communities. But Ignatieff says that the militiamen he talked to were defending their families not their religion; he thinks religious belief in 'such a tumult of self-righteousness' (1998, p. 55) is shallow and inauthentic. The apparent differences don't cause conflict and violence, and it is sham to claim that they do.

Ignatieff says:

> In the first stages, there is rather ambivalence, conflict within identity itself, feelings of difference fighting against feelings of recognition—the very process under way when the Serbian soldier told me that really, the Serbs and the Croats were all the same. It is not a sense of radical difference that leads to conflict with others, but the refusal to admit a moment of recognition. Violence must be done to the self before it can be done to others. Living tissue of connection and recognition must be cauterised before a neighbour is reinvented as an enemy. (Ignatieff 1998, pp. 53–54)

Religious and nationalist sentiment intensified an anxiety of contamination. Ethnic cleansing is cleaning-up a contamination, and that is more primitive than attacking an enemy. It erases the perception of an other and creates a world of delusion that is normalized as ordinary reality by the common-sense idea of hating difference. This aggressive maintenance of an illusory world is deeply confusing because the conscious aim, of defending against an aggressive object, is 'normal' in the sense of well anchored in reality, yet this conscious aim supports an illusory world with its regressive pull into a pre-objectal world. The dread and excitement of this pull is anchored in an apparently real, external world of aggression against the enemy, but the enemy is a virtual object that keeps the regression just this side of psychosis and terror. In line with Freud's reference to the 'most useful service' rendered by the Jews, recent work on inter-war Hungary shows anti-Semitic agitation was directed mainly at Jews who were assimilating to the non-Jewish population (Pók 2006, p. 378).

Conclusion

I have argued that we don't detect differences in the other, and then hate that other for these differences. Instead, we create the other as a psychic reality. Sometimes this psychic reality can be projected into and held in perceived reality, in which difference is reassuring; sometimes it is imposed on perceived reality, more in the order of a hallucination. Hatred then aims to seal this psychic reality in the other, and to destroy it there.

In Nazi imagination, the protean Jew spread everywhere. The ever-present Jew took the conscious form of resentment at Jewish internationalism, international finance, statelessness, Bolshevism, conspiracy and fundamental antagonism to German existence. In the unconscious, however, it would be more accurate to speak of an inner dread of primal catastrophe, projected into the Jews as a people. One can glimpse the confusion of this internal reality with conscious legitimation of virulent hatred of the Jew in Nazi preoccupation with the near impossibility of discerning the Jew in an indigenous population—a modern recrudescence of a centuries-old problem in Christendom (Jacoby 2011). With the assimilation of Jews into society, it was becoming more difficult to detect them (Bartov 1998, pp. 779, 780, 784, 786). The Jew was an uncannily subtle mimic, who could take the shape even of the leaders of a country. American politics, for example, was riddled with this Jewish shadow, a 'fact' confirmed by photographic evidence. Hans Diebow (1941) purported to demonstrate this insinuation into American politics with photographs of New York Governor, Herbert H. Lehman, who could look like any other American, but his Jewishness surfaced with sufficient photographic evidence. Similarly, President Franklin D. Roosevelt surrounded himself with a personal advisory committee, the Brain Trust, composed of Jews. This message was pressed home in an article, 'The Mask Falls', one of series of anti-Semitic tracts in the widely distributed wall newspaper, *The Word of the Week*, controlled by Joseph Goebbels

(Herf 2006, pp. 165–6, 189–97, 201; see the series of plates following p. 166). Churchill and Stalin, like Roosevelt, were said to be tools of the Jews.

This dread lay deep in Nazi leadership, but was also pressed into the minds of Germans, to become what Confino calls the 'imagination of a world without Jews'. In my thesis, the Jew became a psychotic object. Invasion by this object was, therefore, beyond rational control or representation in history or even in race science. It was kept alive as a delusion wrapped in fragments of external reality, a reality that could not be tested because it concealed a delusion that could not be identified and separated from it. That amalgam or agglomeration of delusion and external reality has been captured by historians in ideas such as Kerhsaw's 'working towards the Führer' or Broszat's and Mommsen's recognition that Hitler's dream was not a reality in time and space. One can trace the growing exclusion of Jews from the initial economic and social legislation, through enactment in violence, such as *Kristallnacht*, and finally in a programme of extermination, but the imagination of a world without Jews (Confino) lay outside history as reality, as the very atmosphere in which these attitudes and actions took place. As an unconscious, phantasy object, the Jews were a species that no longer existed: German existence = Jewish non-existence.

When Freud speaks of the special service performed by the Jew, one has to ask whether the hatred of the Jew expressed a particular aspect of entity/identity formation, one which brought out this highly regressive feature. The problem with saying that gypsies, homosexuals, or, today, Islam, have experienced the same hatred as have the Jews, is that it does not discriminate the ultimate forms of hatred. In the German psyche, Jews represented a particular kind of foreign body: one that threatened to be so like them as to be indistinguishable. While assimilation into German culture was often seen by Jews as well as non-Jews to be the way to resolve 'the Jewish question', Jews were reviled for the ease with which they could pass as Germans. They could be absorbed without anyone knowing it was happening, insidiously becoming German. This crypto-assimilation was experienced as a treacherous force that undermined German national character. It was ubiquitous, pressing inwards from everywhere. It was like capitalism: an expanding, supra-national, cosmopolitan agency: the very antithesis of the uniquely ethnic, cultural basis of nationalism. Jews were a massive, centripetal force, threatening to implode the German national and ethnic character. In a paranoid state of mind, the Nazi state could also claim that war against the Jews and their Soviet allies was preventive war (Maier 1988, pp. 67–70).

> The image of 'the Jew' as the state's most insidious enemy by dint of being both distinctly and irreversibly alien and capable of such mental and physical dissimulation that made him appear 'just like us' was a legacy of late nineteenth-century political and racial anti-Semitism...If the new economic forces were anonymous and faceless, Jewish emancipation and assimilation created a new kind of Jew who could no longer be identified as such with the same ease as in the past. Seemingly indistinguishable from his gentile neighbors, 'the Jew' as an identifiable 'other' was disappearing, at the same time that his power, according to the anti-Semitic logic, was expanding immeasurably ... Central to the 'world view' and functioning of the Third Reich was the assertion that its elusive enemies were at once ubiquitous, indestructible, and protean. (Bartov 1998, pp. 779, 780, 785–6)

This usurpation and depletion was happening *inside* German nationalism, and was therefore more like being drawn into an abyss. It was the social equivalent to psychosis: the 'invasion' by the Jews was, psychically, the re-introjection of the fundamental projection into the Jews of the urgent need to infiltrate and possess them. The Holocaust was a violent eruption against this threat, in its paranoid form, and it was against the resurgence of this catastrophe in the form of remembering the Nazi period that a psychosocial defence was organized in post-war Germany.

With 'inside' in mind, remember the scenario that sprang from the unconscious of the young ex- now anti-Nazi, who, as a monstrous animal, had repeatedly to kill the woman who also mirrored him. The idealization of the German people, which was lodged in the *Führerbindung*, sat on the back of this attack on the Jews. And, as Omar Bartov put it, '[t]hat is why Nazism was not only committed to killing all the Jews but was predicated on the assumption that there would always be more "Jews" to kill' (Bartov 1998, pp. 779, 780, 785–6).

Invasion by the Jew as a psychotic object was beyond rational control or representation in history or even in race science. Finally, as Kershaw (2011) says, none of the historical forces, nor the charisma of Hitler, kept the German army fighting relentlessly (as a doomed drive to actualize the German illusion). It was the 'structures and mentalities of his charismatic rule [, which] lasted until his death in the bunker', then dissolved with his death (p. 400).

In the next chapter, we will turn from the delusional object to a dread of catastrophe, to which the creation of the delusional object is the reaction. It is a diffuse, inner state, which can be consolidated as a threat to be attacked and destroyed in the object. In my analysis, German nationalism of the Nazi period was the social form of this reaction, and much of this book tries to draw together historical analyses of the specific targeting of the Jews for extinction, with the psychoanalysis of processes that surface in historians' work. Turning now to the underlying catastrophe, I will draw on Freud's *Das Unbehagen in der Kultur* (The Unease in Culture); on the process of projecting a psychotic object, in order to avoid the catastrophe of psychosis, described clinically and theoretically by Bleger (1967/2013); and on the creation of defensive havens, developed by several analysts, including Steiner (1993), within which individuals feel safe in a psychotic world. They postulate an inner dread, managed by projective processes in relation to objects as their external repositories. This management moves relentlessly to action, often with violence as the motive force.

Notes

1. Just how difficult it is to come to a common understanding on the historical evidence, motivation and ideology among historians is clear in this correspondence between these two eminent historians of this period, in which they hoped to reduce misunderstanding and support a common purpose among historians of the Third Reich and the aftermath.
2. The primacy of the sibling needs qualification for Jacoby. Not only does he imply that there is an Oedipus complex behind Cain's murder of Abel, but also he derives fratricidal violence from an assertion of masculinity

against its loss to the sameness of their siblinghood; in this case, to a feminized brother. The murder of the brother repudiates the male dread of women—the source of the narcissism of small differences for Freud (1918 [1917]). 'A woman', Jacoby says, 'is as familiar – and as strange as a wife or girlfriend' (p. 157).

References

Andrade, V. (2007) The 'Uncanny', the Sacred and the Narcissism of Culture: The Development of the Ego and the Progress of Civilization. *International Journal of Psychoanalysis* 88: 1019–37.
Anon. [Ferenczi] (1933) Ontogenesis. *Psychoanalytic Quarterly* 2: 365–403.
Anzieu, D. (1975) *The Group and the Unconscious*. London: Routledge & Kegan, 1984.
Arlow, J. (1992) Aggression and Vorurteil: Psychoanalytische Betrachtungen zur Ritualmordbeschuldigung gegen die Juden. *Psyche* 46: 1122–32.
Bajohr, F. and Wildt, M. (2009) *Volksgemeinschaft: neue Forschungen zur Gesellschaft des Nationalsozialismus*. Frankfurt am Main: Fischer.
Bartov, O. (1998) Defining Enemies, Making Victims: Germans, Jews, and the Holocaust. *The American Historical Review* 103(3): 771–816.
Bion, W. R. (1957) Differentiation of the Psychotic from the Non-psychotic Personalities. *International Journal of Psychoanalysis* 38: 266–75. In *Second Thoughts: Selected Papers on Psycho-Analysis*. London: William Heinemann, 1967; Karnac, 1984, pp. 43–64.
Bion, W. R. (1962) A Psycho-Analytic Study of Thinking. *International Journal of Psychoanalysis* 43: 306–10; A Theory of Thinking. In *Second Thoughts: Selected Papers on Psycho-Analysis*. London: William Heinemann, 1967; Karnac, 1984, pp. 110–19.
Bleger, J. (1967/2013) *Symbiosis and Ambiguity: A Psychoanalytical Study*. London/New York: Routledge.
Bleger, J. (1974) Schizophrenia, Autism and Symbiosis. *Contemporary Psychoanalysis* 10: 19–25.
Blok, A. (1998) The Narcissism of Minor Differences. *European Journal of Social Theory* 1(1): 33–56.
Blok, A. (2001) *Honour and Violence*. Cambridge: Polity.
Broszat, M. (1970) Soziale Motivation und Führer-Bindung des Nationalsozialismus. *Vierteljahrshefte für Zeitgeschichte* 18(4): 392–409.

4 Delusional Enemies

Broszat, M. and Friedländer, S. (1988) A Controversy About the Historicization of National Socialism. *New German Critique* 44: 85–126.

Burrin, P. (2005) *Nazi Anti-semitism: From Prejudice to the Holocaust.* New York/London: The New Press.

Chasseguet-Smirgel, J. (1985a) *The Ego Ideal: A Psychoanalytic Essay on the Malady of the Ideal.* London: Free Association Books.

Chasseguet-Smirgel, J. (1985b) *Creativity and Perversion.* London: Free Association Books.

Confino, A. (2014) *A World Without Jews: The Nazi Imagination from Persecution to Genocide.* New Haven/London: Yale University Press.

Diebow, H. (1941) *Juden in USA.* Berlin: Franz Eher Verlag.

Figlio, K. (2000) *Psychoanalysis, Science and Masculinity.* London/Philadelphia: Whurr/Brunner-Routledge, 2001.

Figlio, K. (2010) Phallic and Seminal Masculinity: A Theoretical and Clinical Confusion. *International Journal of Psychoanalysis* 91(1): 119–39.

Figlio, K. (2012) The Hatred and Exclusion of Likeness. In Auestad, L. (ed.) *Psychoanalysis and Politics: Exclusions and the Politics of Representation.* London: Karnac.

Figlio, K. (2013) Projective Identification – An Overview. *Encyclopedia of Critical Psychology.* New York: Springer Verlag, 2013.

Firth, R. (1966) Twins, Birds and Vegetables: Problems of Identification in Primitive Religious Thought. *Man, New Series* 1: 1–17.

Freud, S. (1912) On the Universal Tendency to Debasement in the Sphere of Love (Contributions to the Psychology of Love II). *The Standard Edition of the Complete Psychological Works of Sigmund Freud* 11: 177–90.

Freud, S. (1914a). On Narcissism: An Introduction. *The Standard Edition of the Complete Psychological Works of Sigmund Freud* 14: 68–102.

Freud, S. (1914b) Remembering, Repeating and Working-Through (Further Recommendations on the Technique of Psycho-Analysis II). *The Standard Edition of the Complete Psychological Works of Sigmund Freud* 12: 145–56.

Freud, S. (1915) Instincts and Their Vicissistudes. *The Standard Edition of the Complete Psychological Works of Sigmund Freud* 14: 109–40.

Freud, S. (1918[1917]) The Taboo of Virginity (Contributions to the Psychology of Love III). *The Standard Edition of the Complete Psychological Works of Sigmund Freud* 11: 191–208.

Freud, S. (1919) The Uncanny. *The Standard Edition of the Complete Psychological Works of Sigmund Freud* 17: 217–56.

Freud, S. (1930) *Civilization and Its Discontents. The Standard Edition of the Complete Psychological Works of Sigmund Freud* 21: 57–146.

Freud, S. (1939) *Moses and Monotheism. The Standard Edition of the Complete Psychological Works of Sigmund Freud* 23: 3–137.
Friedländer, S. (1997) *The Years of Persecution: Nazi Germany & the Jews 1933–1939.* London: Weidenfeld & Nicholson/Phoenix.
Gabbard, G. (1993) On Hate in Love Relationships: The Narcissism of Minor Differences Revisited. *Psychoanalytic Quarterly* 62: 229–38.
Girard, R. (1988) *Violence and the Sacred.* London: Athlone.
Herf, J. (2006) *The Jewish Enemy: Nazi Propaganda During World War II and the Holocaust.* Cambridge, MA/London: Harvard University Press.
Hinshelwood, R. D. (1991) *A Dictionary of Kleinian Thought* (2nd edition). London: Free Association Books.
Ignatieff, M. (1998) *The Warrior's Honor: Ethnic War and the Modern Conscience.* London: Chatto and Windus.
Isaacs, S. (1940) Temper Tantrums in Early Childhood in their Relation to Internal Objects. *International Journal of Psychoanalysis* 21: 280–93.
Jacoby, R. (2011) *Bloodlust: On the Roots of Violence from Cain and Abel to the Present.* New York/London/Sydney: The Free Press
Jokl, A. M. (1997) *Zwei Fälle zum Thema >Bewältigung der Vergangenheit<.* Frankfurt a.M.: Jüdischer Verlag im Suhrkamp Verlag.
Kaplan, T. P. (2009) *The Language of Nazi Genocide: Linguistic Violence and the Struggle of Jewish Ancestry.* Cambridge: Cambridge University Press.
Kershaw, I. (1999) 'Working Towards the Führer': Reflections on the Nature of the Hitler Dictatorship. In *Hitler, the Germans, and the Final Solution.* Jerusalem: International Institute for Holocaust Research, Yad Vashem; New Haven, [Conn.]: Yale University Press, 2008, pp. 29–48.
Kershaw, I. (2011) *The End: Hitler's Germany, 1944–45.* London: Allen Lane.
Klein, M. (1946) Notes on Some Schizoid Mechanisms. In *The Writings of Melanie Klein,* vol. 3. London: Hogarth and the Institute of Psychoanalysis, 1975, pp. 1–24.
Longerich, P. (2007) *Davon Haben Wir Nichts Gewusst: die Deutschen und die Judenverfolgerung 1933–1945.* Munich: Siedler.
Maier, C. (1988) *The Unmasterable Past: History, Holocaust, and German National Identity.* Cambridge, MA/London: Harvard University Press.
McMahon, P. and Western, J. (2009) The Death of Dayton: How to Stop Bosnia from Falling Apart. *Foreign Affairs* 88: 69–83.
Mitchell, J. (2003) *Siblings.* Cambridge: Polity.
Mommsen, H. (1981) Die Stellung Hitler im nationalsozialistischen Hitler's Herrschaftssystem. In Hirschfeld, G. u. Kenttenacker, L. (Hg.) *Der 'Führerstaat':*

Mythos u. Realität: Studien zur Struktur u. Politik des Dritten Reiches. Stuttgart: Klett-Cotta. English translation, Hitler's Position in the Nazi System. In *From Weimar to Auschwitz: Essays in German History*. Cambridge: Polity, 1991, pp. 163–88.

Mommsen, H. (1983) Die Realisieren des Utopischen: Die 'Endlösung der Judenfrage' im 'Dritten Reich'. *Geschichte und Gesellschaft* 9(3): 381–420; English translation, The Realization of the Unthinkable: The 'Final Solution of the Jewish Question' in the 'Third Reich'. In *From Weimar to Auschwitz: Essays in German History*. Cambridge: Polity, 1991, pp. 224–349.

Murer, J. (2010) Institutionalizing Enemies: The Consequences of Reifying Projection in Post-conflict Environments. *Psychoanalysis, Culture & Society* 15(1): 1–19.

Pók, A. (2006) The Politics of Hatred: Scapegoating in Inter-war Hungary. In Turda, M. and Weindling, P. (eds.) *Blood and Homeland: Eugenics and Racial Nationalism in Central and Southeastern Europe 1900–1940*. Budapest/ NewYork: Central European Press, pp. 375–88.

Rank, O. (1914) *The Double: A Psychoanalytic Study*. Chapel Hill, NC: University of North Carolina Press, 1971.

Rhode, E. (1994) *Psychotic Metaphysics*. London: Karnac.

Schulze, R. (2006) The Politics of Memory: Flight and Expulsion of German Populations After the Second World War and German Collective Memory. *National Identities* 8: 367–82.

Spillius, E. and O'Shaughnessy, E. (eds.) (2012) *Projective Identification: The Fate of a Concept*. London: Routledge.

Steiner, J. (1993) *Psychic Retreats: Pathological Organizations in Psychotic, Neurotic and Borderline Patients*. London/New York: Routledge.

Volkan, V. (1986) The Narcissism of Minor Differences in the Psychological Gap Between Opposing Nations. *Psychoanalytic Inquiry* 6: 175–91.

Volkan, V. (2006) *Killing in the Name of Identity: A Study of Bloody Conflicts*. Charlottesville: Pitchstone Publishing.

Zimmermann, M. (2008) *Deutsche Gegen Deutsche: Das Schicksal der Juden 1938–1945*. Berlin: Aufbau Verlagsgruppe GmbH.

5

Solidarity, Catastrophe and Ambivalence

In this chapter, I argue that the creation of a 'delusional object', described in Chap. 4, is a defence against a primal catastrophe. I describe that imminent catastrophe and its sources. I build my case on two of Freud's powerful concepts: his rich and counter-intuitive concept of the narcissism of small differences, according to which aggressiveness intensifies with closeness; and his *Unbehagen in der Kultur*—an unease or malaise intrinsic to culture, charged with immanent explosive violence. Both of these concepts imply an ever-present catastrophe at the centre of society. There is a convergence among psychoanalytic schools that there is a catastrophe at the origin of psychic life, or in psychic life stripped by psychosis into its elements, and that individual and social organization defend against it through processes, variously called social defence mechanisms, psychic retreats and havens.

The narcissism of small differences implies a dread of dissolution stabilized by concocting a world of imagined differences, delusionally mistaken for external realities, lying beneath Freud's *Unbehagen*. In Freud's theory of the unease in culture, a transformation of the death drive produces an elemental aggression that fractures social solidarity. The superego evolved as an internal agency to manage it, allowing society to survive, by reflecting it back to the ego and holding it there both by its internal aggression and by guilt based on remorse. Individuals, clustered under a common superego, were consolidated into a group. The parallel between individual and group suggests the psychoanalytic idea of a social world with an internal dimension, as we saw in Chap. 3. This 'social subject', like an individual subject, is vulnerable to destruction by internal conflict as well as by external attack.

At an advanced level, the conflict is oedipal, in that the price for being an individual or a civilization is to suffer guilt based on the struggle of love for the oedipal father against aggression against him. Remorse for the aggression, identification with him and, overall, guilt, combine and, along with the conflict evoked under the aegis of the superego, '[appear unrecognized] as a sort of *malaise*, a dissatisfaction' (Freud 1930, pp. 135–6). Guilt follows from ambivalence, in which an aggressive self and a hated object are distinct entities, with love and hate directed towards the same object, but it hints at a deeper vulnerability: a primal catastrophe; an absolute collapse of identity at a more elemental level, rather than aggression in conflict with love. Here, at the limit of experience, there is another reality, in which love and hate are inappropriate terms. Instead, there are elemental and dreadful forces, and they are confused.

At this elemental level, the narcissism of small differences obstructs the collapse of self or group into a 'same' other, by evoking an intensity of repudiation that grows with growing similarity. It implies that society can only form and survive if it can master an originary incoherence. Solidarity is plagued by an imminent catastrophe. Violent conflict, while it threatens to tear the self or group apart, also offers a defence against dissolution. Projective identification transforms internal collapse into an external eroding or attacking force, which can be isolated, kept under surveillance and attacked.

The Dread of (Non-)Existing

The drive to stabilize a psychic structure by projective identification can be seen in patients in confusional states. Remember Bion's case, described in Chap. 2: Bion concluded that '[w]hen the patient glanced at me, he was taking a part of me into him…, as if his eyes could suck something out of me. This was then removed from me, before I sat down, and expelled, again through his eyes, so that it was deposited in the right-hand corner of the room where he could keep it under observation while he was lying on the couch' (1958, p. 67). Through his eyes, Bion's patient blended into him and at the same time held him under rigid surveillance and virtual muscular control. The patient's eyes omnipotently acted both as sense organs that absorbed the object and as motor organs that put it under lock and key. He thereby stabilized an immanent internal dissolution by opposing his impetus to dissolve the object into himself with a projection of this impetus. Now the object threatened him with dissolution from the outside, which he countered by locking it up with his eyes as motor organs.

Rosenfeld (1952) describes the imminence of catastrophe in a moment when the predominance of oral feelings expressed the wish to enter the object. After drinking water, the patient made sucking and chewing movements, which Rosenfeld interpreted as 'introjecting me and my penis [by drinking], and at the same time…projecting himself into me'. The patient was anxious about 'going all the way' in loving someone, because he couldn't then take himself back (p. 115). He then said that 'A big-boned man eats a lot', which Rosenfeld interpreted as greed in his eating up the analyst in his loving wish to get inside him (p. 114). For Rosenfeld, both the chewing and the active sucking attacked the objectal qualities of the object. So there are two currents here, with respect to the inside of the object: (1) getting inside the object *and* having it inside; and (2), at a more primitive level, destroying the very notion of an inside to the object from which one could be outside. The patient unconsciously created an intimacy of total confusion with the object, but could only tolerate this intimacy by also attacking it in order to limit his dissolving into it.

Freud formulated a primal ambivalent stage akin to Rosenfeld's case.

> Preliminary stages of love emerge as provisional sexual aims while the sexual instincts are passing through their complicated development. As the first of these aims we recognize the phase of incorporating or devouring—a type of love which is at one with [*vereinbar*] suspending [*Aufhebung*] the

separate existence of the object and which may therefore be called [*bezeichnet*] ambivalent. (1915, p. 138; translation modified; I have discussed this text more fully in Figlio 2000, pp. 78–82)

The states described above are primal forms of ambivalence. They are not ambivalent in the sense or directing love and hate to the same object, thereby setting up an internal conflict that is resolved through the Oedipus complex, or through working through the depressive position. They are contradictions in the sense of survival itself, between dissolving through an internal collapse and persisting in existence through creating an external object to overcome.

Psychically, the earliest introjection does not retain an object, but incorporates it, making one flesh with the ego. It takes on an objectal character when anal forces transform suspension into expulsion. In that moment, the primally loved object is also a foreign body, the object of aggression. But just before, the object is only in formation, as a transient, virtual object. Such a primal state would characterize the limit of the fragmentation of the ego to the point at which one could no longer speak of an extreme fragmentation. Instead, one can only infer another reality by extending an experience to an imagined limit beyond experience. With Freud, for example, we extend an experience of narcissism, captured in object relational terms as secondary narcissism, to a limit beyond an experience, at which we can speak of an objectless state of primary narcissism. Similarly, for Winnicott, a primal state of unintegration lies behind disintegration. The primal states are on the edge of psychic existence, rather than conflictual states. In that sense, the term 'primal ambivalence' is appropriate.[1]

José Bleger first drew attention to such core state of immanent object relations on the edge of catastrophe in 1967/2013. He called it an 'undifferentiation', a state of disorganization that he identified in working with psychotic patients. These patients needed, for sanity, to dissociate themselves from a psychotic nucleus—an 'agglutinated nucleus'—an entity inside of which no distinction could be made: between self and other, good and bad, different identifications and different stages of development—a kind of agglomerated undifferentiation (pp. 3–6, 79–80, 155, 163). For Bleger, this 'state of primitive undifferentiation is a *particular organization of the ego and of the world*...[It] is not actually *a state* of undifferentiation but a different *structure* or organization that always includes the subject and the subject's environment, though not as differentiated entities' (p. 4; Bleger's emphasis).

A psychic structure with the appearance of sanity can only be maintained if there is a 'depository' for this agglutinated nucleus—a place to put it, from which a distance can be maintained, in order to avoid its forcing its way back into the ego and causing total psychic disorganization. In the clinical situation, establishing and sustaining such a dissociation depends on using the analyst as a depository and rigidly controlling the relationship, so that the nucleus remains immobilized in the analyst. Bleger was concerned both with the description of this symbiotic state and with technique. How could one analyse it, when interpretation—the work of analysis—was experienced by the patient as a forced re-introjection of the projected agglutinated nucleus, and therefore, as a threat to the patient's sanity. 'Loss of the immobilization...of the agglutinated is produced in a *massive*, accessive, *paroxystic way,* provoking or threatening to provoke the *total and immediate annihilation of the subject's ego*' (p. 34; Bleger's emphasis).

Bleger sees the process of immobilizing the agglutinated nucleus as similar in structure to Klein's splitting and projection, but distinct from it. Splitting is characteristic of conflict in the ego between 'good' and 'bad', while immobilization is characteristic of unintegration, against which the ego forms itself by projecting a nucleus of undifferentiated objects. They both bespeak psychotic processes in the loss of perceptual reality, through idealization and denigration in splitting, and unintegration in immobilization, but there is a difference in the psychotic process. Splitting and projective identification detach the ego from reality and produce a psychotic reality in its place, in an attempt to manage the impact of perceptual reality on the ego. Immobilization of the agglutinated nucleus attempts to manage the confusion of unintegration, which the ego confronts as a psychotic loss of identity.

The collapse of the sequestering of the agglutinated nucleus is a catastrophic destabilization of the ego. The cohesion by identification between individuals and their group allows an extrapolation of these clinical findings to the group. The more cohesive the group, the tighter the bond of identification, the more it becomes homogeneous, the more delusional the structure, the more it needs repositories and therefore needs to divide. The narcissism of small differences comes into play.

Catastrophe of Existence Versus Concern for the Object

For Freud, The Oedipus complex was the decisive and inescapable hurdle in psychic development. It structures ambivalence by directing love towards one parent and hate towards the other, but the urge to love and identify with the hated object points forward developmentally, to achieving a resolution of ambivalence. In later thinking (Britton 1989) the resolution of ambivalence includes the recognition of parental sexuality and the conception of the child. But the Oedipus complex is central in another way as well: it also points backwards to elemental states of mind. Bion says that 'the central [oedipal] crime is [not sexual incest, as is usually thought, but] the arrogance of Oedipus in vowing to lay bare the truth at no matter what cost' (1957, p. 86). Pursuing the truth can be done with intelligent curiosity, but Oedipus pursues it single-mindedly in order proudly to discover and denounce the curiosity of the little Oedipus in us all. He is, therefore, stupid with respect to truthfulness. Pride becomes arrogance, and, scattered, along with references to curiosity and stupidly, is evidence of a psychic catastrophe.

Oedipus did not just attack the creative parental couple, and replace father with himself: he attacked at a more primal level the very capacity of the father-object to fathom what was happening. In his curiosity as an analyst, Bion observed a patient who could communicate only through the primitive mechanism of projective identification into an object, which, in the patient's experience, could not tolerate the psychic disruption caused by this mode of communication. In Bion's analysis, getting close to an external object through projective identification was, for the patient, undermined by an obstructive internal object (superego), perceived to be in Bion as an external object. He experienced the analyst-object's curiosity as this obstructive internal object, launching an obliterating attack upon his ego. The central problem was the psychotic conviction that the 'analytic procedure itself is precisely a manifestation of the curiosity which is felt to be an intrinsic component of the disaster…[and the] analytic procedure [becomes] an acting out of destructive attacks launched against the ego, wherever it is discerned' (pp. 87, 88). Bion's clinical observation can be extended to social groups, which are exceptionally reactive against self-observation.

Being an object of curiosity and being open to self-reflection are equated with feeling attacked by an external object. This external object can be identified with another person or with another social group, and this other becomes an intruder that evokes a quick retaliation. Klein's (1946) 'Paranoid-schizoid position' organizes this threatened internal world into illusions of wholly 'good' and wholly 'bad' objects, identified with parts of the self. They assure existence, but in a paranoid, retaliatory world: not a world of benevolent, concerned objects, born of the ego's own concern for the object world.

The loving and hating of the good object without the structure of the depressive position, without the amelioration of destructiveness by reparation, and without the protection of the psychic organization of the paranoid-schizoid position, is a state of elemental terror. I think it can be connected to Klein's understanding of the fixation-point for psychosis. Speaking of the origin of the Oedipus complex in an environment of sadism, she says that defence against libidinal impulses comes later. 'The earliest defence set up by the ego is directed against the subject's own sadism and the object attacked, both of these being regarded as sources of danger. The defence is of a violent kind, different from the mechanism of repression' (1930, p. 232) such as in the normal or neurotic situation. She then turns to the genesis of psychosis.

> The first part of the phase when sadism is at its height is that in which the attacks are conceived of as being made by violence. This is what I have come to recognize as the fixation-point for dementia praecox. In the second part of this phase the attacks are made by poisoning and the urethral and anal-sadistic impulses predominate. This I believe to be the fixation-point in paranoia…My conclusions are in agreement with Freud's hypotheses, according to which the fixation-points of dementia praecox and

paranoia are to be sought in the narcissistic stage, that of dementia praecox preceding that of paranoia. (p. 232)

In Kleinian terms, the fearful version of such a state is paranoid-schizoid anxiety, experienced by an ego threatened by its projected aggression. In her major theoretical statement of 1946, in which she introduced the paranoid-schizoid position, Klein said, 'I hold that anxiety arises from the operation of the death instinct within an organism, is *felt* as *fear* of annihilation (death) and *takes the form* of fear of persecution. The fear of the destructive impulse *seems to attach itself* at once to an object—or rather *it is experienced* as the fear of an uncontrollable overpowering object' (p. 4; my emphasis).

Terrifying as it is, paranoia is a fixation at a later stage than schizophrenia and acts as a defence against psychotic collapse. Although not framed in a Kleinian vocabulary, Winnicott (1949) gives an example from a two-part countertransference dream about a psychotic patient that suggests the same point. In the first part, he lost an arm, which he extended over the edge of the balcony while watching a performance in a theatre; in the second part, he had moved down onto the stage and the right half of his body was missing. He interpreted part one as castration anxiety, a feature of the paranoid-schizoid position; and part two as a more primal loss of self by identification with the patient, who, threatened by terror at any mention of her body, repudiated any acknowledgement of it. In this case, paranoia defended against existential collapse. Winnicott (1974) also says 'we need to use the word "breakdown" to describe the unthinkable state of affairs that underlies the defence organization' (p. 103).

Depressive anxiety is the fearful state of the ego threatened by its aggression with the loss of an object, known to the ego by identification. Beneath these elaborated forms of anxiety, transformed into fearful states, lies primal ambivalence, in which the ego's aggression threatens the ego immediately. The formation of the object that will threaten the ego is itself the effect of this primal ambivalence.

Such a primal state, which in itself lies beyond representation, but may be captured in an organized psychic structure, is what I am calling a catastrophe. Hoffer (1954) introduced the concept of a defensive organization. Building on his work, O'Shaughnessy (1981) defines an enduring 'defensive organization', as distinct from a transient defence, as a refuge that also become a harassing omnipotent delusion of superiority over the object world. She proposes that it 'be reserved for ... a pathological formation when development arouses irresoluble and almost overwhelming anxiety' (p. 366).[2] It appears to benefit from eliminating anxiety from object relations, which can be exploited to become a 'vehicle for the omnipotent gratification of...narcissism and...cruelty' (pp. 364–5). Such an organization gets locked in and perpetuated because its triumphalism, cruelty and robbery maintain the ego at the expense of its objects (pp. 364–5) and can become delusional. Segal (1972) speaks of two main defences against early loss: cannibalism and the faecal empire. But these defensive postures seem to be reformulations, in subject-object language, of the incorporation and expulsion in Freud's account of primal ambivalence.

The weapons of such a defensive organization are degradation, mockery, distortion of the truth, arrogance—in general, a perverse excitement in traduction. They deliver their attack on the object world from the heights of delusional superiority. But attack evokes counter-attack, leaving the ego relieved but also in dread of a primal catastrophe that cannot be fully grasped and managed in object relations. Outside the psychic retreat, the psyche is helpless, possibly immobilized by anxiety and an absence of a sense of self. What I want to focus upon is that very state, which I called a catastrophe, and the projection of this state into the object as a concomitant of the retreat into the retreat.

Psychic Retreats and Social Havens

Many psychoanalytic writers have described various forms of defensive organizations as they appear in the clinical setting (Bleger 1967; Hoffer 1954; Hopper 1991; Jaques 1955; Menzies Lyth 1959; O'Shaughnessy 1981, 1992; Segal 1972; Steiner 1993; Winnicott 1974; Winnicott 1980), including authors who use similar ideas without naming the structure. John Steiner (1993) developed the concept of a 'psychic retreat' most fully. For Steiner, the catastrophe is to be overwhelmed by anxiety pressed into the ego caught somewhere in a spectrum of psychic states organized around the paranoid-schizoid and depressive positions. The psychic retreat offers a haven from impingement by internal and external reality.

In my view, ambivalence is at the core of the catastrophe, and that beneath the oedipal level of a conflict between love and hate, lies a confusional state in which the drive to be (in) the object evokes a dread of dissolution and a repulsion of the object—the two are aspects of the same phenomenon, as in Freud's idea of a 'preliminary stage of love', expressed in an incorporation that loves the object and suspends its separate existence (1915, p. 138), in a primitive ambivalence. Freud's 'suspension' translates *Aufhebung*, which conveys simultaneously obliterating the object and holding it in existence. There has been a convergence in recognizing such a state, variously called 'ambiguity' (Bleger), 'unintegration' (Winnicott), 'annihilation' (Hopper), 'nameless dread' (Bion) or simply 'catastrophe'. I think that Freud pointed to such a non-state as an unanalysable core, shared by males and females, which he called the repudiation of femininity. I take him to mean by a femininity beneath the Oedipus complex, the substrate of identity in the mother as the origin of life. Catastrophe tags an unpresentable pre-identity situation, of which we have an intimation but not an experience. It is captured in the earliest conflictual dynamics of ambivalence and the Oedipus complex.

Segal hints at something of this sort, in stating that ambivalence is built into the very nature of object relating, 'there from the beginning' (1995, p. 159). It is, therefore, in the very foundation of psychic life. Even this ambivalence is a form of internal organization in the contradiction between two currents of affect or of instinctual expression. In that sense, ambivalence defends the psyche against a collapse. The core developmental task is to take on and work through this ambivalence. Otherwise, individuals regress into their psychotic cores, in which they overcome the guilt of ambivalence by deflecting aggression into others, and projecting it as well, thereby creating hateful, threatening, aggressive enemies, over which they omnipotently triumph.

Segal concentrates on psychotic mechanisms to assuage guilt. Indeed, 'a very important function of the group…is to defend individuals against their guilt feelings'. Segal continues, 'but also for that reason, groups find it almost impossible to face collective guilt' (1995, p. 165). When guilt threatens to emerge, they are tempted to opt for a manic solution, which confirms their omnipotence, rather than face the pain. Groups take on this psychotic core by acting in a mad way, often megalomanic and omnipotent, rather than anchored in reality. They restore the sense of normality to group the members, who continue to act psychotically, but with their psychosis assimilated by the group.

While, for Segal, a psychotic core is a haven from guilt, I want to emphasize a disturbance in this haven: an eruption of a psychotic core of confusion rather than of paranoia—a swirl with no appeal to an external reality that might limit it. In paranoia, at least there is an object. External reality has been co-opted by mutually projective, paranoid loops, albeit rooted in projection. Though savage, they promise to anchor the swirl in an enemy persecutor that is attacked. Because the enemy is a projection, the defence exacerbates the danger and fuels further conflict (Klein 1932, p. 150; Segal 1995, p. 164). But in the state to which I am referring, there is no appeal even to this paranoia; there is no stable object, no differentiation. We have no word for it.

The existence of such a state may lie outside experience, so that, clinically, it seems to make no sense to speak of it. Like primary narcissism or the death drive, it may be at the limit of experience: a primal state that adumbrates another reality, one that combines the deepest yearning with the deepest dread, one that does not distinguish them. Such a primal ambivalence occurs at the moment when such a state is hinted at as it is transcended.

This process of group formation intensifies the schismatic pressure to divide into conflicting groups, and, therefore, works towards stabilizing the primal catastrophe. In this model, the ego is born in ambivalence. Ambivalence offers a defence against collapse, bolstered by projective identification, which rids the group of its internal divisiveness by creating an outside group that contains part of the inside of the individual or group. The problem arises when the recipient group, like the analyst in the mind of the patient, cannot bear it and retaliates, creating a mutual, but dangerously conflicted projection system (Bion 1957). The continued recycling leads to intensification of aggression, which can quickly erupt in violence. The process is psychotic in its repudiation of external reality.

As the group grows, it becomes, in Anzieu's (1975) formulation, an archaic mother imago with a limitless oral-incorporative drive to suck into it any trace of individual difference. In the case of Nazi anti-Semitism, this voracious oral incorporativeness was projected into the Jews, and captured in the terminology of the Jews as insects, vermin, parasites, worms, blood-suckers (Bohleber 1997, pp. 585–9).

Social organization—a social frame—is akin to a clinical, analytic frame, in that both offer a defensive organization: a safe, but unstable enclave. The idea that organized defences can form a structure into which the psyche can retreat to escape the impact of depressive anxiety was expanded by John Steiner to include paranoid-schizoid anxiety, in his concept of 'psychic retreat' (1993). But, although defensive organization have been conceptualized as havens from depressive anxiety (sometimes paranoid-schizoid anxiety as well), I am considering them as havens from a primal catastrophe.

In the relationships between groups, there is no equivalent to the analyst in the clinical setting to represent reality or retreat, while monitoring the extent of retreat and the robustness of the haven. Instead, social forces advance and retreat as social groups press against each other. But the aspect I am drawing attention to is not the force with which they intimidate each other, but the use of each other as repositories into which they deposit their anxiety of disintegration. Each builds its delusion of superiority on the success of this projection. Such a process is an essential part of a social, cultural or political understanding of conflict.

The catastrophe, along with the organization that offers a fragile, but safe, haven, is what I have called 'primal ambivalence'; that is, an ambivalence that cannot be organized into the 'good' and 'bad' objects of splitting, because it lies at the embryonic creation of an ego/object world. It is at the cusp between pre-objectal and objectal existence, and therefore also the template of psychotic confusion.

In Bleger's view, ambiguity is also a social phenomenon, and group instability is also a catastrophe of ambiguity, arising from the eruption of the agglutinated (ambiguous) nucleus into the ego and into the 'cohesive group', rather than from the catastrophe of the eruption of bad objects in to the group (1967/2013, p. 207, n. 160). At an elemental level, groups offer protection against catastrophic anxiety because they readily divide and therefore provide repositories into which the agglutinated nucleus can be immobilized by projection. But the cost is inter-group violence, because the repository for projection is an illusion, and the overall structure is unstable.

I have postulated that there is a psychotic core to the individual psyche, held in suspension by social formations that provide repositories for projective identification and, in so doing, build the society—a society that suffers an *Unbehagen in der Kultur*. What is common in a convergence of social with clinical understanding is the idea of a repository of projections that are dreaded and must be kept in the repository, against the dread that something massively undermining might be re-introjected. I have proposed that groups do the same, perhaps even more readily. The fragility of groups as a whole presses them to divide into sectors, which tolerate, or do not tolerate, the imperative of projections between them.

Conclusion

I have tried to show that bondage to the illusion of a homogeneous entity, such as the nation, is an inherently unstable defence against psychotic collapse. But a democratic alternative is endangered by the same threat, because the public forum at the root of a democracy is actualized by inter-subjectivity, and the mechanism of inter-subjectivity is projective identification. A democracy has to recognize this threat to sustained political life by the antagonistic force of projective identification, and bear it. It would have to promote mutual receptivity to projective identification, in order to manage the urge to extinguish interlocutors who automatically become targets.

In succeeding chapters, we will move to post-war Germany, a society rebuilding after the Holocaust and its own devastation. The problem of remembering and tradition comes to the fore: how to build a society that has been blotted by evil memory. Remembering must either find a way to recognize the Nazi period and include it as a reality that drives reparation; or to avoid or overlook it; or, though a defensive organization, aim to both recognize and avoid it at the same time.

5 Solidarity, Catastrophe and Ambivalence

In the aftermath of the Holocaust and in setting up a new state of the Federal Republic of Germany, Jürgen Habermas became the principal advocate of a 'constitutional patriotism', a law-bound patriotism, in which the democratic processes of law-making might replace loyalty to a bloodline or a communality in which nationalism denigrated and attacked an excluded people. Dolf Sternberger introduced the concept of constitutional patriotism in 1979 (see Müller 2006, 2008). He intended it to garner loyalty as a replacement for the nation, but as an equivalent to national loyalty. In that sense, he continued the impassioned conservative thinking of the *Historikerstreit*. Habermas has wanted to shift from loyalty to an entity to a commitment to the limitless processes of struggling to hold together through the process itself of sustaining a political public as a forum of equals (Brunkhorst et al., esp. pp. 377–9).

For post-war Germany, such a nationalism echoed a *Volksgemeinschaft*: the German people as a cultural unity, with blood roots; an enforced 'public' with no trace of a civic space of debate and agreement, which informed government and shaped the state (Bajohr and Wildt; Kershaw 2014).[3] Could a working public and state be crafted from the actuality of working together in a way that reflected an internal honesty, a kind of self-reflective internal discussion that was also reflected in political activity? In psychoanalytic terms, there would be a continuous cycling of the projection of internal self-reflection into social, cultural and political activity, and its re-introjection.

The question posed by post-war Germany is whether democracy could guarantee the conditions of universalization and freedom from prejudice, illusion and superstition, in which truncated, defended, prejudiced positions could not persist. It would, however, be up against the craving for identity embodied in nationalism. Jurgen Habermas has advocated a democratic form that would aim to garner the idealization of nationalism redirected into law and political formations, embraced by a 'constitutional patriotism'. A constitution, though essential to such a democracy, would not symbolize the state or loyalty to the nation, but would articulate a framework for activity: this activity, not the constitution, would embody a democratic public. Habermas (1998) called it 'deliberative politics'. The universal would not be the nation, the people, the religion, but the capacity for this sort of disciplined, honest work, accepted as a struggle against its deterioration.⁴

Such a democratic possibility has to fight against a nation founded on nationalism and, in particular, a *Volksgemeinschaft*, an ideology of magnetic emotional appeal towards a society drawn into thrall. In the following chapters, we will analyse the conflict between a democratic and a nationalistic identity, and the effect it has on memory and, in particular, on remembering as reparation.

Notes

1. Freud (1918[1917]) says, 'It is quite clear that the intention underlying this taboo [of virginity] is that of *denying or sparing precisely the future husband* something which cannot be dissociated from the first sexual act.' Referring to *Totem and Taboo*, Freud considers 'the part played by primal ambivalence in determining the formation of taboo', the genesis of which he finds in 'the prehistoric events which led to the founding of the human family' (pp. 199–200; Freud's emphasis).
2. O'Shaughnessy says that some patients enter analysis 'when they hope not to extend their contact with themselves or their objects, but on the contrary, because they desperately need a refuge from these. Once they are in analysis their first aim is to establish, really to re-establish, a defensive organization against objects internal and external which are causing them nearly overwhelming anxiety' (1981, p. 359). In the analytic setting, the movement out of a retreat, into confrontation with reality and anxiety, and back into a retreat, defines the analytic frame, and the management of the analytic frame is a major task of the analyst.
3. Kershaw (2014) has discussed the importance of the concept of *Volksgemeinschaft* in German historiography. He thinks that the idea of an organic ideology, with the appeal of an ideal of belonging through to a global sentiment of solidarity, has been valuable in understanding the Nazi period. 'The concept of the Volksgemeinschaft has been, and can be utilized to go some way towards capturing this intangible, immeasurable but nevertheless real and vital psychological mobilization that gave Nazism its extraordinary dynamism' (p. 34). At the same time, he cautions against giving too much priority to such a qualitative, overarching sentiment, which would undervalue the detailed study of heterogeneity. 'But a

problem with the *Volksgemeinschaft* concept', he argues, 'is that it makes no attempt to disaggregate the areas where Nazism could gain obvious political support from those in which it evidently faced greater difficulties in overcoming spheres of extensive dissent, even if this could not be translated into outright opposition' (p. 37). I accept his balanced judgement, but my interest has been in the psychological motivation, arising from the power of thrall.
4. Outhwaite (2017) discusses Habermas' concepts of the 'discourse principle' in connection with the 'democracy principle'. Quoting Habermas, '"[O]nly those laws can claim legitimate validity which can achieve the agreement of all citizens in a discursive process of legislation which is itself legally constituted". Law itself provides a necessary complement to morality, especially a post-conventional and therefore critical one' (p. 215).

References

Anzieu, D. (1975) *The Group and the Unconscious*. London: Routledge & Kegan, 1984.
Bajohr, F. and Wildt, M. (2009) *Volksgemeinschaft: neue Forschungen zur Gesellschaft des Nationalsozialismus*. Frankfurt am Main: Fischer.
Bion, W. (1957) On Arrogance. *International Journal of Psychoanalysis* 39: 144–6. In *Second Thoughts: Selected Papers on Psycho-Analysis*. London: William Heinemann, 1967; Karnac, 1984, pp. 86–92.
Bion, W. (1958) On Hallucination. *International Journal of Psychoanalysis* 39: 341–9. In *Second Thoughts: Selected Papers on Psycho-Analysis*. London: William Heinemann, 1967; Karnac, 1984, pp. 65–85.
Bleger, J. (1967) Psycho-Analysis of the Psycho-Analytic Frame. *International Journal of Psychoanalysis* 48: 511–19.
Bohleber, W. (1997) Die Konstrucktion imaginärer Gemeinschaften und das Bild von den Juden – umbewusste Determinanten des Antisemitismus in Deutschland. *Psyche* 51: 570–605.
Britton, R. (1989) The Missing Link: Parental Sexuality and the Oedipus Complex. In Britton, R., Feldman, M. and O'Shaughnessy, E. (eds.) *The Oedipus Complex Today: Clinical Implications*. London: Karnac Books, pp. 83–101.
Figlio, K. (2000) *Psychoanalysis, Science and Masculinity*. London/Philadelphia: Whurr/Brunner-Routledge, 2001.

Freud, S. (1915) Instincts and Their Vicissistudes. *The Standard Edition of the Complete Psychological Works of Sigmund Freud* 14: 109–40.

Freud, S. (1918[1917]) The Taboo of Virginity (Contributions to the Psychology of Love III). *The Standard Edition of the Complete Psychological Works of Sigmund Freud* 11: 191–208.

Freud, S. (1930) *Civilization and Its Discontents. The Standard Edition of the Complete Psychological Works of Sigmund Freud* 21: 57–146.

Habermas, J. (1998) *The Inclusion of the Other: Studies in Political Theory*. Cambridge, MA: Massachusetts Institute of Technology; Cambridge, Polity Press, 1999.

Hoffer, W. (1954) Defensive Process and Defensive Organization: Their Place in Psychoanalytic Technique. *International Journal of Psychoanalysis* 35: 194–8.

Hopper, E. (1991) Encapsulation as a Defence Against the Fear of Annihilation. *International Journal of Psychoanalysis* 72(4): 607–24.

Jaques, E. (1955) Social Systems as a Defence Against Persecutory and Depressive Anxiety: A Contribution to the Psycho-Analytical Study of Social Processes. In Klein, M., Heimann, P. and Money-Kyrle, R. (eds.) *New Directions in Psychoanalysis: The Significance of Infant Conflict in the Pattern of Adult Behaviour*. London: Tavistock Publications, pp. 478–98.

Kershaw, I. (2014) *Volksgemeinschaft*: Potential and Limitations of the Concept. In Streber, M. and Gotto, B. (eds.) *Visions of Community in Nazi Germany: Social Engineering and Private Lives*. Oxford: Oxford University Press, pp. 29–42.

Klein, M. (1930) The Importance of Symbol-Formation in the Development of the Ego. In *The Writings of Melanie Klein*, vol. 1. London: Hogarth and the Institute of Psychoanalysis, 1975, pp. 219–32.

Klein, M. (1932) *The Psychoanalysis of Children*. London: Hogarth and the Institute of Psychoanalysis; revised edition 1975.

Klein, M. (1946) Notes on Some Schizoid Mechanisms. In *The Writings of Melanie Klein*, vol. 3. London: Hogarth and the Institute of Psychoanalysis, 1975, pp. 1–24.

Menzies Lyth, I. (1959) The Functioning of Social Systems as a Defence Against Anxiety. In *Containing Anxiety in Institutions: Selected Essays*, vol. 1. London: Free Association Books, 1988, pp. 43–88.

Müller, J.-W. (2006) On the Origins of Constitutional Patriotism. *Contemporary Political Theory* 5: 278–96.

Müller, J.-W. (2008) A General Theory of Constitutional Patriotism. *I•CON* 6(1): 72–95.

O'Shaughnessy, E. (1981) A Clinical Study of a Defensive Organization. *International Journal of Psychoanalysis* 62: 359–69.

O'Shaughnessy, E. (1992) Enclaves and Excursions. *International Journal of Psychoanalysis* 73: 603–11.

Outhwaite, W. (2017) Reconstructing Social Theory, History and Practice. *Current Perspectives in Social Theory* 35: 211–23.

Rosenfeld, H. (1952) Transference-Phenomena and Transference-Analysis in an Acute Catatonic Schizophrenic Patient. *International Journal of Psychoanalysis* 33: 457–64; In *Psychotic States: A Psychoanalytical Approach*. London: Hogarth, 1965, pp. 104–16.

Segal, H. (1972) A Delusional System as a Defence Against the Re-emergence of a Catastrophic Situation. *International Journal of Psychoanalysis* 53: 393–401. In *Psychoanalysis, Literature and War: Papers 1972–1995*. London/New York: Routledge, 1997, pp. 49–63.

Segal, H. (1995) From Hiroshima to the Gulf War and After: Socio-Political Expressions of Ambivalence. In *Psychoanalysis, Literature and War: Papers 1972–1995*. London/New York: Routledge, 1997, pp. 157–68.

Steiner, J. (1993) *Psychic Retreats: Pathological Organizations in Psychotic, Neurotic and Borderline Patients*. London/New York: Routledge.

Sternberger, D. (1979) Verfassungspatriotismus. *Frankfurter Allgemeine Zeitung*, 23 May.

Winnicott, C. (1980) Fear of Breakdown: A Clinical Example. *International Journal of Psychoanalysis* 61: 351–7.

Winnicott, D. W. (1949) Hate in the Counter-Transference. *International Journal of Psychoanalysis* 30: 69–74.

Winnicott, D. W. (1974) Fear of Breakdown. *International Review of Psychoanalysis* 1: 103–7.

6

Conflicts of Remembering: The *Historikerstreit*

In the previous chapter, I argued that there is an instability in individuals and society, a primal ambivalence, akin to what Freud (1930) called an *Unbehagen in der Kultur*. For Freud, the *Unbehagen* lay partly in unfulfilled instinctual gratification, but more on restraining aggression that would destroy a society from within. I extended Freud's *Unbehagen* into a dread of internal dissolution, stabilized by projective identification into repositories, in a process that creates a delusional enemy. Externalizations of this sort are structured into organizations that provide havens to their members, as inner tension is replaced by conflict between organizations. I now argue that these defensive processes occur in specific historical situations. An *Unbehagen in der Kultur* is quickly divided, projected and distributed into factions in the external world: political, economic, religious, cultural and ideological. Each faction is now threatened by attack from the outside itself, rather than dissolution from the inside, and all are drawn together into a system that acts as a defensive organization. The story of this system is recorded in the interlocking collective memories of these factions.

Post-war Germany has faced a dilemma of how to remember, how to have a collective history and identity, when memory means integration of an unconscionable period of history. This process has been called *Vergangenheitsbewältigung*—the coming to terms with the past. It brought with it the ethical problem of whether it could ever be finished and the political desideratum of forming a state with the capacity to bear its history.

Two unexpected consequences follow from a psychoanalytic approach. First, despite the humiliation of defeat, the division of Germany stabilized its identity by breaking up its idealized, illusory omnipotence and sequestering it in two nations in conflict with each other. This conflict embedded a symmetrical set of defences; in effect, an unconscious collusion to marginalize memory of the Holocaust. Second, the reunification of Germany disrupted this collusive defence and brought out again the need to come to terms with the Nazi period. One strand of this dilemma shows a deep ambivalence towards reparation, embedded in memorialization.

Before following up these consequences, we need to deal with a dilemma in social remembering. On the one hand, the memory that underlies social esteem and cohesion has a moral dimension—the preservation of the good. On the other hand, as memory fades into history, it must be assimilated into reality, including the narrative of the past as the armature of social life. In the process, it comes up against the lure of illusion and the temptation of distortion and falsification. Post-war Germany has lived in both dimensions. The tension between them validates our methodology, because we will focus on a moment of change. The history of post-war Germany is complex, especially given intergenerational conflict. In this chapter, I will concentrate of a specific conflict, provoked into the open by a specific event: the very public *Historikerstreit* of the1980s. This 'debate among historians' centred on the 'historization' of the Nazi past: whether the scholarly researching and writing of its history by professional historians diluted and relativized a horrendous dimension of German culture, which had to be faced and assimilated as part of becoming normal.

The Struggle to Remember and to Forget

From a psychoanalytic angle, remembering is a difficult and compromised process. It is not just a matter of recalling information that has been out of awareness, but of re-integrating clusters of meaning-filled associations into the flow of consciousness—associations not just unnoticed, but held away from consciousness. These dynamically unconscious (Freud 1923, p. 18), virtual memories are distortions and fragments, scattered around the internal terrain of the mind and mixed with the external world by projection and introjection. It is the work of psychoanalysis to restore individual memory from these shards, and of historians to restore social memory and consolidate social consciousness. If remembering is so tortuous in the individual, how much more is it so in social remembering? Social memory ranges from what a few individuals have experienced and might recognize in conversation, to the often raw and immediate representations of events in the media, to disciplined historical research, which forms retrospective, corrected, matured representations that filter back into the society.

A model of individual or social memory, which is based on a concept of a dynamic unconscious, implies that remembering is always in the balance against forgetting. Although it seems almost a tautology, one retains good memories and forgets bad memories, and the continuity of remembering would be easier if it builds on good memories. We will need a psychoanalytic vocabulary to explore the ways that forgetting occurs, and it will include repression, splitting, disavowal and idealization, each to be explained as we come to it.

Building on a Freudian base, my analysis will be principally in the Kleinian/Object relations tradition. In such a model (Greenberg and Mitchell 1983), we would say that the infant—and the nucleus of infantile functioning in the adult—struggles to preserve a 'good' internal object, represented by the breast, against the destructive urges that attack it. In such a state of ambivalence, the psyche suffers from anxiety of persecution by an internal object that has turned bad from attacks that fill it with the ego's projected aggression. It also suffers from the anxiety of having damaged the good internal object, with attendant guilt and the urge to repair it. It swings between what Melanie Klein called the paranoid-schizoid position and the depressive position (Klein 1946). The ego identifies with its objects, and therefore its identity is bound up with the state of its internal object-world. At the social level, this unconscious dimension is held by factions in an organizational/psychosocial enclave, between which internal objects are projected, both to relocate them and to work them over. The collective memory of a faction will tend towards an idealization of itself identified with a good object and projecting bad objects into other factions, along with the struggles to reintegrate them.

This internal world of psyches, shared and bound into a social psyche, is invested in the external world by projection, infusing external reality with the power of phantasy, and external reality is introjected into the internal world, stabilizing it. One could think of national identity as a social ego, with its attributes—what it holds dear to its self-esteem—as its good object, which would be subject to ambivalence as would any internal good object (Hinshelwood 1987; Segal 1995). Any actual society is too diverse, in social class, age, generation, gender, ethnic and religious affiliations, to speak of a coherent social memory. Nonetheless, to the extent that these sectors and the society cohere, they are supported by a social superego-ideal. Individuals identify with each other and, in their superego-ideals, with the leadership or ideology that represents their coherence. In this respect, society has *a* history, no matter how contested among sectors of the society. Since its coherence depends on an superego-ideal held in common, societies aspire to attain a collective memory, supported by a collective history. And it is an idealization.

The wish to have a history supports national esteem, and this national esteem preserves a good internal object. The virulence of the Nazi assault on humanity, unleashed particularly on the Jews as a people, suggests an irrational primitiveness associated with an assault on the good object. The reconstruction of Germany has been riven with conflict over the nature of that assault: internally, over the recognition and response to guilt; externally, over restitution to Jews and to the state of Israel. It erupts in politics and in popular memory, but also in the striving for objectivity, in partisan debates among historians. The *Historikerstreit,* triggered in particular by Jürgen Habermas' intervention in *Die Zeit* in 1986, stands out as such a struggle over remembering. It took place in the public intellectual space of the press (*Die Zeit, Frankfurter Allgemeine Zeitung, Freankfurter Rundschau, Die Welt, Der Spiegel*). Historians' professional work was also a 'project of political pedagogy, implying a large-scale programme of civic education and school reform' (Eley 1988, p. 194; for an overview, see Maier 1988).

Immediately, questions arise: can one say that Germany as a nation has been tarnished by the Nazis; that all Germans through the generations are and will be morally responsible? How can a German identity be reconstituted without incorporating the Nazi period; yet if it is incorporated, how can there be a basis for an identity? The atrocity was so extreme that it can neither be brought into history nor written out of history. In Habermas' view, writing in 1986, even the grandchildren of those too young to have been involved in the Third Reich are part of the identity of the Germany that did include it. 'The simple fact is that even those born later have grown up in a context of life [*Lebensform*] in which *that* was possible' (1986; translated by Maier 1988, p. 57). It was not a matter of shaming a younger generation, innocent of the crimes, but one of its inclusion in national identity, built up by sharing in a 'life-world' of symbols and culture, and a purposeful, rational, functional world. For Habermas, there is a 'contract with the dead' and a history that 'must remain painful' (Maier, p. 59). It is a language of contradiction in an external dimension, but chimes with that of an internal world, one that invites self-reflection among historians equivalent to that of the psychoanalyst (Maier, p. 63).

> Can one become the legal successor to the German Reich and continue the traditions of German culture without taking on historical liability for the form of life in which Auschwitz was possible? Is there any way to bear the liability for the context in which such crimes originated, a context in which one's own existence is historically interwoven, other than through remembrance, practiced in solidarity, of what cannot be made good, other than through a reflexive, scrutinizing attitude toward one's own identity-forming traditions? (Habermas 1986b, p. 236)[1]

There has been, however, a reluctance among historians to make use of psychoanalytic insights, and to engage seriously with the extensive study by Alexander and Margarete Mitscherlich (1967/1975; see also Chap. 3, n. 1). The Mitscherlichs argued that Germans affectively detached themselves from the past—repressed it. A national, narcissistic grandiosity, like that observed in the clinic, had frozen the mourning through which the nation, like the individual, could recover self-esteem and liberation from

6 Conflicts of Remembering: The *Historikerstreit*

the past. The repression of history as national memory, akin to the psychic repression known to psychoanalysts, did not sit well with historians of the Nazi period, some of whom argued that attributing guilt to the nation obstructed the reconstruction of German national identity. Post-war German historiographical tradition broke into a plurality of historical views of German history (Berger 1995; Herf 1997), yet also hungered for German national identity—an identity threatened with the memory of its Nazi history (Eley 1988).[2]

In the context of the *Historikerstreit*, Jürgen Habermas addressed the meaning of national sentiment. He saw a conservative revival based on national identity rooted deep in an imputed essence of German culture—a kind of quasi-religious belonging to a harmonious community of believers whose bloodline was identified with national identity. To these conservative circles, post-war German politics had become left-leaning and had heaped blame and guilt on German society, undermining the self-esteem owing to a self-respecting national identity.

> According to [neo-conservative] interpretations, a moralistic defense against the recent past is blocking the views of a thousand-year history prior to 1933. Without the memory of this national history…a positive self-image cannot be created. Without a collective identity, the forces of social integration decline. The lamented 'loss of history' is even said to contribute to the weakness of the political system's legitimation and to threaten this country's domestic peace and international predictability. This is used to justify the compensatory 'creation of meaning' through which historiography is to provide for those uprooted by the process of modernization. (1986b, p. 235)

Habermas argued that a conservative historiography contained an apologetics for the Nazi period by relativizing it next to movements in history (Nazism as fascist anti-modernization) or by comparing it with atrocities committed elsewhere or upon Germans. He supported an unending, ever-incomplete work of 'critical self-examination' in which a legitimate national identity was established and guaranteed. It would be based on the partial views of sectors of society, and in that sense would not comprise a homogeneous culture, nor would it depend on an illusion of such a social culture. Patriotic sentiment would rest, not in inclusion in such a social culture—perhaps something like what Anderson (1983) means by an 'imagined community'—but in 'constitutional patriotism', a sentiment aroused by belief in law founded on basic principles (Brunkhorst et al. 2009; Müller 2006, 2008).

Habermas saw a collective effort in the public sphere, in which historians played a major role as the representatives of history in a complexity that must neither congeal into a mythic collective national identity, nor evade the specificity of Nazi ideology and actions. 'It is a question of the public use of history' (1986b, p. 237)—which the *Historikerstreit* was.[3] He advocated a democratic politics in which public, democratic debate was essential. Habermas' view brings him close to psychoanalysis, though he rarely mentions it in this debate, despite his extensive writing elsewhere (Habermas 1972, 1988, pp. 93, 180–88).[4]

Habermas' view is consistent with the psychoanalytic concepts of the depressive position and reparation. It is, therefore, consistent with my thesis that remembering is reparation, but can be distorted into a simulacrum—manic reparation—that seems like reparation but is not. Reparation is an unending urge that does not depend on feeling driven by persecution. Manic reparation depends on a sense of an illegitimately imposed guilt with a demand for compensation, mitigated by the claim that it has been paid off. Here we have the two positions of the *Historikerstreit* and its historical ambiance, recast in psychoanalytic language. For conservatives, guilt for the Holocaust was no longer relevant *and* their call for closure evoked the charge of evasion.

As historian, Bern Faulenbach, Chairman of the Social Democratic Party historical commission, put it in 1988:

> There have to be serious doubts as to whether or not complex societies can develop consistent identities at all… There is much to be said in favour of accepting the existence of different identities and developing a historical consciousness that allows for the tension which exists between those different identities, and which encourages critical self-reflection above all. (Quoted by Berger 1995, p. 194)

Yet the yearning for national identity remained. In his overview of historians' attitudes towards nation-building before reunification, Berger said that

> some historians see the determining characteristic of the Federal Republic as its provincialism [and] they have argued [that] the Federal Republic is revealed as an artificial creation of the Allies, bereft of any identity of its own. They see a new German nation-state as a genuine opportunity to transcend the old Federal Republic's alleged lack of historical roots, and write German history from Karl the Great to Kohl the Great (Berger p. 200; also see Eley 1988 on historians of both left and right who argue for recovering a sense of national identity and pride).

Berger points out that it is primarily neo-Prussian historians who see a return to 'the cornerstone of the old *völkisch* nationalism, the idea of ethnicity [in which an] identity derived from ethnic collective memories' will be built (p. 200). But not only right-wing conservatives hold this view. Even the distinguished labour historian and widow of Willy Brandt, Brigitte Seebacher-Brandt, 'criticized the inability of the left to understand the "imponderabilities of the soul of the Volk", and welcome[d] the return of the nation: "The nation remains the natural and normal, the obvious frame of reference for the people, into which they are born"' (p. 201).

The very public *Historikerstreit* was precipitated by the visit by President Reagan to a German military base in Bitburg, West Germany, on 5 May 1985 (see Bartov 1992; Eley 1988; Maier 1988, pp. 9–16; for documents on Bitburg, see Hartman 1986). 'By intention, this was to be an act of symbolic resolution, a closing of the books on the past, the consummation of Germany's long-earned return to normalcy' (Eley 1988, p. 176). The event honoured Germany's fallen soldiers as freedom fighters against communism, but it also brought together the commemoration of German soldiers, including the SS, and the victims of the Holocaust, implying a moral equivalence that cancelled the debt to the victims of the Nazis. The event unleashed fury on all sides, including German nationalists who saw Germany's continuing moral debt as victimization by its enemies. Jürgen Habermas opened the *Historikerstreit* with criticisms of an apologist tendency of some German historians, who wanted to lessen the moral burden of responsibility for Nazi atrocities and to call for recognition of German suffering and victimhood, particularly in the East at the hands of the Red Army. At the heart of it was how to reconstruct a German national identity; whether and how to lay the past to rest, a past that had been corrupted by the Nazi period. Habermas called for a 'constitutional patriotism' based on Western liberal democratic values, as opposed to a völkish nationalist patriotism (Eley 1988, p. 183; Habermas 1989, pp. 227, 256–8, 261–2; Maier 1988, pp. 34–65).

Andreas Hillgruber and the Historikerstreit

The main target of Habermas' critique of an apologist tendency was Hillgruber's, *A Two-Fold Downfall: the Smashing of the German Reich and the End of European Judaism* (1986). Habermas' quick and sharp response, published in Die Zeit (11 July 1986; see 1986a), drew scholars into a very public debate in newspapers, magazines, television and radio. I will dwell on it because it brings out a fundamental issue in historiography. The integrity of historical scholarship demands two attitudes: scientific research and empathic representation. But in historical scholarship of the Nazi period, these two attitudes cancel each other: the historical record, in its very accuracy, can efface the very human experience that it describes; an empathic portrayal may do the same, but in any event, it defies inclusion in a narrative of historical forces. Saul Friedländer (1984, pp. 90–2) gives examples of what he calls exorcism and involuntary evasion in detailed historical scholarship, with all its evidence and so different from Holocaust denial. A narrative can mix, even within one sentence, the ordinary with the horrific and neutralize the experience; for example, 'The Jews of some transports…were not assigned to the local ghettos or camps…These Jews were shot on arrival' (quoting the prominent historian, Martin Broszat). Friedländer says it is an inevitable consequence of historical scholarship, which reaches the limit of what can be expressed.

> And paralysis of language aside, what is the fundamental characteristic of this exorcism? To put the past back into bearable dimensions, super-impose

it upon the known and respected progress of human behavior, put it in the identifiable course of things, into the unmysterious march of ordinary history, into the reassuring world of the rules that are the basis of our society – in short, into conformism and conformity. (106–7)[5]

In the background of the *Historikerstreit* lay a serious discussion among professional historians on the meaning and limits of historicizing events that, as in the case of the Holocaust, were not just inexplicable, but beyond representation. To write history that purported to include them would seem to convey meaning, but would not only grossly fail to represent them: it would also fail their victims, exonerate their perpetrators and distort history. Nonetheless, historical explanation is built on establishing historical facts as the basis of reality-orientated historical narratives. As Hillgruber argues, the pursuit of facts in empirical enquiry, presumed to be free of ideology, endorses the notion of free, unfettered investigation. Indeed, the integrity of historical scholarship demands such an enquiry, with a rigour akin to science, in the historicizing of all aspects of social life.

Another way to bring out this dilemma is to contrast the scholarly narrative of the historian, aiming as much as possible to represent the subjectivity in the narrative, with the memories recalled by the people who are represented. With time, memory gradually gives way to history. The historian's integrity demands that the subjectivity be retained, even as memory is no longer first-hand and as the understanding of the broader forces improves. At the same time, the empiricist claim to pursue any enquiry as the prerogative—even the demand of integrity—might conceal an ideology. A tension remains, one that can be seen in the discussion between Broszat and Friedländer (1988). They agree that historical research should be unfettered and objective, and that the subjectivity of the historical figures is integral to it. They expose a disagreement, in that Broszat sees a special Jewish interest that tends towards a mythologizing, in reaction to which Friedländer sees an ideology concealed in Broszat's objective history. Historical investigation must hold in tension the subjectivity of remembered experience and the objectivity of scientific history. Historians must identify with their subjects and must be objective. To do the former, they must get close to their subjects with their own subjectivity; to do the latter, they must also distance themselves (So it is with psychoanalysis).

Hillgruber makes a case for liberating historical enquiry from a simplified, limiting straight-jacket into a proper history of the Nazi period: the problematic of historicizing the National Socialist period in German history. Historicizing, in the sense of bringing it into a general understanding of historical context and forces seems wholly unobjectionable and, indeed, to be the only acceptable way to conceive of an empirical, scientific history. In the post-war period, there were swings in thinking about the actuality of the Federal Republic of Germany in relation to its situation within the Western alliance: as an independent, self-respecting nation; as the unique lynchpin of East-West relations at the centre of *Mittel Europa*; as a nation sullied by a historically intelligible, fascist anti-modernism. The stakes in the *Historikerstreit* turned on these big questions, on which Hillgruber argued the case for historicizing the Nazi period into the long sweep of German history and the broader power relations to which it had been subjected. Post-war historians, he argued, had focused too narrowly on Hitler and racism.

What fired Habermas' riposte was what he saw to be a smoothing over of the key issue of moral responsibility for the Holocaust and what would become the issue of the 'singularity' of the Holocaust in comparison with other victimizations, including that of the German army of the East. Hillgruber argued that the soldiers on the Eastern front fought relentlessly for their survival and that of German civilians, and that their predicament raised a series of fundamental questions, touching on politics, leadership of the war and morality in a war of annihilation. He argued that historians were obligated by their professional ethos to understand the complexity of life on the ground.

From the outset, therefore, the professional, scientific project of unrestricted enquiry was simultaneously a moral critique. But Hillgruber argued his case solely on the imperative that science must not be restricted—what provoked Habermas was what he saw as the concealment of the moral dimension inside the imperative of science. The idea of historicizing the Nazi period held the scientific and the moral dimensions in a tension, the obscurity of which seemed unresolvable. The very use of words adds to the obscurity. Hillguber implies that the Reich was smashed but Judaisim just came to an end: the true victims were the Germans; the Jews simply vanished. But the very recognition—formulation—of the historical facts from which comparative victimization seems to arise has to be opened to analysis, and this analysis lies outside the historical facts on which Hillgruber makes his case.

For Hillgruber, historical integrity demands that we understand the constraints within which the German army felt impelled to act. But they are also his constraints: he sets up boundary conditions within which the case for unfettered investigation is indisputable. He refers to a commander in the East, who was no National Socialist and who, in 1937, warned the Chief of the General Staff of risks in Hitler's strategy to settle the German territorial question (*Raumfrage*). But when an opportunity arose to return from the Balkans to join the 20 July 1944 [assassination attempt on Hitler], he, instead, returned to protect East Prussia. Nor was he the only commander in the East who possibly chose to act out of concern for the army of the East and the East Germans.[6] The historian must 'take account of the subjective judgment of the situation of the responsible individual on the spot and the action or non-action…that follows from it' (p. 20).

One can see the methodological implication of Hillgruber's position. The historian is driven to identify with actors in their particular setting. History demands the closeness of empathy by the investigator in relation to historical subject. And, in empathizing with the living subject, the historian bears the responsibility of being drawn into the same forced choice as the historical actor: to experience, as a subjective recognition of a fact, the imperative of the moment enforced by the responsibility on the shoulders of the actor. One

> stands before the problem of identification…[I]dentification with the arriving [Soviet Union] was unthinkable. The concept, liberation, implied such an identification with the victors, and naturally it had complete legitimacy for the victims of the National Socialist regime freed from the concentration camps and prisons. With respect to the fate of the German nation as a whole, however, it was inappropriate. (pp. 23, 24)

Here is where he introduces the boundary condition: there can be only one, circumscribed and concrete, identification. The Allies aimed to defeat Germany, not the National socialists; one cannot identify with

Andreas Hillgruber and the Historikerstreit

the victors over one's nation; one cannot identify with Hitler; one can only identify with the people and the army in the East and with the German sailors in the region of the Baltic Sea (pp. 24–5). This identification defines the field of empirical enquiry and historical fact: the professional values of historians require them to identify with the soldiers, by understanding the actuality on the ground without bias intruding into the investigation. It is 'a duty, which belongs to the most difficult that the occupation of the historian bears for the future, and which perhaps is the attempt at an overall view of the collapse of the fronts, the overpowering of Middle Europe, the smashing of the German Reich and the downfall of the German East with all that was bound with it, the last great demand of historical writing' (pp. 35–6). Investigator and object of investigation are tied together by the facts within a science of history.

Hillgruber presents a detailed account of a situation in which, suddenly and without protective resources, the German army and civilian population found itself overrun, before they became aware of it (p. 29). They faced a terror evoked by a Soviet advance bent on revenge for German crimes, but mainly from the reputation of the barbaric character of Soviet conception of war, gained earlier: 1939 invasion of Poland; 1944 in Rumania and Hungary; 1944/45 in northern Czechoslovakia (p. 35).[7]

Richard Evans (2015, p. 348) contradicts these 'facts'. The military abandoned civilians, and *Gauleiters* were even unwilling to evacuate areas threated by the Red army, but the German army nonetheless fought relentlessly and against the clear reality that the war was lost. This dissonance of facts opens the question of the loyalty of the German army to further enquiry. Ian Kershaw (2011) lent some support to Hillgruber's thesis.

> The ideological fight against 'Asiatic hordes' and 'Bolshevik beasts', and even the patriotic defence of the nation, merged subliminally into a desperate attempt to stave off the very obvious threat to families and homes or to avenge the atrocities of the Red Army. Beyond these motives, soldiers fought out of group solidarity for their immediate comrades and, in the last resort, for their own survival. (p. 394)

But Kershaw doesn't leave these facts on their own. He concludes that there was a fanatical loyalty that rested on Hitler (with which Hillgruber might agree), but it was not loyalty to Hitler (p. 400). Hitler's 'mass charismatic appeal had long since dissolved, but the structures and mentalities of his charismatic rule lasted until his death in the bunker'. The willingness to fight to total destruction followed from the structure of the 'charismatic Führer regime'.

> All the other factors – lingering popular backing for Hitler, the ferocious terror apparatus, the increased dominance of the Party, the prominent roles of the Bormann-Goebbels-Himmler-Speer quadrumvirate, the negative integration produced by the fear of Bolshevik occupation, and the continued readiness of high-ranking civil servants and military leaders to continue doing their duty when all was obviously lost – were ultimately subordinate to the way the charismatic Führer regime was structured, and how it functioned, in its dying phase. (p. 400)

From this analysis, there was an imperative driving the army, perhaps especially in the East, but it was an illusion. This illusion spread throughout German society. It was based on the thrall cast by the leader and assimilated by the people, a relationship cogently, economically and beautifully described and explained by Freud (1921; see also Chap. 2). This thrall, with its delusion of enemies necessary to its survival, is what we examined in Chap. 4. Hillgruber ties the historian down to a tightly circumscribed study of identification with desperate people under protection. His boundary condition excludes the structure of Nazi power—a power based on illusion and the delusion that equated German survival with the elimination of an other (Jewish) people. But in fact, what Hillgruber conveys is the sense of being, not just overwhelmed by an external force, but of an unready state in which incursion was so sudden and massive, that it seemed like an eruption in the very midst of the population, civilian and military: a trauma, a view of personal suffering that Hillgruber articulated for the West German pubic (Fulbrook 1999, p. 174).

So began the *Historikerstreit* as an event in 1986. For Hillgruber, the historian must be free to pursue an enquiry, uninhibited by a political correctness, which was intruded into the scientific pursuit of knowledge by revisionist historians. For Habermas, Hillgruber repackaged ideology in support of resurgent nationalism based on a deep immersion in a mystique of identity, enfolding a people with a common root, a *Volksgemeinschaft*. Hillgruber's legitimate claim for a scientific history was simultaneously undermined by the ideological construction of the boundary conditions within which scientific historical methodology operated. This internal tension vexes historical enquiry.

Hillgruber's second theme, anti-Semitism is much the smaller part of the book. In 'The Historical Position of the Annihilation of the Jews', he says that it must be considered in three aspects: historical anti-Semitism in the Christian middle ages; emancipation in the age of Enlightenment and the reaction to it; finally, the 'new' anti-Semitism in Germany from 1918. He asks whether the outcome was foreseeable and predetermined or could have been otherwise. He outlines research on anti-Semitism in Germany from the First World War. Confined to limited sectors of German society up to the First World War, ideologically aggressive, racially radical, detailed proposals for removing rights from Jews rode on a rising tide of anti-Semitism, such that even assimilated Jews would have been aware of their increasingly isolated position (p. 80).

Hillgruber asks, 'Had it [the final solution] not been there to be seen (p. 88)?...To a large part of the National Socialist leadership..., the war was a means of consolidation of the people, a racial reshaping of Europe through emigration and resettlement on a large scale...' (p. 89). The expansion of Germany to include Poland brought an additional 3 million Jews into German territory, which militated against migration as the solution to the Jewish question. Zimmermann (2008, p. 16) pointedly rejects the assumption that the Jews should have known they would have to leave. This shift of blame from perpetrators to victims also ignores the active infusion of Nazi ideology into German society, beginning with progressive exclusion (see Confino 2014, for detailed lists of exclusions; also Zimmermann, pp. 39–40) and persistent propaganda inserted into everyday life (Kaplan 2009) and scripted events. There are many accounts of this marginalization, a preparation for annihilation (Evans 2015; Friedländer 1997; Longerich 2006).

An inquiry into Jewish participation in the military during the First World War was an example of anti-Jewish sentiment based, not on anti-Semitism, but on the suspicion that Jews did not share national interests (11 October 1916 Prussian Ministry of War measure). After the war, in a German nationalist mood, Jews were blamed for a *Dolchstoss* [stab in the back], intruding Jewish Bolshevism and importing an alien [*artfremdig*] democracy.

Hillgruber does argue that the extinction of the Jews could not be conflated with other atrocities; it was not comparable to other war crimes or anti-partisan activity. 'Rather, an arbitrarily selected, large group of people had been declared to be a "deadly enemy" before the war; they were to be physically exterminated' (Hillgruber 1984, p. 121). Nonetheless, he comes to the view that the recruitment of so many people to the extinction of others, leading to the murder of the Jews was not a singular event, but could happen in extreme situations.

> The fact of the direct and indirect cooperation of so many men inside the organizations, jurisdictions and offices, which implemented the murder, and also the acceptance through the mass of the population of the least suspicious foreshadowing of the gruesome happenings, nevertheless points beyond the historical uniqueness of a practice that was possible in line with the constellation of the year 1941. (1986, p. 98)

Historians have repeatedly tried to explain this unorganized collaboration. For Broszat, Hitler was only the 'exponent' of a 'nationalistic psychosis', but also an 'integrating figure of this "movement", without which a threshold into the political could not have been crossed'(1970, p. 402). Mommsen spoke of a 'chiliastic dimension' (1983, p. 237), which gathered different interests (pp. 240–2) and realized what, for Hitler, was a 'timeless programme' (p. 239) 'in the half-light of unclear orders and ideological fanaticism' (p. 251). '[T]he utopian "vision" bound up with the Führer…proved "guidelines for action"' among a people who were 'working towards the Führer' (Kershaw 1999, p. 40). For Confino (2014), the Nazi movement rested on an imagination of a world without Jews. These attempts to explain the Nazi period seem to burst the constraints set by Hillgruber. Even his argument against 'singularity' annuls itself.

Habermas sees in Hillgruber's call to professional duty a mitigation of the victimization of the Jews and a dilution of the singularity of the Holocaust into history.

The *Historikerstreit* and *Vergangenheitsbewältigung*

Recasting Germans from perpetrators into victims has been common (Eley 2004, p. 177; Herf 1997, pp. 82–97, 224; Lüdtke 1993). For conservatives who wanted to preserve national identity, memory was being distorted by youth and a few leftists who opened wounds from the past by exposing a Nazi period that best should have remained concealed (Eley 1988, p. 198). They wanted to finish with Nazism and finish the normalization of German history. Spectacular West German economic growth, a firm democratic structure, embeddedness in the Western Alliance and Western liberal values had already made the case (the comparison with East Germany will be more explicit in the next chapter). Like Hillgruber, Habermas recognized the suffering under the Nazis and the bravery of German troops and civilians in the East, but argued that drawing an abstract moral equivalence between their victimhood and that of the Jews allowed a slippage in which the Holocaust lost its impact in German memory.

West Germany had been cast into a process of *Vergangenheitsbewältigung*. Usually translated as 'coming to terms with the past', this rendering repeats a core post-war German conundrum. Literally, it means 'mastering the past' (Maier 1988, p. 7). It implies overcoming it, getting over it. But to master the past leads away from remembering it in the sense of assimilating it in all its dimensions, including recognition of the victims and of the injury inflicted on them, and a full embracing of them by a benign identification (rather than a claim of equivalent suffering). *Vergangenheitbewältigung* apparently recognized a moral burden of the Nazi past, but also did not recognize it. It was more like management of memory than like Freud's (1914) concept of *Durcharbeitung*—'working through'—in which memory is restored in the sense of an assimilation of the past into the flow of consciousness through repeated tracing of all the aspects of repressed memory in their emotional as well as cognitive dimensions (about which Adorno had already written in 1959; Bartov 1992).

Although post-war historians have concentrated on *Verganageheitsbewältigung* and on historicizing modern German history, into which the Nazi period would find a place and, therefore, a historical meaning, they have generally not thought of the inclusion of the Nazi period as the recovery of memory from repression. There was, it has been argued, no forgetting and there was no repression. The Holocaust was persistently in the public mind, the nation-state was to be restored; the idea that Germany had not mourned its past aimed to create a mythic second guilt that obstructed it (Berger 1995, pp. 201–3; Eley 2004; Herf 1997; Kauders 2003; Margalit 2010, pp. 250–80). Repression and the surmounting of repression have been pinned to the Mitscherlichs and left there (for recent overviews and critiques, see Brockhaus 2008).

Reviewing literature on coming to terms with the past, Geoff Eley (2004) comments that

> [w]hether or not they 'were able to mourn' [referring to Mitscherlich and Mitscherlich 1967/1975], Germans had never been silent about the 1940s, and public talking was vociferously selective rather than merely repressed. Excellent new scholarship has been exploring how these mechanisms of memory worked. By hiding the reality of the full breadth of the support for Nazism, for example, the salient patterns of public remembrance during the 1950s repositioned the German people instead as victims – whether as the oppressed sufferers beneath the Hitler dictatorship, as the GDR's official discourse of anti-fascism proclaimed; or in the Adenauer era's emphasis on the ravages of the Red Army, the forcible expulsion of Germans from Eastern Europe, and the imposing of Communism in the Soviet occupation zone. (p. 177)

Similarly, in his in-depth study of memory in post-war Germany, Jeffrey Herf (1997) follows Adorno's (1959) view that 'the extinction of memory is far more the accomplishment of an all too wide-awake consciousness than of its weakness in the face of the overwhelming power of unconscious processes' (p. 10, quoting Adorno, p. 558). Herf details what he calls 'multiple restorations': the memory that emerged from the varied forms taken by this 'wide-awake consciousness', a divided memory in post-war Germany.

What the *Historikerstreit* revealed was a widely diffused defence against remembering the Nazi period. But it revealed another aspect as well. As Eley and others have shown, Germans were not silent about the Nazi period and as other evidence makes clear, nor did they ignore the demand for reparation. But on both these issues, they refer to *conscious* remembering, *conscious* acts of reparation in the form of compensation, *conscious* action against anti-Semitism, *conscious* acts of contrition. All of these actions are important. But just as the Mitscherlich's thesis has been marginalized, so too has the unconscious dimension in general, including the forms of defence against psychic pain that are common in psychoanalysis.

We needed to work through the detail of the *Historikerstreit* as a crystallization of the German dilemma over remembering, in order to show how it converges with the need of the unconscious dimension. The dialogue between them allows us to situate psychoanalytic thinking in a specific historical setting and, conversely, to include historical explanation in this unconscious dimension. We will turn next to the unconscious dimension of not-knowing and not-remembering, to how one can know and not-know at the same time.

In Chap. 8, we will extend this analysis of unconscious defences against knowing and remembering to the post-war partition of Germany. The partition of Germany, with the ensuing political, ideological and economic separations and confrontations between East and West, also divided and distorted the memory of the Nazi period, specifically of the Holocaust. Each Germany turned the other into an enemy at whose hands each was victimized, and this new history swamped that of the Nazi perpetration. Beneath this victimization lay victimization of the Jews, which was forgotten in the mutual antagonism (Herf 1997, pp. 8, 25, 387), while '[t]he elusive and yet ubiquitous presence attributed to the Jews by the regime played an even more important role in creating an inverted perception of victimhood throughout the Nazi era' (Bartov 1998, p. 784).

Notes

1. Fulbrook (2016) raises a question that we might see as a concrete example of Habermas' point. She asks, 'Do Polish people, for example, have a right to live on what has been described as one mass graveyard of European Jewry without being constantly troubled by memorial landscapes and reminders of the ghosts of the past' (p. 108)?
2. To be more precise, the Mitscherlichs argued that the narcissistic grandiosity essential to the Hitler regime was frozen in place; that the regaining of reality would entail a collapse of this narcissism. Mourning would, therefore, be a catastrophe. This aspect of the inability to mourn is consistent with historical scholarship on the persisting allegiance of the German people to Nazism, based on a bond with the leader. Psychoanalytically, it was an illusion that underlay the relentless refusal to surrender, followed by the immediate collapse of allegiance following the death of Hitler. Ian Kershaw's conclusion, for example, that German allegiance rested on a peculiar bond to a structure of power represented by Hitler, but not embodied in him, supports the Mitscherlich's view that a narcissistic collapse was the dominant mentality in the immediate post-war period (Kershaw 1999, 2011, p. 400).
3. The Historikerstreit was a West German debate, but it will serve the purpose of highlighting the conflict within memory. It has been criticized for exacerbating a moralistic rectitude, which had more to do with intergenerational conflict and an aggressive relocation of the tarnish of Nazi perpetration by the second generation—the 68ers—onto the parental generation of the Nazi period.
Lipstadt (1994) argues that the *Historikerstreit* was a valuable public event, but also that professional historians used arguments that were very close to those of Holocaust deniers, and thereby gave credibility to them.

> Despite widespread criticism, the [historians] debate gave the German media and general public the imprimatur to conduct the kind of discussion about contemporary Germany's relationship to its past that would never have been heard before. Calls for a 'sanitized' version of German history appeared in Germany's most prominent newspapers…Those involved in the current antiforeigner campaign in Germany find this perspective on history particularly inviting. If Germany was also a victim of a 'downfall,' and if the Holocaust was no different from a mélange of other tragedies, Germany's moral obligation

to welcome all who seek refuge within its borders is lessened…These historians are not crypto deniers, but the results of their work are the same: the blurring of boundaries between fact and fiction and between persecuted and persecutor…Relativism, however convoluted, sounds far more legitimate than outright denial. These German historians have created a prototype that may prove useful for the deniers. (p. 215)

It was, in Saul Friedländer's (1993) view, of dubious value. 'In the early sixties signs of a transformation appeared, and that new approach dominated the late sixties and the seventies. From then on various forms of denial and defensive reactions surfaced in a new guise. The Historians' Controversy of the late eighties became an unusual case of acting out' (pp. 124–5). Although Friedländer stands out among historians in his use of psychoanalysis in understanding history, he also does not cite Freud on the psychoanalytic concept of acting-out as an alternative to thinking: acting externalizes and dramatizes; thinking internalizes and reflects. Nor, therefore, does he consider that acting repeats the offence that it aims to mitigate, leading to repetition (and perhaps the seemingly endless futility of the *Historikerstreit*).

LaCapra (1997) notes that prominent historians of Nazi Germany, such as Richard Evans and Ian Kershaw, think the *Historikerstreit* added nothing new, and that it was a form of acting-out. He argues, however, that acting-out can be an essential, preliminary stage in self-reflection. For him, the *Historkerstreit* remains an important preparation for remembering, mourning and reparation.

The history of the Historikerstreit has been surveyed by several authors, including Assmann (2013), Bartov (1992) and Eley (1988). In reassessing the *Inability to Mourn* (Mitscherlich and Mitscherlich 1967/1975), by Brockhaus (2008) sees a shift in German preoccupation with the past, from the guilt and shame of the perpetrator to an identification with the actual victims of Nazi perpetration, which underlies the building of a culture at ease with itself, including its memory. But there is always a tension between a forced enactment of contrition and a spontaneous, deeply held, internalization of a remorseful attitude. This tension surfaces repeatedly, exposing an ambivalence in remembering projects, such as memorialization.

In my view, the *Historikerstreit* remains central to German history as a public process, reinforcing a public, as opposed to the sham public of the

Nazi *Volksgemeinschaft*. And it remains relevant as a moral challenge to possible misuse of facticity in 'scientific' historical methodology.
4. Referring to the psychoanalyst, Edith Jacobson, he speaks of the psychoanalytic insight that 'the process in which we learn to synthesize the initially competing images of the good and bad parents into complex images of the same person is a long and painful one. The weak ego acquires its strength only through nonselective interaction with an ambivalent environment' (1986b, p. 235)—a need that survives in adulthood.
5. Langer(1991) makes a similar point in comparing stark oral Holocaust testimonies with more continuous written narratives. The raw, helpless, unredeemable experiences expressed in the former can seem more managed, hopeful and mitigated by later experience in the latter.
6. Hillgruber is reacting to a claim by Norbert Blüm, that prolonging the war also prolonged mass murders in concentration camps. I have not been able to track down this claim.
7. Hillgruber also has in mind a living myth when he speaks of 'sacrificial efforts of the German army and the German navy in the Baltic Sea, which sought to protect the population of the German East against the orgy of revenge of the Red Army, the mass rapes (*Massenvergewältigungen*), the wilful murders and the enforced deportations, and in the final phase to keep open to the East Germans the escape routes towards the West by land or sea' (Hillgruber 1986, pp. 24–5). The Germans saw 'Tannenberg', a First World War total victory over the Russians, as a reversal of defeat at the hands of the Slavs 500 years earlier—for Hitler, an event that testified to the glory of Germany. The conviction that the German army in the East had the Russian army under control led to being unprepared for the massive offensive. Thus, there are world historical forces behind the scenes in the confined, empirical enquiry.

References

Adorno, T. (1959) The Meaning of Working Through [*Aufarbeitung*] the Past. In *Guilt and Defense: On the Legacies of National Socialism in Postwar Germany*. Cambridge, MA/London: Harvard University Press, pp. 213–28.

Anderson, B. R. O'G. (1983) *Imagined Communities: Reflections on the Origin and Spread of Nationalism*. London: Verso; revised edition 2006.

Assmann, A. (2013) *Das neue Unbehagen an der Erinnerungskultur: eine Intervention*. München: C.H. Beck.

Bartov, O. (1992) Time Present and Time Past: The *Historikerstreit* and German Reunification. *New German Critique* 55: 173–90.
Bartov, O. (1998) Defining Enemies, Making Victims: Germans, Jews, and the Holocaust. *The American Historical Review* 103(3): 771–816.
Berger, S. (1995) Historians and Nation-Building in Germany After Reunification. *Past & Present* 148: 187–222.
Brockhaus, G. (2008) Die Unfähigkeit zu trauern als Analyse und als Abwehr der NS-Erbshaft. In Brockhaus, G. (Hg.) *Ist 'Die Unfähigkeit zu trauern' noch actuell? Eine interdisziplinäre Diskussion. Psychosozial* 31, nr 114 (4) (special issue), pp. 29–39.
Broszat, M. (1970) Soziale Motivation und Führer-Bindung des Nationalsozialismus. *Vierteljahrshefte für Zeitgeschichte* 18(4): 392–409.
Broszat, M. and Friedländer, S. (1988) A Controversy About the Historicization of National Socialism. *New German Critique* 44: 85–126.
Brunkhorst, H., Kreide, R. and Lafont, C. (Eds.) (2009) *Habermas Handbuch*. Weimar: J. B. Meltzer and C. E. Poeschel.
Confino, A. (2014) *A World Without Jews: The Nazi Imagination from Persecution to Genocide*. New Haven/London: Yale University Press.
Eley, G. (1988) Nazism, Politics and the Image of the Past: Thoughts on the West German *Historikerstreit* 1986–1987. *Past and Present* 121: 171–208.
Eley, G. (2004) The Unease of History: Settling Accounts with the East German Past. *History Workshop Journal* 57: 175–201.
Evans, R. (2015) *The Third Reich in History and Memory*. London: Little, Brown.
Freud, S. (1914) Remembering, Repeating and Working-Through (Further Recommendations on the Technique of Psycho-Analysis II). *The Standard Edition of the Complete Psychological Works of Sigmund Freud* 12: 145–56.
Freud, S. (1921) *Group Psychology and the Analysis of the Ego. The Standard Edition of the Complete Psychological Works of Sigmund Freud* 18: 65–144.
Freud, S. (1923) *The Ego and the Id. The Standard Edition of the Complete Psychological Works of Sigmund Freud* 19: 1–66.
Freud, S. (1930) *Civilization and Its Discontents. The Standard Edition of the Complete Psychological Works of Sigmund Freud* 21: 57–146.
Friedländer, S. (1984) *Reflections of Nazism: An Essay on Kitsch and Death*. New York: Harper & Row.
Friedländer, S. (1993) *Memory, History and the Extermination of the Jews of Europe*. Bloomington/Indianapolis: Indiana University Press.
Friedländer, S. (1997) *The Years of Persecution: Nazi Germany & the Jews 1933–1939*. London: Weidenfeld & Nicholson/Phoenix.
Fulbrook, M. (1999) *German National Identity after the Holocaust*. Cambridge: Polity.

Fulbrook, M. (2016) Questionable Concepts: Trust, Distrust and Normalisation. In *Erfahrung, Erinnerung, Geschichtsschreibung: Neue Perspektiven auf die deutschen Diktaturen*. Weimar: Wallstein Verlag, pp. 62–110.

Greenberg, J. and Mitchell, S. (1983) *Object Relations Theory in Psychoanalysis*. Cambridge, MA: Harvard University Press.

Habermas, J. (1972) *Knowledge and Human Interests*. London: Heinemann.

Habermas, J. (1986a) A Kind of Settlement of Damages: The Apologetic Tendencies in German Historical Writing. *Die Zeit*, July 11; English translation in Knowlton, J. and Gates, T. (eds. and translators) *Forever in the Shadow of Hitler? Original Documents of the Historikerstreit, the Controversy Concerning the Singularity of the Holocaust*. Atlantic Highlands, New Jersey: Humanities Press, 1993, pp. 34–44; extended version in Habermas, J. One Sort of Compensation: Apologetic Tendencies in German Historiography. In *The New Conservatism: Cultural Criticism and the Historians' Debate*. London: Polity Press, 1989, pp. 212–28.

Habermas, J. (1986b) On the Public Use of History. *Die Zeit*, November 7. In Habermas, J. *The New Conservatism: Cultural Criticism and the Historians' Debate*. London: Polity Press, 1989, pp. 229–40.

Habermas, J. (1988) *On the Logic of the Social Sciences*. London: Polity Press, 1990.

Habermas, J. (1989) *The New Conservatism: Cultural Criticism and the Historians' Debate*. London: Polity Press.

Hartman, G. (ed.) (1986) *Bitburg in Moral and Political Perspective*. Bloomington: Indiana University Press.

Herf, J. (1997) *Divided Memory: The Nazi Past in the Two Germanies*. Cambridge, MA/London: Harvard University Press.

Hillgruber, A. (1984) War in the East and the Extermination of the Jews. Yad Vashem. https://www.yadvashem.org/untoldstories/documents/studies/Andreas_Hillgruber.pdf. Accessed 31.5.2016.

Hillgruber, A. (1986) *Zweierlei Untergang: Die Zerschlagung des deutschen Reiches und das Ende des europäischen Judentums*. Berlin: Seidler.

Hinshelwood, R. D. (1987) *What Happens in Groups: Psychoanalysis, the Individual and the Community*. London: Free Association Books.

Kaplan, T. P. (2009) *The Language of Nazi Genocide: Linguistic Violence and the Struggle of Jewish Ancestry*. Cambridge: Cambridge University Press.

Kauders, A. (2003) History as Censure: 'Repression' and 'Philosemitism' in Postwar Germany. *History & Memory* 15(1): 97–122.

Kershaw, I. (1999) 'Working Towards the Führer': Reflections on the Nature of the Hitler Dictatorship. In *Hitler, the Germans, and the Final Solution*.

Jerusalem: International Institute for Holocaust Research, Yad Vashem; New Haven, [Conn.]: Yale University Press, 2008, pp. 29–48.

Kershaw, I. (2011) *The End: Hitler's Germany, 1944–45*. London: Allen Lane.

Klein, M. (1946) Notes on Some Schizoid Mechanisms. In *The Writings of Melanie Klein*, vol. 3. London: Hogarth and the Institute of Psychoanalysis, 1975, pp. 1–24.

LaCapra, D. (1997) Revisiting the Historians' Debate: Mourning and Genocide. *History and Memory* 9(1/2): 80–112.

Langer, L. (1991) *Holocaust Testimonies: The Ruins of Memory*. New Haven/London: Yale University Press.

Lipstadt, D. (1994) *Denying the Holocaust: The Growing Assault on Truth and Memory*. New York: The Free Press.

Longerich, P. (2006) *Davon Haben Wir Nichts Gewusst: die Deutschen und die Judenverfolgerung 1933–1945*. Munich: Siedler.

Lüdtke, A. (1993) 'Coming to Terms with the Past': Illusions of Remembering: Ways of Forgetting Nazism in West Germany. *The Journal of Modern History* 65(3): 542–72.

Maier, C. (1988) *The Unmasterable Past: History, Holocaust, and German National Identity*. Cambridge, MA/London: Harvard University Press.

Margalit, G. (2010) *Guilt, Suffering, and Memory: Germany Remembers Its Dead of World War II*. Bloomington/Indianapolis: Indiana University Press.

Mitscherlich, A. and Mitscherlich, M. (1967/1975) *The Inability to Mourn: Principles of Collective Behaviour*. Munich: Piper & Co. Verlag; English translation, New York: Grove Press.

Mommsen, H. (1983) Die Realisieren des Utopischen: Die 'Endlösung der Judenfrage' im 'Dritten Reich'. *Geschichte und Gesellschaft* 9(3): 381–420; English translation, The Realization of the Unthinkable: The 'Final Solution of the Jewish Question' in the 'Third Reich'. In *From Weimar to Auschwitz: Essays in German History*. Cambridge: Polity, 1991, pp. 224–349.

Müller, J.-W. (2006) On the Origins of Constitutional Patriotism. *Contemporary Political Theory* 5: 278–96.

Müller, J.-W. (2008) A General Theory of Constitutional Patriotism. *I•CON* 6(1): 72–95.

Segal, H. (1995) From Hiroshima to the Gulf War and After: Socio-Political Expressions of Ambivalence. In *Psychoanalysis, Literature and War: Papers 1972–1995*. London/New York: Routledge, 1997, pp. 157–68.

Zimmermann, M. (2008) *Deutsche Gegen Deutsche: Das Schicksal der Juden 1938–1945*. Berlin: Aufbau Verlagsgruppe GmbH.

7

Remembering and Not-Remembering

Introduction

Post-war Germany was a period of catastrophic loss: loss of the war, loss of national pride, loss of national identity, partition into two Germanys. All these losses might have promised to come to an end with reunification in 1990. But while reunification brought a restoration of German identity, it also undermined an unconscious stabilizing organization, which I call a psychosocial enclave or haven. This enclave was built from an unconscious complex of defences, shared across the two Germanys. It had brought a haven of paranoid 'security', now lost; and with this loss also came the depressive anxiety of internalizing the destroyed object and the psychotic anxiety of internalizing the German-Jew as a returning, retaliatory object. They brought two dreads: of dissolution of identity and of remembering the Nazi period as unredeemable perpetration.

In order to develop this theme, we need briefly to review the difference between perceptual and delusional reality, from Chaps. 3 and 4, and tie them to forms of remembering. We will then be ready to take up the themes of memorialization as remembering and remembering as reparation in the Chaps. 9 and 10.

© The Author(s) 2017
K. Figlio, *Remembering as Reparation*, Studies in the Psychosocial,
DOI 10.1057/978-1-137-59591-1_7

Perceptual and Delusional Realities

A perceptual difference between people is a difference in ordinary reality of the senses, which includes characteristics that we associate with groupings, such as skin colour, stature, the conformation of the face and the anatomical differences between male and female. Delusional difference is a phantasy of a defining characteristic, which invents a grouping as essentially other. For the thesis of this book, we could say that there are features that we call Semitic in perceptual reality and there were phantasy features that, for the Nazis, defined a Jew as *essentially* non-German. The difference between these two 'realities' is complicated by the way a delusional difference rides inside a perceptual difference, which appears to anchor it in the ordinary reality of the senses. A Jew then becomes essentially non-German on the basis of a set of characteristics that anyone could 'see', if they attended to them carefully. The Jew, so defined, is a creation of anti-Semitism, not an other in perceptual reality, who attracts anti-Semitism.

I based this distinction between realities on Freud's concept of the 'narcissism of small differences'. Sameness, not difference, is the target of hatred. The differences on which hatred is pinned are the anchors of delusional difference, which allow the delusions to parade as observable by anyone who looks. Delusional differences are creations of narcissism, not of the senses. The sensory differences are, in this respect, charades. That goes for the bedrock difference between male and female. They are visibly—anatomically—different, but this difference to the senses is, in itself, of little consequence. The delusional difference that it anchors, however, fuels antagonism as a defence against dissolution: the catastrophe that I described in Chap. 5.

There are, therefore, two forms of identity. The one is based on living in reality, in relation to perceived others. The other is an omnipotent phantasy of self-creation: 'narcissism' in psychoanalysis. At one pole, identity is formed through living in reality among others whose differences—male from female; parent from child—carry no delusional charge. At the other, all beings are (so to speak) male, in the sense of living in a delusional phantasy of masquerading with an omnipotent phallus as a repudiation of femininity. In this reality, there are no differences between the sexes or between generations (Chasseguet-Smirgel 1985b; Freud 1910, p. 173). Ultimately, it is an omnipotent phantasy of self-creation.

In delusional reality, there must be an object, the annihilation of which carries away the dread of dissolution. The dread becomes an internal tension, as in Freud's *Unbehagen der Kultur*; the internal tension becomes an identity threatened by an internal enemy; projection casts it out; internal stability returns as the enemy is extinguished; the dread recurs and the process is repeated. As the historian, Omar Bartov put it, 'Nazism was not only committed to killing all the Jews but was predicated on the assumption that there would always be more "Jews" to kill' (Bartov 1998, pp. 779, 780, 785–6).

The Ambivalence of Not–Remembering

The same holds for memory. In ordinary, perceptual reality, remembering means not only recollecting accurately but also the recognition and toleration of others in relationships. In narcissistic reality, it means creating a delusional memory. In post-war Germany, remembering has meant recognizing the existence of all German people in German society in history, including 1933–1945. That includes remembering the aim to annihilate the Jewish people, along with the guilt and the urge for reparation. But it also has meant retaining the Jew as delusional enemy and the annihilation of the memory of the Jewish German people, dreaded for its threat to national identity of the equally delusional *Volksgemeinchaft*, and annihilating the memory of this aim. I will speak of 'remembering true' for the former and 'remembering false' for the latter. The falseness of remembering, which annihilates it, is carried inside apparently normal, 'remembering true', just as the delusional enemy is carried inside a people with observable characteristics. The charade creates an inherent ambiguity and ambivalence in remembering and in reparation as a form of remembering.

We need to explore the forms of not-remembering before we move on to reparation and memorialization in Chaps. 9 and 10. I will consider three psychoanalytically defined forms of not-remembering, which are relevant to post-war Germany: undoing, disavowal and splitting. They work together, but I will separate them here in order to describe them clearly.

We begin with a blunt fact.

> On May 8, 1945, 8 million Germans were members of the Nazi party. They and their friends and families would constitute a formidable voting bloc opposed to any serious efforts at post-war judicial reckoning or frank public memory…The lesson was that one could speak openly about the Nazi past or win national elections, but not both. (Herf 1997, pp. 202, 203)

We will focus mainly on the Federal Republic of Germany (FRG) in this section, because, as we will see in Chap. 8, the German Democratic Republic (GDR) renounced Nazism and reparation, as problems of the West. The political landscape of the emergent West German state enacted a contradiction in remembering and reparation. In 1949, Konrad Adenauer ran for the post of the first Chancellor of the new FRG. Although himself of 'unassailable' anti-Nazi credentials during the Nazi period (Herf 1997, p. 270), and committed to a Germany that remembered its Nazi past as part of becoming a liberal democracy, Adenauer was nonetheless clear that the FRG could have memory or democracy, and he would lose if he favoured memory (Herf 1997, pp. 267–300).

In his first address to parliament on the state of the government, Adenauer spoke of 'the question of amnesty', adding that

> 'The government…, in the belief that many have subjectively atoned for a guilt that was not heavy, is determined where it appears acceptable to do so to put the past behind us. On the other hand, it is absolutely determined to draw the necessary lessons from the past regarding all those who challenge the existence of our state whether they come now from right-wing radicalism or left-wing radicalism.' This last statement was greeted with shouts of 'bravo!' and 'Very good' [presumably at the mixing of extremisms, into which Nazism was diluted] (Herf 1997, p. 271).

In 1950, Adenauer demanded of the Allies sovereignty for the FRG, an apology for slandering Germany, release of German war criminals and an apology to German soldiers. Jumping forward to 2004, the Central Council of Jews suspended participation in the Foundation for Saxon Memorial Sites, which administered memorials to the victims of Nazi and Communist persecution, because the foundation tended to equate Nazi with Communist crimes (Beattie 2006, p. 147). This reaction has to be seen in the context of discord over a motion put to the German parliament by the conservative Christian Democratic Union (CDU), which alleged that insufficient attention was paid to Communist tyranny and that there should be commemoration of victims of both 'totalitarian dictatorships'.

The opposition was led by the Social Democrat, Kurt Schumacher. He doubted that the government thought very much about the Jewish question. He said, about the gaping wound inflicted, that much depended on Jewish sensibilities, but that the future was bleak when Jews saw the extent of complicity with the Nazis (Herf, p. 277).

Remembering is caught in a tension between recognition and rejection of reality. Making-good in post-war Germany has included nationalism and magical restoration, which has infiltrated the reparative urges towards the damaged object. Thus, the FRG's economic miracle was not only a material success but also a magical creation of a new history. This restoration illusion can be seen in the popular publication of rubble photography (*Trümmerfotographie*), which shows the removal of rubble and rebuilding as if nearly instantaneous—as if by magic (Fuchs 2012, Chap. 2). Sebald (2003), who reproduced rubble photographs from the period, felt troubled by people who seemed out of touch with the horror, offering bland accounts of everyday post-war life or seeing in the devastated cityscapes the dawn of a new age. Similarly, Jager (2002) speaks of the use of photographs as a 'collective visual memory of German culture' (p. 287). German cities had been sick and weak from age. The ruins left after Allied bombing were the 'foundations of the search for an identity rediscovered through the destruction' (p. 294). This reconstruction of the German state and its material substrate combined omnipotent phantasy with observable reality, to fashion an ambiguous reality of a new Germany.

We are speaking, not just of forgetting, but of a wish—unconscious—to forget. As James Young (1993) states, '[t]o the extent that we encourage monuments to do our memory-work for us, we become that much more forgetful. In effect, the initial impulse to memorialize events like the Holocaust may actually spring from an opposite and equal desire to forget them' (p. 5). And individuals do not forget on their own: they group together—coalesce—to forget. Furthermore, in the collective act of forgetting, in the very process—in the memorializing—of remembering and rebuilding a collective identity, perpetrators forget defensively.

Ambiguous Remembering

Memorials as symbols capture the movement towards and away from reconciliation, and they touch raw nerves. They are, in particular, seen as evidence of intention. Indeed, the more innocuous and agreeable the manifest message, the more clues are sought to the latent message. They become either the truest expression of reconciliation or the most suspect expression of malice. In the post-1945 German context, they have been the foci of discord in the midst of overt and public dedication to overcoming the Nazi blight on collective memory. This discord suggests an intense need to uncover the motives that lurk in the underground of a culture.

One of the most moving embodiments of remembering and of reparation towards the Jews, of universal suffering, and also of the dilution of the specific atrocity of the Holocaust, is the sculpture Mother with Her Dead Son by Käthe Kollwitz (Fig. 7.1). It is housed in Berlin in the *Neue Wache* (the new guardhouse), a neo-classical building designed by Karl Friedrich Schinkel in 1816 for the troops of the Crown Prince of Prussia. Used as a memorial in the GDR, which dedicated it to the victims of fascism and militarism, the *Neue Wache* site is now a memorial in reunified Germany. The Kollwitz statue was placed there after unification and re-dedicated, in a ceremony officiated by Chancellor Kohl, to all victims of war.

Outside the memorial was a moving dedication of the Neue Wache, adapted from a speech by the West German Federal President, Richard von Weizäcker, on the 40th anniversary of the end of the war. The commemoration began:

Today we commemorate in sadness all dead of the war and the tyranny.

Fig. 7.1 Kollwitz, Pietà, Neue Wache, Berlin

> We remember especially the six million Jews who were killed in German concentration camps.

By comparison, the new wording demonstrates the conflicted memories lying just beneath the surface:

> The Neue Wache is a place of remembrance and commemoration of the victims of war and tyranny. We remember all nations/peoples who suffered in war.

For Harold Marcuse (1997), historian of German memorials, there should be no simplification either of the complex situation of a reunified Germany struggling with its past or of the use of Kollwitz to represent it:

> Kollwitz was a socialist artist, close to the proletariat. She was ridiculed by the Nazis…[a]nd she is unquestionably one of Germany's greatest artists… She created this sculpture in 1937, twenty years [after her son's death in the First World War]. In her diary she wrote: '**The mother sits and has the dead son lying between her knees. It is no longer pain, but reflection.**' Later she added: it is '**a kind of Pietà. But the mother is not religious…She is an old, lonely and darkly reflecting woman**' (Marcuse's emphasis).

Marcuse continues:

> This mother is not displaying the martyred body of her dead son, but is enveloping it, taking it back into her womb. She is not merely *mourning*, she is filled with *regret*, with the wish to be able to do it over again differently…The only appropriate relationship for Germans to the Nazi past, I think, is sadness and regret. That is well expressed by Kollwitz's sculpture. (Marcuse's emphasis)

In Marcuse's view, symbols themselves do not do the work needed to achieve an appropriate relationship to the past. He writes, '[if] Helmut Kohl or his successor kisses the ground at Yad Vashem [the Israeli Holocaust Memorial], as Brandt knelt in Warsaw in 1970 [and] [i]f Netanyahu came to the Neue Wache afterwards, I would have a more positive assessment of the role of symbolic politics in forging a more peaceful world.' Memorials do not perform this work of reparation—akin to *Aufarbeitung* or *Durcharbeitung* rather than *Vergangenheitsbewältigung* (mastering the past)—but they recognize the fact of it, and sadness and regret are part of reparation.

We might think of the Neue Wache memorial as a sculpture of a collective mind. It portrays not only humanity and worthy memories but also an avoidance of memories of inhumanity. Regardless of the intention of the artist, it reflects not only a hope for a unified German future but also a dissonance in German collective consciousness that can be traced from shortly after the war and into the present. Remember that Konrad Adenauer, running for office as the first chancellor of the new FRG, decided that Germany could have democracy or memory of the Nazi period, but not both (Herf 1997, pp. 267–300). This reaction has to be seen in the context of discord over a motion put to the German parliament by the conservative CDU to commemorate of victims of both East and West 'totalitarian dictatorships'.

It is not surprising that memorials have stirred intense controversy. Remembrance includes recognition of an immense German suffering, which in Andreas Hillgruber's (1986) account was an unimaginable, overwhelming experience inflicted by the indiscriminate Soviet onslaught on civilians and soldiers alike. It also includes accounts of the bombing of Dresden by the British and Americans (which we will take up in Chap. 10). But the denunciation of the Allies for bombing Dresden began with Nazi propaganda during the war and an annual commemoration includes a long-standing apologetic line, seeking to mitigate responsibility for Nazi atrocities and to bring the Nazi period into the post-war historical narrative without accepting these atrocities (see Niven 2006). Creating images out of context, divorced from the history of the Holocaust, Hillgruber (1986) and the nationalist remembrance of Dresden (see Fuchs 2012) serve the aim of apologetics, not of apology or reparation.

Beneath Ambiguity

Ambiguity in remembering allows perpetrators to gain equivalence to their victims. In an extensive study of German memorials of expulsion, Luppes (2010) argues that the memorials carry a political message: that Germans were the innocent victims of the loss of homeland at the end of the war. He writes of an 'aesthetics of innocence' and notes the large number of monuments that feature women and children as emblems of undisputed innocence. He grants that many Germans expelled from neighbouring territories were innocent, but nonetheless criticizes the decontextualized presentation of suffering from 1945, which implied an atrocity committed against innocent Germans.

James Young (1993) writes, 'instead of allowing the past to rigidify in its monumental forms, we would vivify memory through the memory-work itself – whereby events, their recollection, and the role monuments play in our lives remain animate, never completed' (p. 15). Perhaps the most profoundly evocative memorial sites are the Nazi concentration camps, which have been converted into memorial sites in which the monuments include the actual structures in the original camps. Young states:

> For Germans who experienced both the economic boom during Hitler's Reich and the destruction of their cities during the war, who knew both total military victory and unconditional surrender, memory of this time encompasses much more than the images of liberated concentration camp prisoners by which the era has so often been epitomized in America and England. Indeed, the piles of corpses in German camps seemed to reflect back to many Germans their own total devastation, the masses of dead in German cities and on the front. At first, the German's only nexus of identification with Jewish victims lay in the destruction they now seemed to share, not in what they had wrought in Hitler's name. (p. 5)

At these sites, therefore, there are at least three groups of memories: of the Jews, of the Germans, and of the American and British Allies. No doubt, the Germans could be divided into Nazi supporters, Nazi resisters and bystanders—and bystanders could be further divided into degrees of complicity with the Nazis. Despite recognizing the groupings of 'rememberers' at memorials, Young aims to 'break down the notion of any memorial's "collective memory" altogether, and to focus on "collected memory", the many discrete memories that are gathered into common memorial spaces and assigned common meaning'. He argues that a 'society's memory cannot exist outside of those people who do the remembering [and that] individuals cannot share another's memory…They share instead…the meanings in memory generated by [the] forms of memory' (p. xi).

I share his view, both that memorials vivify remembering while monuments tend to freeze memories into preconceived messages and that individuals cannot in a literal sense share memories as specific experiences. His work provides extensive documentary material and analyses through which he demonstrates the wish in Germany in the decades after 1945 to evoke memory-work through memorials, rather than frozen, prescriptive messages. I differ with him, however, on two related aspects of his interpretative stance. Firstly, he sets his case against 'ascribing psychoanalytic terms to the memory of groups'; secondly, he rejects the 'consequent tendency to see all the different kinds of memory in terms of memory-conflict and strategies for denial' (p. xi).

On the first point, regarding the idea of collective memory, the question as to the applicability of psychoanalytic interpretation is not whether individuals share a mind, in the sense that society as a whole can be viewed as a collective subject or agent. Rather, the question pertains to the ways in which individuals coalesce into imagined unities through group processes. In fact, Young's vocabulary points to just such a process of coalescing, for example, in the phrases 'socially constructed' (p. xi), 'collective meaning' (p. xii), 'shared experience and destiny' (p. 2), 'shared memory' (p. 6), 'common spaces' (p. 6), the creation of a 'common past' (p. 6), groups that 'become communities precisely by having shared (if only vicariously) the experiences of their neighbors' (p. 7). The mentality that underlies that process presses historians of collective life to include the study of memory, itself an established discipline, in their methodological repertoire (Kansteiner 2002). They need explication of collective memory, and, I would say, psychoanalytic explication. I have explored this topic in detail in Chap. 3 (on the idea of community, see Bohleber 1997). One needs also to remember that the aim of the Nazis was to eliminate Judaism: a people, not every individual Jew, but a people and the extinction of this people was equated with the restoration of the German nation—the Germans as a people—as in Friedländer's concept of 'redemptive anti-Semitism' (Friedländer 1997/2007, pp. 73–112).

On the second point—avoiding concepts of defence, such as denial—I do not think one can do without the idea of a socially buttressed exclusion or distortion of memory of the perpetration of, or complicity with, events and attitudes that corrupt a group's identity. The divergences and conflicts of memory at memorial sites bespeak not just differences of memory: they bespeak the aim of one version to suppress another, thereby contradicting the aim to integrate them into a common memory.

For the historian Charles Maier, '[t]he writing and reading of history must rest upon intellectual sociability', a common effort that can overcome ideological partisanship (1988, p. 63). He believes that the self-reflection required is equivalent to the psychoanalyst's own analysis. I would add that the psychoanalyst's inquiry into defensive 'forgetting' must work together with the historian's investigation of the 'multiple restorations' of memories (Herf 1997, pp. 10–11).

We are speaking, not just of forgetting, but of a wish—unconscious—to forget. As Young states, '[t]o the extent that we encourage monuments to do our memory-work for us, we become that much more forgetful. In effect, the initial impulse to memorialize events like the Holocaust may actually spring from an opposite and equal desire to forget them' (1993, p. 5). And individuals do not forget on their own: they group together—coalesce—to forget. Furthermore, in the collective act of forgetting, in the very process—in the memorializing—of remembering and rebuilding a collective identity, perpetrators forget defensively. We will now turn to specific mechanisms of not-remembering.

Not Knowing While Knowing: Disavowal and Undoing

By disavowal, I am referring to Freud's concept, *Verleugnung*, by which he defined a state of disowning what one simultaneously knew, and it depended on dividing the mind into two parts. The organization of the split mind held underlying unconscious dread in place. The dread was a phantasy, in which difference vanishes. Freud's theory of the division of the mind was based on his analysis of fetishism (1927, 1940[1938]). In my rendering of his theory, male and female threatened to absorb each other when the possibility entered the mind that the phallus—the decisive marker of difference—might not be essential and might not offer a fortress for identity. Mutual rebuke between the sexes, which found expression variously, as in the taboo of virginity (Freud 1918[1917])), anchored an assurance of difference by offering each sex an object of hatred in the other, which could also be observed in the external world of perception. I argued in Chap. 4 that the implosion of identity in the erosion of sex difference was a form of the narcissism of small—delusional—differences (cf. Klein 1932, p. 67).

Looked at from the angle of unconscious defence, we see disavowal, which allows two contradictory currents of belief to be held. One current recognizes the reality of evidence from the senses and from reasonable connections. The other is omnipotent. It overrides the judgement of reality in line with illusion or delusion. Sometimes, as we saw in Chap. 4, it masquerades inside evidential reality, remaining uncorrected by it. In Nazi Germany it fostered an omnipotent phantasy of German society, based on the imagination of a world without Jews, and of a kind of kinship between the individual and the nation and with the *Führer*: not as Hitler himself, but of the people merged with an ego-ideal, forming an ideal-ego. This phantasy of the people cannot bear reality: reality can only be tolerated, if at the same time, it is replaced by omnipotence. Unconsciously, the claim for national pride was based on the omnipotent phantasy of a German heroic identity, not on the working-through of German perpetration and the reparation that follows with 'remembering true'. The phantasy says that Germany is innocent in its transcendence over reality.

Phantasy also repudiates the reality of German loss. Germany did not triumph over the Jews, nor did they become victims in place of them. The reality was absolute defeat, the destruction of German cities, rampant poverty, mass dislocation of people. The Nazi regime brought loss, including loss of Jews, truth bent by the equation between the suffering inflicted by Germany and the Allied defeat of Germany, mangling the reality of the Jews and of the non-Jewish Germans.

The following clinical vignette by Werner Bohleber (1992) makes this point vividly:

[In this session, Peter, an adolescent who identifies with a Nazi past, which he seeks to exonerate] mentions a newspaper report on the interning by the SS of Italian soldiers unwilling to fight in the Second World War. I also read this report and know that the soldiers were shot, not interned. At this point in the therapy we have worked through mainly Peter's steady avoidance of unpleasant feelings and his insecurity through extensive daydreams. In the transference at that time I was not a father who helped him to deny the reality through daydreaming, but someone who supported him in recognizing it. I therefore confronted him at this point with the reality. To my amazement be doubted the correctness of the newspaper report. When I then commented on the SS criminality, he erupted, 'The others have also committed crimes, the English bombed Dresden.' He paused and was silent. Then he spoke of a 'conflict' in his head and continued, 'I know full well that everything does not correspond to what I say. But in my feelings the version that I want always pushes through' (p. 697).

Katharina Rothe (2009, 2012) conducted psychoanalytically informed small group sessions with, as well as interviews of, non-Jewish Germans, who, as children, had observed the deportation of Jews from their school. One of the striking features of her work was the way the participants began to remember what they seemingly did not remember or did not know, sometimes contradicting themselves within one contribution to the group. Various themes would spread through the group, as they coalesced into a group of non-Jewish Germans self-defined as not-Jews, but occasionally divided among themselves as they prompted each other to remember more truly. She shows how they could not remember having contact with Jews, while having regular contact; or seeing the deportations, but not knowing that they were Jews (2009, pp. 186–205).

In these group sessions, one theme coalesced around the statement, 'We Nordic men' (pp. 107–16). To this 'we', Jews simply did not figure in their memories. They did not think of Jews as subhuman, though it is interesting that they used that term, while stating that Jews were simply not in their experience. There was discussion at school about degenerate art and music and about the Nordic race, but nothing about Jews. They were members of youth groups and part of the collective 'we' Germans. They never had contact with Jews (pp. 186–9). As one participant said, 'I never knew a Jew…never, never. Only after the war' (p. 187). In another case, a man went on from never knowing a Jew to describing how his father, a doctor who opposed the regime, told him to take a certain man to the basement and await a signal to bring him to his father's surgery (p. 188). Another revealed that his family doctor was a Jew, who later disappeared (p. 190). Another had fond memories of, to him, Opa (Grandfather) Peterson, whose son had fallen in the First World War, and who was taken to Theresienstadt, though a man of nearly 90. He also reported that, when they, 10- and 11-year-old children, looked out of the window, they often saw 'Opas und Omas' (grandfathers and grandmothers). What sort of people they were, was another matter (p. 193).

One man did speak of the Holocaust, but noted that he used to exclude Hitler from any knowledge of it (apparently no longer). He blamed '*diese kleine Schweine*' (these little swine, such as Himmler and Goebbels). But his language is important. Hitler, he said, 'probably knew nothing of these *Schweinereien* [filth, but literally pig matters]' (p. 141).

Remember Young's concluding that the impact of piles of corpses in concentration camps was the 'German's only nexus of identification with Jewish victims'. Rothe's finding on the same theme suggests more of a disavowal. One interviewee reported having watched a film about the concentration camps, probably made by the Americans, which included a 'corpse mountain', supposedly of Jewish victims. He watched it three times, and began to concentrate on the background rather than the foreground. He could detect ruins in the background. There were no ruins in concentration camps: what he saw must have been, he claimed, not Jewish corpses in a concentration camp, but German corpses in Hamburg, devastated by the Allies. The film was a fraud: Germans, not Jews, were the victims in the war (pp. 119–22).

Similarly, in their clinical experience after the war, the Mitscherlichs (1967/1975) found a type of not-knowing, sufficiently common for them to speak of it as a collective defence. Germans did not know of their victims whose absence would evoke mourning, or of their own loss, which would also evoke mourning. Instead, they 'knew' of the lost war and of their lost position in the world. Their loss, if that is the right word, was a collapse of narcissism (see Chap. 6, n. 2).

In a case reported later by Margarete Mitscherlich, a German officer did not know, at first, of the Nazi victimization of the Jews. In fact, he was not a convinced Nazi, and though otherwise restrained in manner, he publically poured contempt on Germany and National Socialism. He was part of an occupation force in Holland, in whom, 'one after the other, memories surfaced of events of which he was ashamed and had for the most part forgotten or repressed... It also came to light that he had 'requisitioned the home of a Jewish family for his officers in Poland. He had never seen the family and had no idea what happened to them... There were thousands and thousands of requisitions, carried out in a similarly unempathic way.' It was relatively insignificant next to Nazi atrocities and he was just a middle-ranking German officer—yet 'everyone executing such measures knew that there was more than the "emigration" of a Jewish family'. Unlike the lively memories of the war period, the memories that now forced themselves on him seemed strange. He was exposed to devastating knowledge inside an envelope of not-knowing. His treatment was also 'suddenly no longer disturbed by an individual resistance of the patient against the surfacing of unpleasant feelings, but by a collectively justified resistance, in which he could feel himself to be a participant' (Mitscherlich 1987, pp. 106–8).

What these Germans 'knew' was actually a delusion of omnipotence, the aim of which was to not know the actuality of the Holocaust. It was an inversion of knowing and not-knowing in the usual situation, in which one knows what one perceives and what makes reasonable sense; one does not know what lies beyond their experience. Instead, they 'knew' they had a right to think and do what they did. Just beneath, they also 'knew' they were living in a fragile illusion of survival based on extermination of the Jews. They 'un-knew' the actuality of perpetration: the unconscious meaning of extermination as German survival through the extinction of an alter-identity; the delusional creation of an enemy; the Jews as Germans; the identification (not the equivalence) with them in their suffering).

What we find when we bring together detailed historical scholarship and the elaboration of subtle forms of defence is that there are ways of managing the memory of the past that are unconscious and compatible with an apparent acknowledgement of what is also repudiated. In disavowal, the Jews are both despised and idealized, hated and envied, to be annihilated yet kept alive in order to be annihilated, absent and ever-present, weak and all-powerful, wholly other and the mirror of the German. Germany was proud, but shameful; strong in the external reality of military power, but fragile in internal reality.

Other defences have also been identified in post-war Germany. Domansky (1993), for example, argues that commemorative rituals in Germany, consciously aiming to remember, recognize and atone, actually 'undo' the very remembering that they consciously express. Psychoanalytically, 'undoing' is an unconscious defence mechanism that, for Freud, was characteristic of obsessional thinking and rituals. His expression was, literally, *ungeschehen machen*—to make something not to have happened (1926, p. 119; original in *Gesammelte Werke* 14: 149). Domansky (1993) uses exactly the same expression, without citing Freud or 'undoing' as a psychoanalytically recognized defence mechanism. She says that, since the end of the 1960s, people in the FRG have participated in Holocaust rituals, 'not because they accept their past, but because the can use them retrospectively to undo it (*nachträglich ungeschehen machen möchten*)' (p. 192).

But Domansky omits more than a citation: she misses the implication of an unconscious defence: undoing is a form of omnipotent thinking. That is why it expresses remorse for recognized perpetration while, simultaneously, not only eliminating it but also eliminating the very grounds for it. That is why, as well, it must be repeated: for every act of defence is also a new act of perpetration, calling for a renewed undoing.

Perhaps the most significant repudiation of memory in post-war Germany involved an unconscious collusion between the political division of Germany and splitting as a defence. The Allies partitioned Germany after the war, imposing the formation of two states. Each state coalesced (more or less) into the politics and culture of its 'protector', laying down memories consonant with its situation. But because the partition was imposed, it could conceal an unconscious defensive function beneath conscious resentment and aggression between the two states. We turn to this unconscious organization in the next chapter.

References

Bartov, O. (1998) Defining Enemies, Making Victims: Germans, Jews, and the Holocaust. *The American Historical Review* 103(3): 771–816.

Beattie, A. (2006) The Victims of Totalitarianism and the Centrality of Nazi Genocide: Continuity and Change in German Commemorative Politics. In

Niven, B. (ed.) *Germans as Victims: Remembering the Past in Contemporary Germany.* Houndmills: Palgrave Macmillan, pp. 147–163.

Bohleber, W. (1992) Nationalismus, Fremdenhass und Antisemitismus: Psychoanalytische Überlegungen. *Psyche* 46: 689–709.

Bohleber, W. (1997) Die Konstrucktion imaginärer Gemeinschaften und das Bild von den Juden – umbewusste Determinanten des Antisemitismus in Deutschland. *Psyche* 51: 570–605.

Chasseguet-Smirgel, J. (1985b) *Creativity and Perversion.* London: Free Association Books.

Domansky, E. (1993) Die gespaltene Erinnerung. In Köppen, M. (ed.) *Kunst und Literatur nach Auschwitz.* Berlin: Erich Schmidt Verlag, pp. 178–96.

Freud, S. (1910) A Special Type of Choice of Object Made by Men (Contributions to the Psychology of Love I). *The Standard Edition of the Complete Psychological Works of Sigmund Freud* 11: 163–75.

Freud, S. (1918[1917]) The Taboo of Virginity (Contributions to the Psychology of Love III). *The Standard Edition of the Complete Psychological Works of Sigmund Freud* 11: 191–208.

Freud, S. (1926). *Inhibitions, Symptoms and Anxiety. The Standard Edition of the Complete Psychological Works of Sigmund Freud* 20: 75–176.

Freud, S. (1927) Fetishism. *The Standard Edition of the Complete Psychological Works of Sigmund Freud* 21: 147–58.

Freud, S. (1940[1938]) Splitting of the Ego in the Process of Defence. *The Standard Edition of the Complete Psychological Works of Sigmund Freud* 23: 271–8.

Friedländer, S. (1997) *The Years of Persecution: Nazi Germany & the Jews 1933–1939.* London: Weidenfeld & Nicholson/Phoenix.

Fuchs, A. (2012) *After the Dresden Bombing: Pathways of Memory, 1945 to the Present.* Basingstoke: Palgrave Macmillan.

Herf, J. (1997) *Divided Memory: The Nazi Past in the Two Germanies.* Cambridge, MA/London: Harvard University Press.

Hillgruber, A. (1986) *Zweierlei Untergang: Die Zerschlagung des deutschen Reiches und das Ende des europäischen Judentums.* Berlin: Seidler.

Jager, J. (2002) Fotographie-Errinerungen-Identität.Die Trummeraufnahmen aus deutschen Stadten 1945. In Hillmann, J. und Zimmermann, J. (hrsg.) *Kriegsende 1945 in Deutschland.* München: Oldenberg Verlag, pp. 287–300.

Kansteiner, W. (2002) Finding Meaning in Memory: A Methodological Critique of Collective Memory Studies. *History and Theory* 42(2): 179–97.

Klein, M. (1932) *The Psychoanalysis of Children.* London: Hogarth and the Institute of Psychoanalysis; revised edition 1975.

Luppes, J. (2010) *To Our Dead: Local Expellee Monuments and the Contestation of German Post-war Memory* (Unpublished doctoral thesis). University of Michigan.

Marcuse, H. (1997) The National Memorial to the Victims of War and Tyranny: From Conflict to Consensus. Paper presented to the German Studies Association Conference, September 25, 1997, Washington, DC. Retrieved from http://www.history.ucsb.edu/faculty/marcuse/present/neuewach.htm. Accessed 22.6.2011.

Maier, C. (1988) *The Unmasterable Past: History, Holocaust, and German National Identity*. Cambridge, MA/London: Harvard University Press.

Mitscherlich, M. (1987) *Errinerungsarbeit zur Psychoanalyse der Unfähigkeit zu trauern*. Frankfurt aM: Fischer.

Mitscherlich, A. and Mitscherlich, M. (1967/1975) *The Inability to Mourn: Principles of Collective Behaviour*. Munich: Piper & Co. Verlag; English translation, New York: Grove Press.

Niven, B. (2006) The GDR and Memory of the Bombing of Dresden. In Niven, B. (ed.) *Germans as Victims: Remembering the Past in Contemporary Germany*. Basingstoke: Palgrave Macmillan, pp. 109–29.

Rothe, J. (2009) *Das (Nicht-)Sprechen über die Judenvernichtung: Psychische Weiterwirkingen des Holocaust in mehreren Generationen nicht-jüdischer Deutscher*. Giessen: Psychozial Verlag.

Rothe, K. (2012) Anti-semitism in Germany Today and the Intergenerational Transmission of Guilt and Shame. *Psychoanalysis, Culture, and Society* 17(1): 16–34.

Sebald, W. G. (2003) *On the Natural History of Destruction*. London: Hamish Hamilton.

Young, J. (1993) *The Texture of Memory: Holocaust Memorials and Meaning*. New Haven: Yale University Press.

8

The Unconscious Division of Germany

The post-war occupation zones crystallized into two states, one closely allied to the Western democracies, and the other to the Soviet Union, followed by reunification in 1990. We have, therefore, a case of the political, economic, ideological and administrative splitting of a nation, followed by a reintegration. In this chapter, I argue that this division also realized an unconscious psychic splitting of the German people. By 'splitting', I refer to the psychic mechanism described by Melanie Klein (1946), which organizes psychic reality in the form of an omnipotent ego in relation to two, opposite, phantasy objects, one purely 'good' and one purely 'bad'. In this 'paranoid-schizoid' position, the ego retreats from engagement with external reality, in which it would suffer the recognition of damage to a good object, with guilt and an urge to repair it, which Klein called the 'depressive position'. Instead, it lived in a paranoid world of threat to itself by bad objects and an equally psychotic phantasy of a haven within its good objects.

But splitting in the paranoid-schizoid position also confers stability on an ego struggling for order, by imposing a dichotomized structure on a fundamentally psychotic core. In Chap. 5, I described this core in the social world, against which splitting also operated. I spoke of this internal relationship as a primal ambivalence, which covered the dread of dissolution (the catastrophe) and fomented internal aggression (as in Freud's *Unbehagen*). The explosion of violence aimed to project this internal aggression and the underlying catastrophe into a delusional enemy (see Chap. 4).

In Nazi Germany, the Jews as a people were the target object for systematically forcing out this primal ambivalence, while aggression was also projected everywhere, as the unconscious dimension of Germany's push to expand its borders without limit. The division of post-war Germany provided each nation with a bad object in the other and a haven of a good object in itself. In this unconscious collusive state, the total system allowed a paranoid-schizoid retreat from the depressive reality of damage to its actual good objects, embodied in remembering. Instead of remembering, both Germanys could feel threatened by its enemy object and safe within itself inside its alliance. The shared position brought stability but was at base psychotic and therefore prone to explosive, apparently retaliatory behaviour.

The common unconscious aim of the divided Germany was to marginalize the Holocaust through an unconscious collaboration. The GDR, now part of the Soviet alliance that had fought the Nazis, regarded itself as essentially anti-fascist. It projected its Nazi underbelly into the FRG, where it was surrounded by capitalist success. It identified the FRG with capitalism and, through capitalism, with Nazism and with Judaism, and the GDR was, therefore, relieved of guilt. The FRG, now part of the Western alliance, created a miracle of capitalist success, which in itself demonstrated well-being untrammelled by guilt, but which also held the GDR in place. It projected its Nazi underbelly into the GDR, where it was surrounded by Soviet tyranny. The FRG identified the GDR, not only with Soviet tyranny but also with tyranny itself, including Nazi tyranny. Together, East and West unconsciously collaborated in creating a psychosocial enclave, a haven from guilt and from the dread of dissolution.

It is also the case that, since the end of the war, anti-Semitism in Germany has declined as a secular trend, especially among young people—more so in the former GDR than in the former FRG—and has concentrated in a small group of right-wing extremists (Bergmann

1997). One explanation is that public policy has not tolerated it, and that xenophobic resentment has shifted from a deep ethnic and racial base to competition. But the reasons for the decline also differed between the two states. The GDR not only had suppressed anti-Semitism, but would not engage with any recognition of it, such as guilt and reparation. It refused to recognize or pay reparations to Israel, and supported the Arab cause against Israel. It pushed the issue of German guilt into the West. Despite conscious recognition of the Holocaust, it had in effect included the Jews, along with West Germans and Western Allies, as the capitalist enemy. The state persecuted the 'cosmopolitans' in their midst as dangerous agents of international capital, regardless of their socialist credentials; and righteous anti-fascism had replaced their 'memory' of perpetration. Fascism was, for them, a crisis of capitalism, not a feature of German history (Herf 1997, esp. Chaps. 4, 5). Within the Soviet sphere, the Real Socialism of the GDR was to be the bulwark against its Nazi past.

For West Germany, embedding the nation in the tradition of the Western democracies with their capitalist base was the only way the Germans could prevent a resurgence of fascism and restore their respect as a civilized people. The West German state paid restitution to Jews, supported the Israeli state and engaged extensively in self-searching into the origins of the fascist state and responsibility for the Holocaust. For the FRG, splitting had made the GDR, along with its Soviet ally, into the socialist enemy. Its own spectacular economic success and democratization stoked a triumphalism in relation to 'dictatorship' in the East. Overall, these relationships implied an equivalence between the Third Reich and GDR/Soviet Union (Eley 2004, pp. 181, 184, 188).

But although democracy, spectacular economic success, embeddedness in the Western alliance and staunch opposition to the cold-war communist threat subdued the guilt of Nazi perpetration, it carried a darker side with it. 'Indeed, with the growth of prosperity, a German self-regard is being revived that is often not greatly removed from the values and standards of the Third Reich' (Mitscherlich and Mitscherlich 1967/1975, p. 51). These general 'values and standards' can also be pinned down to Nazi personnel continuing in the FRG (Fulbrook 2016; Perels 2015). At the same time, Adenauer's aim to establish democracy at the core of the state and of political consciousness also ran counter to reparation and memory, while engagement with its Nazi past also opened a channel for anti-Semitic expression (Herf 1997, pp. 179–200; Kurthen 1997, p. 47).[1]

For both East and West Germany, the cold war marginalized Jewish concerns (Herf 1997, pp. 83–4, 163, 171–2, 261, 276), albeit with the differences outlined above. German success in reconstruction and the fight against victimization transformed both Germanys from dishonourable perpetrators into honourable defenders of the nation. But

> [t]he Holocaust was a tragedy without redemption. It did not fit into any optimistic theory of history or post-war policy of reconstruction, whether it promised the first socialist society in Germany in the East or an 'economic miracle' in the West. In both West and East, those who focused only on a bright future saw no place for an evil past. (Herf 1997, p. 392)

Moreover, German optimism was buttressed by putting Germans alongside the Jews as victims of the tragedy and, as a muted repetition of the Nazi aim actually to eliminate them, now destroying the memory of this aim. Omar Bartov (1998) said

> [i]t has been noted that Germans experienced the last phases of World War II and its immediate aftermath as a period of mass victimization. Indeed, Germany's remarkable reconstruction was predicated both on repressing the memory of the Nazi regime's victims and on the assumed existence of an array of new enemies, foreign and domestic, visible and elusive. Assertions of victimhood had the added benefit of suggesting parallels between the Germans and their own victims. Thus, if the Nazis strove to ensure the health and prosperity of the nation by eliminating the Jews, post-war Germany strove to neutralize the memory of the Jews' destruction so as to ensure its own physical and psychological restoration. (p. 788)

The living 'memory' of German victimization in the war even turned them into fighters against Jewish atrocities, rather than perpetrators of atrocities against the Jews. In unconscious terms, this reversal is evidence of projection. If the projection were withdrawn, the atrocity would be inside the Germans, with guilt for the attacks on the Jews.

8 The Unconscious Division of Germany 169

The elusive and yet ubiquitous presence attributed to the Jews by the regime played an even more important role in creating an inverted perception of victimhood throughout the Nazi era...Soldiers tended to ascribe massacres perpetrated by their own units to Jewish criminality, even when the actual victims of such atrocities were Jews, and civilians in the rear similarly attributed the destruction of cities by aerial bombing to Jewish thirst for revenge. (Bartov 1998, p. 784)

Fulbrook (1999) refers to the accepted early post-war view in Germany, that the real catastrophe was the 'bitter defeat and division of the fatherland'. 'For all the public anguish about national humiliation, there was little evidence of a sense of real guilt or concern for real victims' (p. 118). Similarly, historians such as Broszat, Confino, Friedländer and Mommsen detail the specific historical setting in which these defensive systems operated. One general feature of a defeated and humiliated post-war Germany, East and West, was the craving for success without memory; an omnipotent illusion of a continuous history of German superiority untarnished by horrific disregard for humanity.

Fulbrook (1999) also brings out the symmetry between East and West Germany, in their mutual creation of an enemy, each of the other. Postwar, for both Germanys, was an *Aufbaugeneration*, a generation of work and restoration (p. 163). Although there were differences between the two Germanys, there was 'an extraordinary mirror-image symmetry about the ways in which the interpretations of professional historians sustained the broader historical pictures...of the identification of villains, victims and heroes, and the location of the present in the long sweep of German and European history' (p. 107). In both Germanys, the *Volk* were innocent at the hands of the Nazis (pp. 113–14). The Holocaust was not discussed in either Germany (pp. 110, 115). This situation began to change in the 1960s, coming to a head in the West in the 1980s with open conflict among historians, which, in 1986, 'exploded into public confrontation, in what soon became known as the *Historikerstreit*' (pp. 103–41; 125; see also Chap. 6).

Focusing more specifically on a shared defensive structure, Domansky (1993) argues that, despite the separate pasts fabricated by their different social structures, both parts of Germany handled their 'once common past in an identical way' (p. 185). She also brings out the systematic, *collaborative*, defensive character of the division of Germany.

> The Third Reich was eliminated from the respective history of each state and manoeuvred into the history of the other. In both states, we find only resistance fighters and victims of German politics and history, but no perpetrators. In addition, both states took a share in the memory of genuine victims of National Socialism – or else their forgetting of it – in order for their respective national integration and finding identity to function. They thus continued in memory, albeit in different ways, the injustice committed against the victims: their persecution and elimination from German society had already in the Third Reich served the purpose of creating a new – in that case 'racially pure' – *Volksgemainscahft*. In the 1950s and 1960s, the foundation for the often invoked 'unity of the German nation' lay in the creation of a divided memory, which the divided Germany bound into a gigantic common repression-effort. Its form preserved the memory of the substance of what was to be forgotten: those who had been eliminated from the society of the Third Reich would now be excluded from memory. (p. 185)

Domansky suggests an unconscious dimension, which we must now bring to the fore. Conscious resentment at the division of Germany only more firmly anchored an unconscious splitting that entrenched an evasion of guilt at the remembering of perpetration. Resentment at Allied authority was conscious, easy, satisfying and repetitive; recognizing a defence against guilt was painful. One sees a similar disparity between conscious and unconscious levels in the intergenerational antagonism provoked by the events of 1968 (p. 185). The younger generation challenged the view that their parents were resistance fighters and were largely unaware of Nazi atrocities. They forced the recognition of Germans as participants, albeit as bystanders, not as perpetrators. This shift in West German memory politics increased the distance from the East, where there was no change. But at the same time, the unmasking of German participation in the West, along with a greater awareness of Jewish suffering, continued to leave perpetration out of the picture there as well. Each Germany continued to marginalize perpetration in its own way, now extended by concentration on the Jews and memory of the Holocaust

(p. 188; Fulbrook 2016). Splitting remained, and one could speak of an unconscious collaboration, whereby both Germanys signed up to replacing complicity with the victimization of the Jews by a sense of righteous honour in triumph without ambiguity, each over the other.[2]

Around the same time, on the basis of extensive clinical evidence, Alexander and Margarete Mitscherlich reported that post-war Germans emotionally detached themselves from their involvement in Nazism (1967/1975). They spoke of denial and a consequent failure to mourn, but they also implicated the splitting of Germany. The West Germans replaced their dependence on Hitler with dependence on the United States, and given that the United States was so much larger than the FRG, the FRG shifted the rivalry evoked by that dependence to the GDR (p. 49).[3] Later, writing of the FRG in 1987, Margarete Mitscherlich saw a drive to maintain a division between the two power blocs, each containing part of Germany, in which '[t]he existing chasm between the West and the Soviet Union is certainly not to be attributed to the ex-Nazis, [and] also certainly not to be hindered in being widened and deepened. The aggressive-projective component of Nazi ideology continues with the help of emotional anticommunism, through which every differentiated perception of the East up to now is blocked and with it every *Ostpolitik* that rightly carries that name' (pp. 24–5).

Collective Memory and a Psychosocial Enclave

I have argued that the history of post-war Germany—distorted, broken, displaced by division—was a vehicle for an unconscious history fashioned by 'defence' in the psychoanalytic meaning of the word. Repression is not simply forgetting: it is the breaking-off and displacement of affective investment in ideas, leaving them unconscious (Freud 1915; see also example in Chap. 1). In addition, there are more primitive, more elemental defences. Splitting divides the psyche, so that memory is carried away in disowned psychic fragments. Such fragments are 'projected' into another (projective identification), and not recognized (Klein 1946; on splitting vs repression, see Hinshelwood 2008). They can be delusional, using the external world as an apparent reality within which to masquerade. In the phenomenology of projection, unaccepted parts of the self *are* expelled and *do* reside in the other. The division of Germany into two states, each supported by a power bloc, each bloc aggressively confronting the other, not only divided the nation: it consolidated a splitting. This splitting—of the nation and of the psyche—prevented a catastrophic re-introjection of the massive aggression and the dread of dissolution that had been exported into enemies, internal and external. Much as the geographical splitting separated individuals from relatives and friends, especially after the construction of the wall in 1961, it also provided an idealized object for identification inside each Germany and another object as a repository for projection in the other Germany.

This way of thinking about defence is common in clinical psychoanalysis, and it applies to groups as well as to individuals. Indeed, groups can facilitate splitting through the opportunity offered by another group to reduce its internal complexity by projection (see Chap. 3; Segal 1987, 1995). Groups need each other as repositories and easily act that way for each other. The system of mutual projection stabilizes all the components. Systems of this sort are called 'social defence systems' (Hinshelwood 1987) or 'psychic retreats' (Steiner 1993), which act as psychosocial enclaves.

Post-war German national experience, as a collective identity buttressed by splitting, shared between the two states as an unconscious collusion, was such a psychosocial enclave. It depended on a collective illusion of being rooted in German national soil and having grown robustly until it was infected, then recovering its robust growth after the Nazi infection was removed into the other Germany. Post-war collective memory avoided the core identity of perpetrator, an identity that had previously been essential to an illusion—even conscious—that German survival depended on it. In other words, a complete *volte-face* was needed for the formation of an organized retreat into post-war stability.

Each Germany, in its grandiosity, trumpeted its success in comparison with the demeaned other. The fact that each used the other in this way condensed the range of unconscious defences against remembering the Holocaust into competition between the two German states as resistance fighters against oppressive forces, whether they be fascism, Nazism, capitalism, Bolshevism or the occupying Allied forces. So we come to the particular character of splitting between the two Germanys. The East or West German nation functioned as a superego-ideal for its own people, with which the people as a group identified. In this case, the nationalist core in the life of the country is a collective illusory state of mind, with both an allure and dread of dissolution.

On the surface, citizens of each state knew they belonged in an economic, military and power bloc that opposed an antagonistic bloc. Bearing disavowal in mind, we could say that they 'knew' that the antagonist structure of the German nation was built on denying perpetration of the Holocaust, and they 'knew' that they were protected inside their own block. The organized structure of antagonism allowed them, on both sides, to feel a normal fear of a rebound of the Nazi illusion with its defeat, or paranoid persecution, rather than dread of internal collapse.

In order to firm up the hypothesis that the division of the German nation into two Germanys enabled the consolidation of a defence against the memory of the Holocaust, we need to look at the reunification of Germany. The hypothesis would predict an unease, taking the form of an increase in right-wing extremism because the pressure to split and project rather than to tolerate ambiguity. It would find expression through extremist hatred and divisiveness. It would find once again in the Jews the apt repository for this projection, and it would act rather than think; that is, it would be prone to bellicose demonstrations and violence. In general, one would expect the psychosocial retreat, which was based on splitting, to be threatened. Once again, a denigrated other, including the Jews, would become the enemy, this time replacing the lost 'other' Germany.

Reunification and the Collapse of the Psychosocial Enclave

Reunification was a mixed blessing to the Germans. Eley (2004) speaks of the wave of nationalistic enthusiasm, with '[p]atriotic expressions of belief drawing upon national history, which increasingly risked venturing even into the forbidden territory of the Third Reich… [But as] it turns out, public memory in unified Germany remains highly contested' (p. 176). Germans were brought into an alliance with a suspect society and enemy. It fulfilled the dream of restoring German nationhood, but the stabilization achieved by the division of the nation dissipated in the (partial, to be sure) collapse of splitting, leaving Germany exposed to its past. For Michael Ignatieff (1994), the 'two states offered both sides the necessary negative image of each other'. With reunification, 'the negative image is the nation, the people themselves … Now that the state has vanished, the people itself – the nation – are blamed for its ever having existed' (p. 49), and the FRG assimilated into itself the disdain for the GDR state as the GDR people joined them to reform Germany (pp. 49, 63, 69, 71). Both former cultures lost their repositories for projection, through which each could bear the loss of national self-esteem and defend against the recognition of perpetration, which more fundamentally sullied their self-esteem.[4]

Reunification also brought back the dread of remembering the Holocaust and, beneath it, the dread of dissolution, on which redemptive anti-Semitism was built. But layered on top of recognizing the disaster visited upon the Jews and identifying with them as a way to understand them, as opposed to compete with them, was the self-absorption in the loss of an ideal. From a West German perspective, Maragrete Mitscherlich-Nielsen (1992) put it this way.

> Mourning the Hitler-period has [for us] been primarily mourning the loss of our own ego- or we-ideal, along with individual and collective self-esteem. I believe that fellow countrymen from the former GDR feel similarly after re-unification. A loss of self-worth can be observed – individual and well as collective – which again must be repressed or projected, in order to bear it. (pp. 413–14)

The GDR tried simply to disown its Nazi past by projection into the West. Reunification brought them face-to-face with it, but they sought a 'political cleansing', rather than focusing on unambiguous criminality (pp. 414–15), but meanwhile, 'We West Germans sometimes seek to practice in the East that *Vergangenheitsbewältigung* which we never achieved ourselves' (p. 415). The quest for projection remained.

There were also several objective indicators of the collapse of the psychosocial enclave with the fall of the wall and the process of reunification. Holocaust denial increased (Wetzel 1997, p. 161). West German politicians engaged in a 'zealous pursuit...of communist injustice after 1990[, which the historian, James McAdam attributed to] "uneasy memories about the handling of an only marginally more distant period in German history – National Socialism"' (Eley 2004, p. 181). Right-wing extremism increased (Kurthen et al. 1997, p. 8). Reunification was followed by a small, but consistent increase in anti-Semitism (Weil 1997). As Kurthen documents, German trends were in line with European trends, so we have to focus on the particular relationship in Germany between right-wing extremism and identity, including principally its anti-Semitism and its identification with the Nazi period. The substantial increase in right-wing incidents and violence after reunification peaked in 1993, but remained higher than pre-unification rates. The majority were directed against foreigners, and the rate correlated with the increase in numbers of asylum seekers. Anti-Semitic aggression, though lesser in numbers, showed the same trend, but differed, in that the increase continued for another year before declining, which suggests that it was to some extent a distinct phenomenon (Kurthen et al. 1997, p. 8; Bergmann 1997, p. 34).

In another survey, respondents were clustered into four groups according to their response to the question: 'Do not want too much to do with' (Turks/asylum seekers/Jews/Blacks; then, within each cluster, their responses were given to the question with respect to the other three, with the addition of 'Arab'). Thus 34% of 721 respondents said they didn't want too much to do with Turks. Of them, 66% said it of asylum seekers, 64% of Arabs, 50% Blacks, 25% of Jews. If the 'test question' referred to Jews, only 13% of 273 said they did not want to have much to do with them, but the percentage with respect to the sub-groups was higher: 88% with respect to Turks, 84% Arabs, 80% Blacks, 80% asylum seekers. In other words, though a smaller proportion of Germans admit to anti-Semitism, they are more other-phobic. Anti-Semitism seems to be more fundamental than xenophobia (Bergmann 1997, p. 36; Bergmann suggests the perpetrator groups are different, p. 34). It may also be significant that damage to Jewish property has been 'almost exclusively directed towards monuments, memorials or Jewish cemeteries' (pp. 34–5). Bergmann sees it as 'an iconoclastic redefinition of these artworks or institutions more than attacks against existing Jewish communities' (p. 35). But these objects are not just artworks: they are the embodiments of identity, including ideals. To attack them is to aim to project into them a core anxiety of dissolution and to destroy it in the object.

Right-wing extremist publications continue to be anti-Semitic as well as xenophobic (Wetzel 1997). Benz (2001) has shown that public language, such as broadcasting, can be laced with anti-Semitic stereotypes, despite a decline in anti-Semitism as a personal attitude. Anti-Semitism is more rooted in seeing Jews as anti-German than, xenophobically, as economic competitors (Kurthen et al. 1997, pp. 10, 12). '[A]nti-Semitism', Bartov argues, 'even when it was least discussed, served along with economic anxiety and hardship, fear of revolution, a longing for national unity and greatness, and a generally xenophobic climate as an important adhesive that kept together an otherwise incoherent and irreconcilable ideological hodgepodge' (1998, p. 783). In my view, this ill-defined concoction of all that threatened from within indicates a core psychotic anxiety. Interestingly, post-unification support for treating Jews as a special case, on account of the Nazi past, was stronger in the East than in the West (40%/30%), as was support for Jewish and Israeli claims for compensation (57% rejected these claims in the East; 75% rejected them in the West) (Kurthen 1997, p. 49). The figures suggest a rebound after reunification: the West from being the repository of guilt; the East taking some of it on.

Finally, Human Rights Watch Helsinki (1995, pp. 12–20) gathered research on right-wing extremism in Germany, including anti-Semitism in the 1990s. I will report just one finding: overall crimes associated with right-wing extremism rose from 1991, as did specifically anti-Semitic crime. Looking at 1993, the overall figure, not including anti-Semitic crime, was 12, 793. Anti-Semitic crime totalled 728, which seems a small figure next to non-anti-Semitic crime. But if we factor in the Jewish population, the level of anti-Semitic crime becomes more alarming. Unfortunately, the systematic data available to me are for 2010, when the Jewish population in Germany was 230,000 or .3% of the German population (Pew Research Center 2012). Nonetheless, allowing a huge margin of error in applying this figure to 1993, we could still multiply anti-Semitic crime figure by at least 100 for comparison with the non-anti-Semitic crime rate, giving a comparative figure of 72,800 anti-Semitic crimes next to the 12,793 non-anti-Semitic crimes.

Surveys give a broad-brush picture of a lingering core *Unbehagen*. Clinical work gives a deeper insight into the unconscious dimension. Bear in mind that, unlike historians who have written on the form of non-engagement with the Nazi past, the Mtischerlichs (1967/1975) based their appraisal on the clinical records of 4000 patients. But also bear in mind that a single clinical case gives an incomparable insight into the workings of the internal world. I will sketch one clinical vignette, in which the appeal of right-wing extremism to a deprived boy also carried an identification with the Nazis of his grandparental generation. Streeck-Fischer (2000) presented the case of a 16-year-old Nazi skinhead. His alcoholic mother abandoned him when he was three years old; his father treated him as if dead; his maternal grandmother, who cared for him until he was 12 years old, died, leaving him with his father and paternal grandfather. The grandfather was a soldier in the war, and the boy idealized his stories as 'reports from a better world'. A background silence on the 'traumata of war, such as the death of comrades, hunger, freezing, death anxiety, humiliation', left them outside his awareness. His grandfather was, for him, a 'powerful, potent person whom he feared and whose sympathy he sought, while father seemed to him weak and unfit as a model' (Streeck-Fischer 2000, p. 58; Bohleber 1992, 1995 presents strikingly similar cases; see also the cases presented in Chap. 4). Streeck-Fischer sees his case as typical. The youth of the GDR were turning to right-wing extremism as an identification with the Nazi period, which would reassert national pride and power. She concludes:

> In retrieving right-wing extremist ideologies, the youth seek to recover, on the one hand, a piece of history, which members of the GDR and the FRG could hold in common [but which] must, on the other hand, make them aware of being the dupe of history, of a history that indicated in the example of its repetition, that they as Germans with dignity were nevertheless always on the losing side. The grievance of many unresolved problems after the destruction of their social structure leads to the call to law and order in

familiar totalitarian structures, which right wing ideologies offer. (Streeck-Fischer 2000, pp. 68–9; cf. Mitscherlich and Mitscherlich 1967/1975)

Reintegration, Memory and Reparation

Reunification meant losing control of the psychosocial enclave, including control of the other Germany as a repository for projection. Losing control meant re-introjection, remembering, guilt, but also loss of an orientation in the world of reality and of the delusion of defining and sustaining national identity. Losing, the Mitscherlichs argued, had to be mourned; to be mourned, it had to be remembered. But remembering is the backbone of it all: not recall, but the assimilation of the ambivalence, including the perpetrator's love and hatred of the good object. For Germans, this good object had been replaced by the idealized Nazi object, the love of which had to be recognized along with complicity, followed by hatred and separation from it; then recognition of love and hatred of the Jewish object (Mitscherlich-Nielsen 1992). Anti-Semitism remained a unique type of defence against internal catastrophe: the object that had to be attacked, torn to pieces, in order to create an illusory, idealized German nation object, born into collective memory for collective adulation.

At reunification, 'West Germans and East Germans had few common experiences and memories left apart from National Socialism, the Second World War and the uprootedness many suffered as a consequence of these' (Schultze 2006, p. 376), but this depletion of common experience was in consciousness. The unconscious experience was different. Here, what they shared in common was the psychosocial enclave, which relieved them of persecutory, depressive and psychotic anxiety, and they now shared its weakening. As a result, each now 'remembered' that underneath the two competing German identities, there was a German people, responsible for the post-war situation in which they found themselves, with the critical issue of perpetration denied.

The collective memory of a *Volksgemainschaft* is always unstable. It is always drawn towards factionalism and conflict because it exposes the *Unbehagen in der Kulture* that unsettles collective identity. Successful, democratic, collective identity is informed by the disenchantment delivered through historical debate and a political forum, as in a democracy; in general, by whatever undercuts idealization. These democratic essentials had been foreclosed in Nazi Germany, where the *Volksgemeinschaft* was anything but a public sphere as we think of it in a democracy. Reunification brought, at least in the West, both the aim to establish a democratic, reflective identity and a *Volksgemeinschaft*. Truthful memory is the backbone of successful collective identity. It is won through hard, self-reflective work towards shared memory with its rough edges. It is reparative, not as a final product, but as a process. Reunification challenged the defensive retreat offered to both East and West by the division of Germany, and brought out a reparative possibility through 'remembering true' and an opposing current bent on 'remembering false', garnering the illusion of the *Volksgemeinschaft*.

Post-war Germany—at least in the West—has been preoccupied with reparation, but the underlying question has been when would there be enough, so that the nation could put the Nazi period behind it, repair its history and move on. On the conservative side, it has been more a demand than a question, following quickly upon the end of the war, and reappearing from then on. Maier (1988, pp. 121–39), for example, sees it in debates over establishing historical museums, in which visitors will see their past. It was there at Bitburg (Hartman 1986), where commemoration, conceived as an act of reconciliation between the West and the FRG, brought fallen German soldiers, including the SS, into an equivalence with the victims of the Holocaust. A similar debate was evoked by establishing a German memorial in 1993, in a historic military building, with the sculpture by Kathé Kollwitz, *Mother with Her Dead Son*, at the centre. Dedicated to all victims of tyranny and torture, it seemed again to draw a moral equivalence (Marcuse 1997; though it is not his language, he thinks that it does promote reparation).

Now we turn squarely to the theme of reparation. Remembering, memorializing, compensating, restoring (to), commemorating—all can be forms of reparation. My aim is to show that 'remembering true' is reparative. But our analysis of defensive organizations leads to the suspicion that what looks like reparation might actually negate reparation. We have already seen that confidence in overcoming the past might also express splitting and idealization, in which success is, in this defensive dimension, an illusion; that repeated acts of commemoration might enact an undoing—a making 'not to have happened'; that the *Historikerstreit* was not only an attempt to engage with the contradictory aims of bringing the Nazi period into History without diluting its inconceivable traduction of history into radical evil, but was also an acting-out. Similarly, reparation could be shadowed by its negation. In psychoanalytic thinking, the anti-reparative counter-current is called 'manic reparation'. In the next chapter, we will explore in detail the character of reparation and manic reparation. And, as in the book as a whole, we aim to hold in dialogue the psychoanalytic dimension—clinical and theoretical—with the specific historical situation of post-war Germany and its interpretation(s) by historians.

Notes

1. Bergmann (1997) argues that the anti-fascist policy and self-image of the GDR, along with the conviction that fascism and anti-Semitism were problems of the capitalist West, invalidate 'the psychoanalytic model, which theorizes that something can be overcome by being worked through, does not apply to societies as a whole' (p. 24). Not only is Bergmann's conclusion unjustified, but also it contradicts his own historian's explanation, which links GDR ideology with transporting culpability to the West. In fact, his conclusion implies the very defensive retreat we have been examining, based on splitting within an organized social defence, with the further implication that reunification would undermine it and bring with it the pressure identified by psychoanalysis, either to work through the past, or to find another repository for the projection.
2. I cannot go into other shifts evoked by intergenerational conflict of the 1960s. They included a recognition in the FRG of German responsibility for the partition of Germany and the cleansing by the younger generation of the Nazi-tarnish of the parental generation, thus repeating the latter's detachment from the Holocaust (Domansky, pp. 189–90).
3. In my view, the Mitscherlichs have made a major contribution to understanding the structure of German society in the post-war period, based on an anticipated catastrophe of losing a narcissistic illusion of German identity. The 'inability to mourn' refers to an unbearable recognition of, and

responsibility for, inconceivable damage to the 'good object', embodied both by German culture without illusion and to the victims of German perpetration. Mourning builds on and promotes ego-reality in place of ego-illusion in an ego-merger with the ego-ideal. In its reparative dimension, ego-reality bestows reality on the object in a recognition of damage to it. Reciprocally, it reinforces an ego-capacity to be better, to bear the recognition of reality and an urge to make the object better. This process can be identified by the defences against it. For recent interdisciplinary assessments of the Mitscherlich thesis, see Brockhaus (Hg.) (2008).
4. 'Reunification' does not convey the relationship between the two former states. The former FRG in effect assimilated the GDR, perpetuating a condescension towards it.

References

Bartov, O. (1998) Defining Enemies, Making Victims: Germans, Jews, and the Holocaust. *The American Historical Review* 103(3): 771–816.

Benz, W. (2001) Anti-semitism and Philosemitism. In Klessmann, C. (ed.) *The Divided Past: Re-writing Post-war history*. Oxford/New York: Berg, pp. 149–70.

Bergmann, W. (1997) Antisemitism and Xenophobia in Germany Since Reunification. In Kurthen, H., Bergmann, W. and Erb, R. (eds.) *Antisemitism and Xenophobia in Germany After Unification*. New York/Oxford: Oxford University Press, pp. 21–38.

Bohleber, W. (1992) Nationalismus, Fremdenhass und Antisemitismus: Psychoanalytische Überlegungen. *Psyche* 46: 689–709.

Bohleber, W. (1995) The Presence of the Past – Xenophobia and Rightwing Extremism in the Federal Republic of Germany: Psychoanalytic Reflections. *American Imago* 52: 329–44.

Brockhaus, G. (2008) Die Unfähigkeit zu trauern als Analyse und als Abweher der NS-Erbshaft. In Brockhaus, G. (Hg.) *Ist 'Die Unfähigkeit zu trauern' noch actuell? Eine interdisziplinäre Diskussion. Psychosozial* 31, nr 114 (4) (special issue), pp. 29–39.

Domansky, E. (1993) Die gespaltene Erinnerung. In Köppen, M. (ed.) *Kunst und Literatur nach Auschwitz*. Berlin: Erich Schmidt Verlag, pp. 178–96.

Eley, G. (2004) The Unease of History: Settling Accounts with the East German Past. *History Workshop Journal* 57: 175–201.

Freud, S. (1915) Repression. *The Standard Edition of the Complete Psychological Works of Sigmund Freud* 14: 141–58.

Fulbrook, M. (1999) *German National Identity after the Holocaust*. Cambridge: Polity.

Fulbrook, M. (2016) Questionable Concepts: Trust, Distrust and Normalisation. In *Erfahrung, Erinnerung, Geschichtsschreibung: Neue Perspektiven auf die deutschen Diktaturen*. Weimar: Wallstein Verlag, pp. 62–110.

Hartman, G. (ed.) (1986) *Bitburg in Moral and Political Perspective*. Bloomington: Indiana University Press.

Herf, J. (1997) *Divided Memory: The Nazi Past in the Two Germanies*. Cambridge, MA/London: Harvard University Press.

Hinshelwood, R. D. (1987) *What Happens in Groups: Psychoanalysis, the Individual and the Community*. London: Free Association Books.

Hinshelwood, R. D. (2008) Repression and Splitting: Towards a Method of Conceptual Comparison. *International Journal of Psychoanalysis* 89: 503–21.

Human Rights Watch/Helsinki (1995) *'Germany for Germans': Xenophobia and Racist Violence in Germany*. New York and elsewhere: Human Rights Watch.

Ignatieff, M. (1994) *Nationalism and the Narcissism of Minor Differences*. Milton Keynes: The Open University.

Klein, M. (1946) Notes on Some Schizoid Mechanisms. In *The Writings of Melanie Klein*, vol. 3. London: Hogarth and the Institute of Psychoanalysis, 1975, pp. 1–24.

Kurthen, H. (1997) Antisemitism and Xenophobia in United Germany: How the Burden of the Past Affects the Present. In Kurthen, H., Bergmann, W. and Erb, R. (eds.) *Antisemitism and Xenophobia in Germany After Unification*. New York/Oxford: Oxford University Press, pp. 39–87.

Kurthen, H., Bergmann, W. and Erb, R. (1997) Introduction: Post-unification Challenges to German Democracy. In Kurthen, H., Bergmann, W. and Erb, R. (eds.) *Antisemitism and Xenophobia in Germany After Unification*. New York/Oxford: Oxford University Press, pp. 3–17.

Maier, C. (1988) *The Unmasterable Past: History, Holocaust, and German National Identity*. Cambridge, MA/London: Harvard University Press.

Marcuse, H. (1997) The National Memorial to the Victims of War and Tyranny: From Conflict to Consensus. Paper presented to the German Studies Association Conference, September 25, 1997, Washington, DC. Retrieved from http://www.history.ucsb.edu/faculty/marcuse/present/neuewach.htm. Accessed 22.6.2011.

Mitscherlich, A. and Mitscherlich, M. (1967/1975) *The Inability to Mourn: Principles of Collective Behaviour*. Munich: Piper & Co. Verlag; English translation, New York: Grove Press.

Mitscherlich-Nielsen, M. (1992) Die (Un)Fähigkeit zu trauern in Ost- und Westdeutschland. Was Trauerarbeit heissen könnte. *Psyche – Zeitschrift für Psychoanalyse* 46: 406–18.

Perels, J. (2015) *Die Nationalsozialismus als Problem der Gegenwart*. Frankfurt aM: Peter Lang.

Pew Research Center (2012) Global Religious Landscape. http://www.pewforum.org/2012/12/18/global-religious-landscape-jew. Accessed 9.5.2017.

Schultze, R. (2006) The Politics of Memory: Flight and Expulsion of German Populations After the Second World War and German Collective Memory. *National Identities* 8: 367–82.

Segal, H. (1987) Silence Is the Real Crime. *International Review of Psychoanalysis* 14: 3–12. In *Psychoanalysis, Literature and War: Papers 1972–1995*. London/New York: Routledge, 1997, pp. 143–56.

Segal, H. (1995) From Hiroshima to the Gulf War and After: Socio-Political Expressions of Ambivalence. In *Psychoanalysis, Literature and War: Papers 1972–1995*. London/New York: Routledge, 1997, pp. 157–68.

Steiner, J. (1993) *Psychic Retreats: Pathological Organizations in Psychotic, Neurotic and Borderline Patients*. London/New York: Routledge.

Streeck-Fischer, A. (2000) Vergangene und gegenwärtige Traumatisierung – jugentliche Skinheads in Deutschland. In Opher-Cohn, L. et al. (eds.) *Das Ende der Sprachlosigkeit? Auswirkungen traumatischer Holocaust-Erfahrungen über mehrere Generationen*(2nd edition). Giessen: Psychosozial Verlag, pp. 51–70.

Weil, F. (1997) Ethnic Intolerance, Extremism and Democratic Attitudes in Germany Since Reunification. In Kurthen, H., Bergmann, W. and Erb, R. (eds.) *Antisemitism and Xenophobia in Germany After Unification*. New York/Oxford: Oxford University Press, pp. 110–42.

Wetzel, J. (1997) Antisemitism Among Right-Wing Extremist Groups, Organizations, and Parties in Post-unification Germany. In Kurthen, H., Bergmann, W. and Erb, R. (eds.) *Antisemitism and Xenophobia in Germany After Unification*. New York/Oxford: Oxford University Press, pp. 159–73.

9

Reparation

Reparation in Psychoanalysis

In this chapter, I will set out the psychoanalytic background for the thesis that 'remembering true' is a form of reparation and that there is a traduced form of remembering-false-as- manic reparation ('true' and 'false' will come clear in the discussion of reparation; Klein 1937, pp. 311–13, 1940, pp. 348–9; Segal 1981, pp. 147–58). They look the same, but reparation is based on concern for the other, while manic reparation is based on narcissistic aggrandizement and contempt for the other. Remembering as reparation includes an awareness of an attack upon an object, which drives a reparative process. By contrast, remembering as manic reparation controls memory, one form of which is to recast it into a defensive, narcissistic memory organization. Any actual remembering is an ambivalent mixture of the two.

We will then be ready to continue our psychoanalytic-historical dialogue by addressing the problem of remembering and repairing in German memory of the Nazi period. Sites of remembering portray this ambivalent reparative intention and gather conflicting views and factions around them. To make this case, I will clarify the concepts of reparation, manic reparation, introjective identification and projective identification. I align reparation with introjective identification and manic reparation with projective identification.

Reparation is driven by guilt. To remember as reparation is to suffer guilt. It is also to be drawn into falsifying memory in order to avoid guilt: reparation can then take on a manic-reparative colouring, and symbols of reparation can become ambiguous as they become foci for different, conflicting groups.[1] They can become enclaves of memories that differ from each other and depend on these differences. Each enclave can remember in its own way because another remembers differently, at the expense of a convergent memory. Symbols of remembering, such as memorials, are sites of ambivalence, used differently by different groups. They represent both reparative and manic-reparative intentions, as well as intellectual, emotional and political conflict.

Reparation cannot be engineered. It must make its own path. External constraints divert it, and behaviour is not its measure. Murdered victims cannot be repaired, but reparation nonetheless takes place through them, perhaps through identification with them by those who survived them, but also by the perpetrators and by the community that identifies with either group (cf. Maier 1988, who addresses the issue of German responsibility to everyone who identifies with German nationality).

Reparation is an essentially psychoanalytic concept, in that it refers to an internal reality that can be expressed through an external reality, but cannot be reduced to it: one can repair a damaged object without reparation and reparation can occur without a clear object. It has, therefore, an observable, social meaning and an invisible subjective meaning. Moreover, the secular concept of reparation entered psychoanalytic and social vocabularies around the same time: mainly through Klein in psychoanalysis and the Treaty of Versailles in social discourse. In both arenas, a range of meanings bespeaks the ambiguity between, on the one hand, an act and, on the other, a subjective state that registers a change for the better in the relationship between subject and object. Such an idea is hard to grasp, and one is tempted to reconfigure reparation as an act, the measure of which is time. In my view, a psychoanalytic concept of reparation lies outside time, and expressions such as 'Time heals' or 'He/she will get over it in time' are very misleading. There is no time when enough has been done.

Reparation as a psychoanalytic concept also brings out the paradox of referring to an internal state in a vocabulary generated from its social environment. For the Germans, following Versailles, reparation was a debt that could be settled and Germany could be redeemed, or it could be opposed as a victor's illegitimate charter. In this case, the idea of compensation also—and maybe principally—would then include some form of atonement, assuaging guilt, eliciting forgiveness or showing a moral renovation. For the Jews, however, it has been a process without closure, leaving the issue of guilt untouched. The immense atrocity of the Holocaust has challenged the very idea of reparation, which now must be seen through the relationship of Germans to Jews (Goschler 2008, p. 7).[2] Israel has replaced reparation with the Hebrew expression, *Shilumin*, which, in the Old Testament, meant a payment or retaliatory measure unconnected with forgiveness or pardon (Frohn 1991; Goschler, p. 12). This difference of view starkly pulls making better, in the subjective sense, apart from compensation, and the issue of guilt from restoring a lost good, as in 'goods', to a dispossessed owner. Time divides them, in that compensation takes time, but can be completed: redemption cannot.

Psychoanalysis has worked over the relationship between these two forms of reparation, though not explicitly, and it is to this implicit project that I now turn. The fear of retaliation in a persecutory environment drives the need of a fragmented ego to compensate a fractured object for what has been taken or damaged. In contrast to this meaning, remorse and guilt drive the urge of a whole ego for reparation of a whole object in an environment of concern. The shift from hate, persecution and control to remorse for aggressiveness and to an opportunity to love and to identify with the damaged object needed a new vocabulary, in which change replaced stasis and identification replaced the management of an alien and persecuted object by paying it off. A vocabulary to cover this complex territory includes 'undoing injury', 'compensation', 'restitution', 'reparation' and 'manic reparation'. The more the ego is composed of identifications, the more reparative its orientation, and the more it grows in a process of unending, continuous development through the transformation of largely hostile object relations to largely loving object relations.

The essential link between reparation and guilt, as opposed to related concepts to do with compensation or restitution, is immanent in Freud's distinction between a controlling identification with a demeaned object in melancholia and identifications as the core of the ego. In the latter direction, Freud (1913[1912–1913]) articulated the idea of 'taboo conscience' in *Totem and Taboo*, as the earliest form of conscience and the concomitant of identification with the oedipal father, thereby discriminating a different relationship of ego to object from the need to compensate.

> [The] mob of brothers were filled with the same contradictory feelings which we can see at work in the ambivalent father-complexes of our children and of our neurotic patients. They hated their father…; but they loved and admired him too… A sense of guilt [*Schuldbewußtsein*] made its appearance…They revoked their [murderous] deed [and] created out of their filial sense of guilt [*Schuldbewußtsein*] the two fundamental taboos [that] corresponded to the two repressed wishes of the Oedipus complex [parricide and incest]. (p. 143)

Along with reparation, Freud nonetheless speaks of a grievance for which we feel we are owed compensation. 'We all think we have reason to reproach Nature and our destiny for congenital and infantile disadvantages; we all demand reparation for early wounds to our narcissism, our self-love' (1916, p. 315). But the word translated from Freud's German by 'reparation' is not the usual word for what we now call reparation, '*Wiedergutmachung*': it is '*Entschadigung*', which literally means the removal of an injury.

In his paper on the loss of reality in neurosis and psychosis, Freud (1924) referred to restoration, less as returning something taken, than of healing a damaged relationship to reality. In comparing psychosis with neurosis, he discerned a two-stage process in both: in the first, the ego was 'dragged away' from reality by the id; in the second, the ego struggled to reinstate reality. In both cases, stage one led to a compromised reality. In stage two, the ego reasserted reality against the id with varying success: in neurosis, by a compromise, allowing a certain reality while satisfying the id with wish-fulfilling phantasy; in psychosis, by creating an alternative, hallucinated, reality. Both scenarios aimed to re-establish a reality for the belaboured ego.

But let's look at Freud's language, especially with respect to the recovery of reality in psychosis. The second stage, he said, 'would try to *make good the damage* done [to reality] and re-establish the subject's relation to reality at the expense of the id' (p. 184; my emphasis); stage two 'is indeed intended to make good the loss of reality' (p. 184). In the first of these two extracts, he uses the common expression, *wieder gutmachen*; in the latter, he uses '*Realitätsverlust ausgleichen*': here the emphasis is on loss, not damage, and he calls the recovery '*ausgleichen*', which means to balance out, or to settle, as with a debt. So, there is a mixed language: making good for damage and settlement of a loss. He goes on to say that this process has the character of a reparation (pp. 184, 185). What stands out here is that he introduces the actual word, 'reparation', into the German text.

Reality for Freud is both the reality of the reality principle—the external actuality, experienced through perception—and the oedipal reality of child with the father and the mother. The resolution of oedipal reality takes place in two stages: first, the deflection of oedipal wishes by castration anxiety or its equivalent; second, the loving identification with father or mother, with remorse for injury to them, in what he saw as the beginnings, in a 'taboo conscience', of conscience and the 'fearful sense of guilt' that it produced (1913[1912–1913], pp. 67, 68). The former is like compensation—it requires that the boy give back father's penis or girl give back mother's position; in the latter, he/she, in remorse and by conscience, is moved to heal the injured parent along with him/herself. Reality as oedipal reality is recovered as reparation for injury to a good object.

What I want to draw attention to is that there are two dimensions and two vocabularies in this evolution of the concept of reparation, both clear in Freud. In the first, there is the idea of taking and returning, of recompense or reimbursement; in the second, there is the idea of injury or damage: something that cannot be replaced. Of the former, one could say that property was stolen, and then returned; or that the owner was reimbursed or compensated for the loss. Of the latter, one speaks, not of property, but of injury. It is not like stolen property—it cannot be returned, nor can the 'owner' be reimbursed. Damaged personhood can only be made better. While a theft creates a debt that can be repaid and the account settled, an injury creates an indebtedness, an obligation, a responsibility to an other. One might add that the former is mostly driven by hate and the fear of retaliation in hatred; the latter by love, empathy and identification. If we take Freud's four expressions, they span the range from reimbursement at one end to making better at the other: *Ausgleichen* (settling an account), *Wiederherstellung* (re-establishing the original state), *Wiedergutmachung* (making good again), reparation (making better as an internal urge).

A similar dual vocabulary is used by the psychoanalyst, Joan Riviere, in her 1929 paper on 'Womanliness as Masquerade'. Against the background of the typical meaning of restitution as the recovery of reality, Riviere speaks of the woman's defensive posture with respect to her castrating attacks on men, and her rivalry with women, but she also speaks of love-making as a restitution of her own self-esteem (p. 307). The love-making was in part from the position of the masquerade woman, whose mask of femininity reassured the man that he still possessed the (stolen) penis and reassured herself that her sadism in her supremacy over both parents was not in evidence. But in speaking of the restitution of self-esteem, Riviere implies that the girl also suffers injury and aims for restitution. In this case, the injury to the man is made better along with the injury to herself, which implies an identification between herself and the man as an injured, good object. Further back, the mother was the original good object. The penis was stolen from her along with the nipple and milk and everything maternal. Restoring the penis was not enough restitution: the daughter's 'efforts to placate and make reparation by restoring and using the penis in the mother's service were never enough' (p. 311).

I draw attention to the word, reparation, in the difficult and inadequate attempt at restoration of the mother described by Riviere. It suggests the dual vocabulary of reparation that I have delineated: giving back what has been stolen and healing or making better an injury. The overall process is far from perfect, but its fundamental driver is love and identification, not the agency of the penis. The essential nature of the internal world, in its capacity for love and goodness, is the source of reparation.

But in addition, this essential, good nature depends on an identification with a good object: reparation by identification with a good object, as made explicit by Melanie Klein. Reparation is a reciprocal process between a better (good) ego and a good object.

But to step back to Klein's original use of reparation: at first, she meant giving back what had been stolen. Her first published use of the word 'reparation' was in 1928, commenting on a dream presented by Douglas Bryan, in which a male patient was accused by his mother of taking and destroying money that belonged to her. He was a rent collector, and had in fact stolen rent money paid only by women. Klein said

> It seems evident that the patient took the money for the purpose of throwing it down the lavatory pan [in] his anxiety to make reparation, to restore to the mother (or the womb) represented by the lavatory pan, that which he had stolen. (p. 256)…[T]he thefts of the money [were] a repetition of the early anal-sadistic desires to rob the mother, but they were also brought about by the compulsion…to make reparation for these early thefts and to restore that which had been stolen…by throwing away the money into the lavatory pan [mother]. (p. 257)

In this case, reparation meant restitution, a settling of accounts, a giving back what had been taken, in order to bring a grievance to an end. It is as if mother's womb contained objects, including father's penis, which could be restored to her.

A year later, in her paper on the work of the painter, Ruth Kjär, Klein (1929) uses reparation clearly to speak of injury.

> It is obvious that the desire to make reparation, to make good the injury psychologically done to the mother and also to restore herself was at the bottom of the compelling urge to paint these portraits of her relatives…The daughter's wish to destroy her mother, to see her old, worn out, marred, is the cause of the need to represent her in full possession of her strength and beauty. By so doing, a daughter can allay her own anxiety and can endeavour to restore her mother and make her new through the portrait. (p. 218)

The combined restoration of subject and object is clear in *The Psychoanalysis of Children* (1932).

> [T]he boy's desire to restore his mother's body and his desire to restore his own interact, the fulfilment of the one being essential to the fulfilment of the other... An adequate belief in the 'good' contents of his body which neutralizes, or rather opposes, its 'bad' contents and excrement seems to be necessary in order that his penis, as the representative of his body as a whole, shall produce 'good' and wholesome semen. This belief, which coincides with his belief in his capacity to love, depends upon his having sufficient belief in his 'good' imagos especially in his 'good' mother and in her unimpaired and wholesome body. (p. 277)

Picking up the thread from Freud, we can see that this affect-driven process is also an urge to recover a connection with reality. For Bion (1957) as well, the ego struggles to mend its object world, one aspect of which is to mend itself. A fragmented ego lives in a fragmented, persecutory object world; an integrated ego lives in a whole-object world.

Reparation in the psychoanalytic sense is, therefore, a peculiar kind of action. It has no time-scale. The ego may be urged to repair damage in the external world, but the 'force' that impels it is identification with good internal objects and its good capacity to identify with them. The dimension of reparation is different from the typical dimension of action, which implies force and time. More generally, there are the following times: metric time (the time of the ordinary material world, including the second law of thermodynamics); repetitive time (obsessional undoing); hopeful time (incomplete reparation); manic time (complete, failed reparation). Dimensions outside time include narcissistic annulment (Kernberg 2009); the abolition of time and space in psychosis (Bion 1962, p. 113); reparation as a moment of love and identification.

There is a contradiction at the heart of reparation. The call to action to realize reparation occurs in time, but as manic, and therefore failed, reparation. The urge to reparation occurs outside time and the corresponding dimension of space and force. It occurs in the internal dimension of guilt, conscience, identification and the superego. The way this contradiction has vexed our understanding of reparative processes can be seen more clearly in the social world. There are countless situations that call out for compensation to victims, which also aim for some kind of accountability and renovation, but which run in circles of mutual accusation and evasion. None more vexes an understanding of reparation than the Holocaust. Regardless of one's point of view, the Holocaust has become the primal form of an atrocity. It demands compensation in all forms, and they are forever inadequate.

Reparation and Identification

In her paper, A Contribution to the Psychogenesis of Manic-Depressive States, Klein (1935) introduces the concepts of the paranoid-schizoid position and the depressive position. Restitution based on fear of retaliation is a feature of the paranoid-schizoid position; reparation-based guilt is a feature of the depressive position. Paranoid anxieties and the attempt to placate them are of the form of 'dangerous monsters' inside; depressive anxieties are of the form of 'sorrow and anxiety for the object' (p. 272) and concern for the 'loss of the whole object' (p. 275). 'The ego feels impelled (and I can now add, impelled by its identification with the good object) to make restitution for all the sadistic attacks that it has launched on that object' (p. 265). In the depressive position, the perpetrator suffers along with the victim, made worse because the perpetrator cannot compensate the victim, cannot give anything back that will relieve the pain of either the victim or the perpetrator.[3]

Reparation is not accountability in a juridical sense but acceptance of responsibility in psychic reality. As an aspect of the 'depressive position', an internal psychic moment in which an internal good object is experienced as damaged by the ego and in which 'depressive anxiety' at the state of the object, guilt arouses an urge to repair it (see Klein 1935, 1940; Hinshelwood 1991, pp. 138–55). Guilt is intrinsic to reparation. The object remains blemished and can never again be as it was, so the reparative process remains incomplete. Sadness at the loss of the object and remorse at the attack upon it engrave themselves into the psyche. One might say that the object eventually is found to be good, as a discovery rather than as an achievement—something we notice when we stand back and attend to what has happened, and is likely to happen, to the object. I think that this state of 'found to be good' is a form of Klein's idea of gratitude (1957) and that hope is an appropriate word for an anticipation of it (Hinshelwood 2007, p. 202).

This understanding can be applied at the social level, without having to assume that society is a subject or agent, which feels guilt and acts as an individual writ large. But one can give a parallel description and use it as a model. In psychic reality, as it appears in the clinical process, guilt evokes reparation. Evidence of reparative intention is therefore also evidence of guilt. Similarly, a national purposiveness in reparative activity gives evidence of national guilt and also of the urge to recover a convergent memory from the shards and distortions of memory. Political accounts of this reparative activity are needed to understand post-1945 Germany, but such accounts also require the language of perpetration, guilt, defence and reparation. It cannot be coerced from outside.[4]

In this respect, my view differs from that of C. Fred Alford (2006). He argues for a 'reparative natural law' that would provide a foundation for a natural law of ethics and that would be incomplete if it did not garner an ethical commitment to the actual victims of unethical behaviour (see also Vetlesen 2005, pp. 104–44). Without the honing of commitment by generations of social life, it would remain an abstract force that could as well drive an aesthetic, even narcissistic, preoccupation as inspire a concern to improve the situation of people who suffer. I agree that one needs to distinguish between concern for the object and the narcissism of feeling good, but I will stress here the importance of internal objects in relation to external objects. The commitment of successive German governments to make good the damage inflicted in the Nazi period provides an example of embedding a reparative attitude into social life, a commitment that has continually to be remade and that is also continually challenged as no longer relevant to later generations. Nonetheless, reparation takes its own path and does not easily translate into action. Based on an identification between ego and object, perpetrator and victim, which is rooted in depressive concern for the object, it is more loving than doing. Making the object better involves making the ego-perpetrator better (a topic intensively explored by Schwab [2010], drawing on her experience as a German and a psychoanalyst). Ego and object impart beneficence to each other as a continuing urge to make better. By contrast, narcissistic identification is not properly an identification, but

Reparation and Identification 195

swells up with pride, while secretly denigrating the object. In that sense it is manic.

Clinical psychoanalysis has studied the reparative process in detail, offering thereby perhaps the deepest insight into its nature. As an example, I choose the following clinical vignette published by the psychoanalyst, Haydee Faimberg (2005) from the case of an intergenerational transmission of trauma, in this instance passed from a father during the Nazi period to his son. I have condensed the narrative of a session into a diagram of the reparative process in relation to identification (Fig. 9.1). The interpretation is mine.[5]

The analysand, Mario, seemed almost lifeless for some time in his analysis. In the background was his father, a Polish refugee (presumably from the Nazis) in Argentina. Father had sent money during the war to support

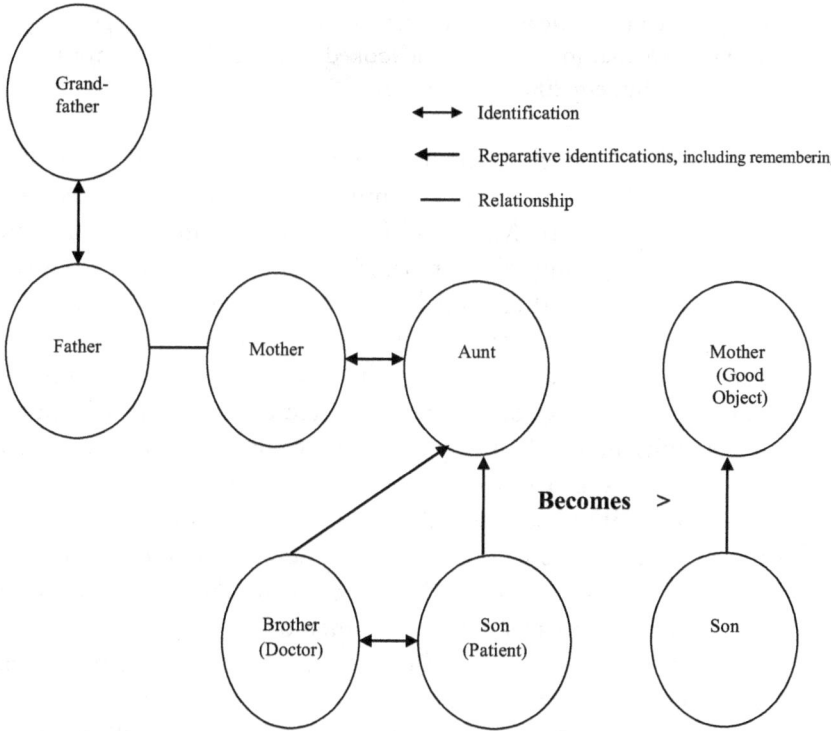

Fig. 9.1 Diagram based on Faimberg 2005

his natal family in Poland, but to no avail, the implication being that they had perished. Now, in his analysis, Mario speaks of (re)discovering that his mother had a sister who had been 'forgotten' and left in a mental hospital:

> I asked my mother about Auntie Rita. [Mother] was quite surprised at my knowing of her existence and asked me how I knew about her. I remembered her. I don't know if I had always remembered her, but in the last few years I realized I knew about her. My mother told me that Rita was confined to a psychiatric hospital. I asked her how long ago had she been sent there and she told me it had happened when she (my mother) was expecting my brother. I was five at the time. My mother never went to see my aunt and never talked about her…I found out where she was and I asked my brother, who is a doctor, to see if she was well taken care of. I have been visiting her, telling her all that has happened in the twenty-five years she has been isolated from the world. I've taught her to wash [he said, pointing to his own shoes that for the first time looked clean] and I've set myself as an example. (Faimberg 2005, pp. 13–14)

Note the background: the patient's father, as the son of his own father, tried to make his father and father's family better, a reparative task now unconsciously taken on by Mario as his son. Mario brings his aunt into his memory, as the beginning of reparation. His mother and her sister together represent a mother who had lost her memory and her self-esteem. In getting in touch with his aunt, then, Mario brings his aunt as mother and himself as son together. Furthermore, 'son' is divided between himself and his brother, a doctor who is enlisted to make 'mother' (in the form of his aunt) better. In bringing 'mother' and 'son' back together, mother's memory is also restored. It is a reparative scenario, in which mother—the patient's good internal object—is looked after, made better. In his repeated references to her, she was remembered, and the making better, including being remembered, restores the mother's internal world, repairing her self-esteem and her missing memory.

The reparative process was based on identifications. In the beginning of the analysis, the patient was almost lifeless, but he remembered his aunt, got in touch with her and in the process not only came alive himself but also brought her, as 'mother', alive. Sent to a mental hospital during mother's pregnancy, his aunt had been destroyed as a mother. The mother's pregnancy had been attacked—a primal attack on her reproductive capacity. The two sons, together, represent her son, in both a doing mode (the doctor) and a loving mode (the patient): 'he' as son draws her as mother into identification with 'his' restorative character. Guilt for the attack on maternal reproductive capacity (in the ostracized aunt) drives the reparation. Stated in a condensed formulation, a son-ego felt impelled to repair a damaged-mother-object and the means of reparation became identification between a getting-better ego and a getting-better object.

In this form of identification—introjective identification—the ego and object are brought together, each enriched by the process. By contrast, in projective identification, the ego intrudes a part of itself into the object, both to control the object through this part-ego and to evacuate this part-ego from the ego. Klein (1957) offers a clinical example; a patient reported the following dream:

> He was in an upstairs flat and 'X', a friend of his, was calling him from the street suggesting a walk together. The patient did not join 'X', because a black dog in the flat might get out and be run over. He stroked the dog. When he looked out of the window, he found that 'X' had 'receded'. (p. 227)

In Klein's interpretation, the friend, X, is a part of the patient, an aggressive part that recedes from him. X takes with him the patient's aggressive danger to the dog-analyst, who must be protected, stroked, by the ego that stays behind in the flat. The patient's aggression is managed by projective identification into X; that is, X is identified with, and controlled by, the part-ego that has been projected into him, forming a part-ego-object unit under part-ego control, which is moved into the distance, carrying the ego's aggression with it. The bulk of the ego, now freed of aggression, protects the dog-analyst.

In this case, the menace to the ego was the aggression that would target the object, evoking guilt and a depressive reaction in the ego. This patient's concern for the analyst was near the surface. The scenario approaches a wish for reconciliation between the ego and object and between the ego and its aggressiveness. Here, introjective identification holds ego and object, as well as aggression, together, in that the patient can represent the situation to himself in the internal scene of the dream. In other cases, however, hatred seethes self-destructively inside the ego. In such instances, projective identification, reinforced by an annihilating attack on the part-ego-object aims at extinguishing the hated aspect. The attack on the object saves the perpetrator, something that happens in the manic phase of manic-depression or in murder as an unconscious alternative to suicide (Williams 1998, pp. 41–51). In virulent cases, the object of projective identification must be annihilated in order to eliminate the internal aggression that otherwise could overwhelm the ego, or, as in Chap. 5, would re-expose the ego to internal collapse.

Collective Memory and Reparation

As I said earlier, reparation cannot be engineered or completed within a discrete time frame. We saw in Chap. 7 that Adenauer was already pressing for a normalization of Germany shortly after the end of the war. Time means duration and challenges the capacity for toleration. It frustrates, provoking a call to dismiss the project of reparation. In 1946, Roger Money-Kyrle worked for the Allied Control Commission, assessing Germans for suitability for employment in the new, democratic West German state, on the basis of Nazi characteristics. In 1950, shortly after the creation of the Federal Republic of Germany and the German Democratic Republic, with the consolidation of the antagonism between the Western Allies and the Soviet bloc, Money-Kyrle (1951) was concerned that this new threat to West Germans could weaken their belief in reparation to the new, democratic, social good object.

> [In 1946, there was] the obvious manifestation… of a widespread sense of collective guilt of a genuinely depressive kind…There could be no doubt that the tragedy of such men was that they felt they had devoted their aggressiveness…to the defence of something which in their inmost hearts they themselves felt to be mainly sinister and evil. It was therefore often of great therapeutic importance to them as individuals – and probably also for

the future of their society – to be allowed to participate in the protection of what they could feel, both consciously and unconsciously, to be a better object. The idea of Western culture threatened from without had already begun to play the rôle of an object of this kind, and in the idea of its defence they had begun to seek an outlet for an unconscious reparative impulse. But there was also a tendency to turn against these new ideas in… despair [and] very many Germans…were in a depressive phase which could be succeeded either by an impulse to constructive reparation or, if this failed, by a renewed paranoidal attack on the objects they had injured… (pp. 243–4)[6]

Money-Kyrle was speaking of a Germany made better in its capacity and willingness to remember its Nazi past, to embrace a reparative attitude towards it and to work to achieve it, but note his referring to protecting the good object, as if it were already present, and action was needed to defend it, not to produce it. It is, therefore, an example of identification between a making-better ego and a making-better object, in which time means something like time-enough; for example, for the withdrawal of projections. But it also evokes a paranoid response to despair, which sets up an enemy to overcome. As we saw in Chap. 8, with an external enemy to combat, time as a scarce commodity defeats memory and guilt. To live in time-enough, without regard to overcoming it, would be to harbour memory and guilt. What we hear, from Adenauer to the present, is a complex of remembering and overcoming, and one of the hallmarks of overcoming has been the proclamation that the time has come to end the devotion to reparation and to demand that Germany be accepted as a normal state.

There have been key moments at which this contradiction has exploded into consciousness to become a conflict between sectors of German society. The *Historikerstreit* over national history, identity, moral renovation and pride in post-Holocaust Germany, which we discussed in Chap. 6, was a public debate over whether it could bear the burden of the past and integrate the Nazi period into its collective memory, or whether it had to fall into isolated enclaves of distorted, conflicted memory (Maier 1988, pp. 34–65). This event became a marker of the progress of reparation, as something either incomplete or complete. For the liberal left in Germany and for the Jews, it was incomplete; for conservatives and for Chancellor Kohl, it was complete. In my view, the conflict, as anchored in time, allowed the nature of reparation to recede. Reparation is something that eventually is recognized to have been adequate—a different dimension, one that is incompatible with time. And here is the dilemma: how can it be an ingredient of social reality, documented in history and yet be outside time, outside the actions of responsible agents? But the question can also be reversed: 'How can there be an adequate history without this dimension?'

We need them both. Reparation lies outside time, as an internal frame of mind and an orientation towards the object. These aspects can be observed in the psychoanalytic setting. The reality of the world we live in, and our own reality to ourselves, proceeds in time. Thinking psychoanalytically is also a reality, one that brings out the immediacy of our relationship to the object, both individually and in our comprehension of the external world.

We can identify a reparative process in depressive features, both in the analytic setting and in the social world, as in the case of post-war Germany. In either case, it is a retrospective discovery that a reparative moment has occurred. That is what historical research reveals, no matter how much action has been documented. We see the features and conditions of reparation and defences against it, in the consulting room. We see the historical dimension more clearly in the social world. We define the qualities of reparation in the social world on the basis of psychoanalytic investigation, but while psychoanalytic observation brings out the detail of internal states and changes, it can't get totally outside the historical reality of society. Language, including the language of psychoanalysis, is embodied in the history of social reality. We can't begin to formulate the concept of reparation without the history that is embedded in the word, but we can't understand the word as an account of social reality without the psychoanalysis of it. I have tried to show that the two are wrapped together, but can be analytically discriminated.

Remembering in post-war Germany has reflected an acute sensitivity about the intentions behind symbols of reparation. In particular, this sensitivity has stemmed from ambivalence and from an undercurrent of anti-reparative feeling beneath the dedicated reparative aim towards the

Jews. This ambivalence-driven sensitivity surfaces in memorialization. I will take up this theme in Chap. 10, but I want briefly mention it now, in order to consolidate the theme of collective memory as reparation. Memorialization begins as a site for remembering, whether or not centred on a physical object, such as a monument. For example, one might see the Historikerstreit was a kind of memorial, perhaps concretely located in Bitburg, but then transferred to the virtual space of public debate in the press and in collected contributions (Hartman 1986; Knowlton and Cates 1993). But, following Noam Lupu (2003) and James Young (1993), I differentiate memorials and memorialization from monuments. Monuments are material objects, which freeze memories, confining them into ideological portrayals; memorials are sites of remembering, often differently, by different groups, but around which remembering is alive and ongoing. Bitburg was closer to the former, the *Historikerstreit* to the latter.

Remember James Young's point, that 'instead of allowing the past to rigidify in its monumental forms, we would vivify memory through the memory-work itself – whereby events, their recollection, and the role monuments play in our lives remain animate, never completed' (1993, p. 15). While I differ from him on a couple of issues (see Chap. 7), I share his view, both that memorials vivify remembering while monuments tend to freeze memories into preconceived messages, and that individuals cannot in a literal sense share memories as specific experiences.

We can now move on to exploring memory as reparation, occasioned by memorialization. In particular, I will link 'remembering true' and reparation with mourning, and link 'remembering false' and manic reparation with melancholia. This distinction builds on Freud's contrasting identification of the ego with the object in mourning with a totalizing identification, creating something more like an identicality between ego and object in melancholia. Of the former, he says that the ego is composed of identifications with lost objects (1923); of the latter, he says that the ego is locked together with a kind of negative (shadow) object, which is rigidly controlled (1917[1915]). In a manic swing, this object is denigrated as the ego soars above it. The relationship between the ego and the object in the former case is reparative ; in the latter case, manic reparative.

Notes

1. Guilt is often used in too indefinite a way. While it does convey an ineffable inner ache, with which we are all familiar but cannot adequately describe, it typically also includes an anxiety of being discovered, shamed, rebuked, exiled, persecuted—what Freud called 'social anxiety'.

   > [A] person feels guilty (devout people would say 'sinful') when he has done something which he knows to be 'bad'... even when a person has not actually *done* the bad thing but has only recognized in himself an *intention* ...[H]e must have had a motive for submitting to [an] extraneous influence[,which] is easily discovered in his helplessness and his dependence on other people...[At] this stage the sense of guilt is clearly only a fear of loss of love, 'social' anxiety. In small children it can never be anything else, but in many adults, too, it has only changed to the extent that the place of the father or the two parents is taken by the larger human community...A great change takes place only when the authority is internalized through the establishment of a super-ego. The phenomena of conscience then reach a higher stage. Actually, it is not until now that we should speak of conscience or a sense of guilt...[T]he fear of being found out comes to an end; the distinction, moreover, between doing something bad and wishing to do it disappears entirely, since nothing can be hidden from the super-ego, not even thoughts...The super-ego torments the sinful ego with the same feeling of anxiety and is on the watch for opportunities of getting it punished by the external world. (1930, pp. 124–5; Freud's emphasis)

   Freud adds that the ego is also driven by remorse at the stage. Klein takes Freud's distinction further. She distinguished between persecutory anxiety and depressive anxiety or guilt; the former characteristic of the paranoid-schizoid position, the latter of the depressive position; the former seized by anxiety at its own annihilation, the latter by anxiety based on concern for the object and remorse for attacks on it. The former is expressed in manic reparation, the latter in reparation.

2. The German word, *Wiedergutmachung*, seems to have come to prominence in the twentieth century. Grimm's dictionary, completed in 1893, does not include it. In the socio-political context, it primarily refers to compensation owed a victorious state by a defeated state. It is, for

example, the German equivalent for reparation in the *Treaty of Versailles*. In psychoanalysis, the common term for reparation is *Wiedergutmachung* (rather than the range of other terms reviewed in the text above), and both terms emphasize the subjective, internal urge, driven by guilt, to make a damaged object better. Freud uses 'reparation' in his German text, rather than the common *Wiedergutmachung*, when speaking of remorse for injury to the oedipal father and of the recovery of reality. His reversing its usual meaning, as in compensation for damage in war, seems to emphasize the more internal dimension of reparation (1913[1912–1913], p. 143, 1924, pp. 184, 185).
3. That helpless inadequacy runs in two directions: one way, the subject and object get better together; the other way pushes for a paranoid-schizoid resolution by attacking the victim again as a monster that got inside.

For an immediate post-war analysis of external calls for accountability versus internal, uncompelled, spur to reparation, see Jaspers (1946, pp. 33, 39, 59, 90, 96ff, 108–9, 112–17). Schlink (2009) defines responsibility in terms of strictly juridical accountability and an embedded responsibility for one's people. In trying establish the distinction between the law in its properly protective and sanctioning functions, on the one hand, and processes that provide an illegitimate haven for ex-Nazi's, he both holds these two agencies in a discriminating balance and moves closer to Habermas (1986; see also Chap. 6) view.
4. For a fuller interpretation, together with interpretations by other authors, see Figlio (2012).
5. Money-Kyrle's observation of a depressive mood in post-war Germany reinforces the Mitscherlich's (1967/1975) analysis of the inability to mourn. They observed a defence. Money-Kyrle points to the fragile, depressive inclination at the core of the defence.

References

Alford, C. (2006) *Psychology and the Natural Law of Reparation*. Cambridge: Cambridge University Press.
Bion, W. R. (1957) Differentiation of the Psychotic from the Non-psychotic Personalities. *International Journal of Psychoanalysis* 38: 266–75. In *Second Thoughts: Selected Papers on Psycho-Analysis*. London: William Heinemann, 1967; Karnac, 1984, pp. 43–64.

Bion, W. R. (1962) A Psycho-Analytic Study of Thinking. *International Journal of Psychoanalysis* 43: 306–10; A Theory of Thinking. In *Second Thoughts: Selected Papers on Psycho-Analysis*. London: William Heinemann, 1967; Karnac, 1984, pp. 110–19.

Faimberg, H. (2005) *The Telescoping of Generations: Listening to the Narcissistic Links Between Generations*. London: Routledge.

Figlio, K. (2012) Devaluing and Repairing the Internal World. *Psychoanalysis, Culture and Society* 17(1): 87–91.

Freud, S. (1913 [1912–13]) Totem and Taboo. *The Standard Edition of the Complete Psychological Works of Sigmund Freud* 13: 1–165.

Freud, S. (1916) Some Character-Types Met with in Psycho-Analytic Work. *The Standard Edition of the Complete Psychological Works of Sigmund Freud* 14: 309–31.

Freud, S. (1917[1915]) Mourning and Melancholia. *The Standard Edition of the Complete Psychological Works of Sigmund Freud* 14: 237–58.

Freud, S. (1923) The Ego and the Id. *The Standard Edition of the Complete Psychological Works of Sigmund Freud* 19: 1–66.

Freud, S. (1924) The Loss of Reality in Neurosis and Psychosis. *The Standard Edition of the Complete Psychological Works of Sigmund Freud* 19: 181–8.

Freud, S. (1930) Civilization and Its Discontents. *The Standard Edition of the Complete Psychological Works of Sigmund Freud* 21: 57–146.

Frohn, A. (1991) *Holocaust and Shilumin: The Policy of Wiedergutmachung in the Early 1950s. (German Historical Institute Occasional Paper 2)*. Washington, DC: German Historical Instiute.

Goschler, C. (2008) *Schuld und Schulden: Die Politik der Wiedergutmachung fur NS-Verfolgte seit 1945* (2nd edition). Gottingen: Wallstein Verlag.

Habermas, J. (1986) On the Public Use of History. *Die Zeit*, November 7. In Habermas, J. (1989). In *The New Conservatism: Cultural Criticism and the Historians' Debate*. London: Polity Press, pp. 229–40.

Hartman, G. (ed.) (1986) *Bitburg in Moral and Political Perspective*. Bloomington: Indiana University Press.

Hinshelwood, R. D. (1991) *A Dictionary of Kleinian Thought* (2nd edition). London: Free Association Books.

Hinshelwood, R. D. (2007) Review of Alford, C. (2006) *Psychology and the Natural Law of Reparation. Psychoanalysis, Culture and Society* 12(2): 199–202.

Jaspers, K. (1946) *The Question of German Guilt*. New York: Fordham University Press, 2000.

Kernberg, O. (2009) The Destruction of Time in Pathological Narcissism. In Fiorini, G. and Canestri, J. (eds.) *The Experience of Time: Psychoanalytic Perspectives*. London: Karnac, pp. 155–74.

Klein, M. (1928) Note on the Preceding Communication. *International Journal of Psychoanalysis* 9: 255–58.

Klein, M. (1929) Infantile Anxiety-Situations Reflected in a Work of Art and in the Creative Impulse. In *The Writings of Melanie Klein*, vol. I. London: The Hogarth Press and the Institute of Psychoanalysis, 1975, pp. 210–19.

Klein, M. (1935) A Contribution to the Psychogenesis of Manic-Depressive States. In *The Writings of Melanie Klein*, vol. 1. London: The Hogarth Press and the Institute of Psychoanalysis, 1975, pp. 262–89.

Klein, M. (1937) Love, Guilt and Reparation. In *The Writings of Melanie Klein*, vol. 1. London: Hogarth and the Institute of Psychoanalysis, 1975, pp. 306–43.

Klein, M. (1940) Mourning and Its Relation to Manic-Depressive States. In *The Writings of Melanie Klein*, vol. 1. London: Hogarth and the Institute of Psychoanalysis, 1975, pp. 344–69.

Klein, M. (1957) Envy and Gratitude. In *The Writings of Melanie Klein*, vol. 3. London: Hogarth and the Institute of Psychoanalysis, 1975, pp. 176–235.

Knowlton, J. and Cates, T. (eds.) (1993) *Forever in the Shadow of Hitler?: The Dispute About the Germans' Understanding of History, Original Documents of the Historikerstreit, the Controversy Concerning the Singularity of the Holocaust*. Atlantic Highlands, NJ: Humanities Press.

Lupu, N. (2003) Memory Vanished, Absent, and Confined: The Counter-Memorial Project in the 1980s and 1990s. *History and Memory* 15(2): 130–64.

Maier, C. (1988) *The Unmasterable Past: History, Holocaust, and German National Identity*. Cambridge, MA/London: Harvard University Press.

Mitscherlich, A. and Mitscherlich, M. (1967/1975) *The Inability to Mourn: Principles of Collective Behaviour*. Munich: Piper & Co. Verlag; English translation, New York: Grove Press.

Money-Kyrle, R. (1951) Some Aspects of State and Character in Germany. In *The Collected Papers of Roger Money-Kyrle*. Strath Tay: Clunie Press, 1978, pp. 229–44.

Riviere, J. (1929) Womanliness as a Masquerade. *International Journal of Psychoanalysis* 10: 303–13.

Schlink, B. (2009) *Guilt About the Past*. St Lucia, Qld: University of Queensland Press.

Schwab, G. (2010) *Haunting Legacies: Violent Histories and Transgenerational Trauma*. New York: Columbia University Press.

Segal, H. (1981) *The Works of Hannah Segal: A Kleinian Approach to Clinical Practice*. New York: Jason Aronson.

Vetlesen, A. J. (2005) *Evil and Human Agency: Understanding Collective Evildoing*. Cambridge: Cambridge University Press.

Williams, A. H. (1998) *Cruelty, Violence and Murder: Understanding the Criminal Mind*. London: Karnac.

Young, J. (1993) *The Texture of Memory: Holocaust Memorials and Meaning*. New Haven: Yale University Press.

10

Remembering, Memorialization and Reparation

As individuals, we institute sites and occasions for mourning, for remembering and for reparation. Think of days put aside for these purposes; of objects that we preserve; of photographs; of letters; of dedications, enacted outside, and preserved internally. As social groups, we do the same, through memorials, archives, official recognition of special places, such as historic buildings. In both instances, we can speak of there being a private and a public dimension. In the course of this chapter, I will define what I mean by these two dimensions to mourning in the service of remembering as reparation. I distinguish between 'remembering true', a form of repairing the good object, and remembering 'false', an attack on the good object. What I call 'private mourning' restores memory and is reparative, what I call 'public mourning' is prone to the distortion of memory and to a distorted reparation, called by Hannah Segal, 'manic reparation'. Memorials become ambiguous locations for remembering and for the distortion of remembering, for private mourning and for public mourning.

Memorials in Conflict: Vietnam

There are three Vietnam war memorials in Washington, DC. The first is a plain wall with the name of each US soldier who died in Vietnam. This memorial evoked fierce controversy and a demand for something more traditional, which was satisfied by a statue of three soldiers. A demand for recognition of the role of women led to the commissioning of a third statue. For our theme, we need refer only to the first two memorials. The difference between them is striking. The Wall reminds the viewer of each lost, individual US soldiers among the massive total of 58,272. The latter confronts the viewer with three individual figures who seem designed to evoke an emotional response, in particular to the tragedy of sacrificing the young. The Wall invites contemplation and, for anyone who knew an individual soldier, private mourning. The statues invite public responses, perhaps mourning for the tragedy of Vietnam, but also a rededication to sacrifice, sacrifice that supports a heroic myth of war through a celebration of heroism.

People argue over the aim of memorials and the adequacy with which they commemorate and advocate their ideals. In the case of war memorials, the meaning of personal sacrifice comes together with the ideals of the nation, and together they divide people into groups of conflicting, passionately held conviction. But, apart from political controversy, the Wall is ambiguous. For the historian, Kristin Hass (1998), the inscribing individual names of Vietnam veterans on the wall remembers not only the individual who was lost but also the unfathomable magnitude of loss—a loss that is also the nation's loss. The impulse to remember individual soldiers began in the immense internal upheaval of the American Civil War. But this remembering could not embrace the 'intensity of the crisis of finding a place in the culture [to] heal the radical rupture the[Vietnam] war created between so many citizens and the nation' (p. 62).

One remarkable feature of the memorialization inspired by the Wall has been the leaving of a multitude of objects by people who come to the wall in an active relationship between the bereaved citizen and the lost loved one or the lost national ideal. Hass goes on to say that

> [T]he design of this memorial [the Wall] comes out of the history of memorial design that has been driven by the problem of representing

Memorials in Conflict: Vietnam

Fig. 10.1 Vietnam Veterans Memorial Wall, Washington, DC

Fig. 10.2 The three soldiers memorial, Washington, DC

individual sacrifice in the name of an imagined national community. In departing from that tradition, I have argued, the Wall makes a place for private grief and powerful resentment and a whole range of funerary practices based on the idea of an active relation between the living and the dead to seep into the crack in civic and patriotic tradition. (pp. 85–6)

The Memorial Wall is a site of unsettling feelings, meanings and aspirations.

> Americans coming to the Wall have not forsaken the idea of the nation; they are struggling to salvage it and its place in their identities. They are not simply expressing the antiwar movement's rage or the hawks' pride; they are participating in a struggle of politically diverse, ordinary citizens to make a memory of the war that will allow them to reclaim their place in the culture. These things [left at the Wall] do not mark the death of the nation or patriotism; on the contrary they mark a tremendous effort to reconstitute the nation and the citizen's faith in it. (p. 102)

At the Wall, private grief struggles with public solidarity; the citizen's individual loss with the nation's loss; the loss of person with the loss of an ideal. Next to the Wall, the statue of the soldiers seems less ambiguous, less internally uneasy and tense; less an occasion for private grieving, remembering and reflecting; more a call to honour the nation, its actions and those who implement them. These two processes of remembering seem too different for 'mourning' to cover them both. Public mourning seems closer to expressing what the historian George Mosse called the 'myth of war experience', a kind of thrall kept alive through an appeal to images of heroism, manliness and salvation of the nation. Private mourning, by contrast, is an internal, contemplative—reparative—process, whether or not in the presence of other people.[1]

Memorials in Conflict: Hamburg

In Hamburg, a memorial site with two adjacent memorials brings out this comparison between nationalistic and reparative impulses in memorialization clearly: the first, erected by the Nazis in 1936, celebrates

Fig. 10.3 Nazi memorial, Hamburg

militarism through a column of marching soldiers[2]; next to it, commissioned as a rejoinder, is a memorial made of scenes of devastation of human life and hope, begun in 1985 but not completed. A tablet stands between these two memorials, outlining their history. The history begins with a memorial by Ernst Barlach, a tall stele with a mother and child inscribed into one side, completed in 1931 and standing outside Hamburg city hall. The Nazis wanted something more heroic, and commissioned the massive stone block, surrounded by the marching soldiers cut into its sides (Culpepper 2014). The post-war monument, by contrast, speaks to the devastation to which that triumphalism leads and it evokes remorse and compassion. At the same time, it is built in and around the pieces of a broken swastika, so that it carries, along with tragedy, a warning of retaliation. In doing so, it is not only cacophonous but also reveals the subtle merging of the two dimensions of mourning, as a commentary on the

10 Remembering, Memorialization and Reparation

Fig. 10.4 Counter-memorial, Hamburg

militaristic monument next to it. Together, these two memorials portray two impulses—one triumphal, the other desolate and sad. They not only merge in mourning but also pull in two different directions.

Such a contrapuntal memorialization is hard to achieve, politically, economically and artistically, mainly because it is nearly impossible to create an occasion for reparative remembering; maybe also because reparative remembering includes a defensive triumph over the guilt and recognition of reality associated with mourning. Memorials serve a public function, and while Nationalistic celebration can salve open wounds when grief is near the surface, it can maintain a distance from an enemy and a ready aggressiveness that suppresses mourning for losses. If a nation mourns the losses suffered by an enemy along with its own losses, the certainty of purpose that undergirds aggression dissolves. At the end of the Falkland War, Robert Runcie, Archbishop of Canterbury, remembered

Argentinean as well as British dead in a service at St Paul's Cathedral. Later, Prime Minister Thatcher, presumably believing she was speaking for the country, was angered (Church Times 2013). Nationalism in this case required mourning to be restricted to British losses. Similarly, American grief at the Vietnam War has been about the impact of the war on Americans not on the Vietnamese, Laotians or Cambodians (Hass, p. 151, n. 7).

Concern for the enemy comes later. Memory can be recovered and corrected. Vietnam is no longer an enemy of the United States. The ravaging of its land and people can be looked at more squarely, alongside mourning of the US casualties. Robert McNamara, Secretary of State at the time, later acknowledged that the United States mistook a war of liberation for a communist threat (Morris and McNamara 2003). But it took time. Many might recall with disbelief President Johnson's announcing an escalation of the conflict on the grounds that the Vietnamese navy had attacked the US Seventh fleet. Indeed, in the 'Gulf of Tonkin Incident', three North Vietnamese patrol torpedo boats did launch torpedoes at the destroyer, USS Maddox. Two were damaged, the third destroyed, while the Maddox was unscathed. An alleged second incident never occurred. President Johnson then announced the escalation on national television. It would be 11 years before that war ended (Morris and McNamara 2003; Paterson 2008).

War provides the most striking example of the contradiction between mourning and the celebration of the aggressive acts that produce more mourning. Fallen soldiers are memorialized, but wartime victory is commemorated at the same time. The one can move imperceptibly to the other. This ambiguity in memorialization allows an insight into a hidden connection through which one war justifies another war. Let's cast a psychoanalytic eye on this phenomenon.

Hannah Segal (1995) argued that an incitement to war builds on unassuaged guilt from the destructiveness of a previous war. This psychoanalytic angle, which began with Edward Glover's 1947 book on war (followed by Money-Kyrle 1951; Fornari 1966; Wangh 1968; for an overview, see Richards 1987), requires that guilt be considered a force in history along with politics and economics. The guilt that cannot be assimilated and worked through is beaten away by another round of aggression, in the same way as an individual might stave off guilt and persecution by projecting phantasized aggression into another person and righteously attacking that person. An occasion for mourning turns into a triumphal repudiation of mourning, in which a society's internal unease is projected into an enemy and quelled.

Such a repudiation of mourning is different from the comfort people find with others who have suffered the same loss. They are mourning with fellows they know, each of whom, individually, mourns the same person; or empathically, they mourn together for their separate losses. The public in which they congregate is not abstract but a group of mourners sharing individual grief. In Melanie Klein's thinking, mourning in the present is also mourning for all the losses of one's life, including the normal losses in development, from the original good object of the breast onwards. People gather to share their separate griefs supporting each other in knowing what it is to mourn without knowing the different individual objects of mourning, because they have all mourned from infancy to the current moment.

Perhaps the most moving sites for mourning are the *Stolpersteine* in several German cities. Literally, stumbling stones, they are cobble-sized, square cement blocks with Brass plaques, giving the name, dates and fates of people who lived at that location and were persecuted by the Nazis. One stumbles unexpectedly into a personal tragedy; no grand monument to a group or a cause: just a moment when one is seized, not just by that person's tragedy, but by sadness at loss. For example, see https://www.stolpersteine-berlin.de.

What I am calling public mourning, by contrast, refers to a group that supervenes in the particular gathering. This public is an abstraction, like the nation, the elderly, Christians, and it gathers to commemorate an abstraction: Labor Day, Thanksgiving Day, Guy Fawkes Day. Group processes work against mourning. They promote splitting, which delusionally polarizes reality into idealized and contemptible. And although idealization can support self-esteem through restoring the relationship with the good object or ideal, especially in recovering national pride following a disaster, it can also entrench a sense of superiority based on contempt and an acute sensitivity to loss because it is not ordinary loss, but the vanishing of idealization. Normal recovery feels like rejuvenation after mourning, the return of life after grief, when the world again seems fresh and one's spirits are reanimated. It does not trumpet a triumph over hostile forces that caused despair, but expresses a grateful appreciation of life restored. But idealization, as in extreme nationalism, calls for allegiance to the project of reasserting pride against the forces believed to have thieved it. It is proud of its strength and sure of its enemies. Its pride is outside any measure, because it is based on immeasurable idealization.

The Silence of Trauma

Such a confusion and cacophony between mourning and triumphalism occurred in the German response to the destruction of its cities by Allied bombing. In *The Natural History of Destruction*, the novelist and observer of culture, W. G. Sebald (2003), said that the Allied devastation of German cities had been a trauma that could only be followed by silence. Silence was the only voice that could be given to massive trauma, a silence that only recently could be broken. His accounts are horrifying and he reproduces photographs of the destruction. His aim was to convey the experience of suffering massive, unthinkable destruction, in order to '... cast some light on the ways in which memory (individual, collective and cultural) deals with experiences exceeding what is tolerable' (p. 79).

But this unspeakable experience was not just a German trauma, inflicted on Germany, but a pressing for recognition as victims, a scenario already promoted during the war. Fuchs (p. 73), and Margalit (pp. 267–80), rejecting the claim that the Germans were silent in shock until a few individuals broke the silence, argue that they were vocal about their own suffering. For Margalit, the myth of post-war silence has been constructed and perpetuated by writers such as Sebald and Gunther Grass. In doing so, they have elevated German suffering. Germans then remember being victims of atrocity equivalent to the sufferers of their perpetration and consequently conceal German perpetration and the suffering inflicted on its victims.

'Silence' is a complex idea. Certainly there has been a kind of not-speaking about the Nazi period since the end of the war. But what we see in this myth of breaking a traumatic silence is not the surfacing of the trauma of perpetration, but the eruption into consciousness of the trauma of German suffering. The myth of breaking the silence began with the publication in 2002 of *The Conflagration: Germany in the Bombing War 1940–1945* by Jörg Friedrich. Friedrich gives a graphic account of the destruction of German cities, history and culture by the Allied bombing campaign. The Friedrich myth gained power by being confined to 1940–1945, by documenting only the effect of Allied bombing and by seeming, finally, to overcome a German reticence. In doing so, he could be interpreted as freeing Germans to speak of their suffering and loss at the hands of the Allies. The photographs reproduced by Sebald and his account of the incineration and suffocation of Germans in their bunkers could be seen as supporting the same, documentary, style (see Moeller 2006 for a detailed account of Friedrich as the myth-maker of breaking the silence).

Margalit, by contrast, asserts that there was no silence to overcome and that anti-Semitic language could find its way around legislative bans. He suggests that the Germans knew full well what they had done and were unrepentant. Moreover, the myth of silence can be exploited by right-wingers.

> Grass and Sebald do not claim, as the extreme right does, that the Allies and their German lackeys imposed such a taboo. In their view, it was a product of self-censorship growing out of a sense of guilt. [But] [t]he word 'taboo' evokes a highly loaded political slogan of Germany's extreme right. After 1945, Germany's political discourse developed ways of circumventing sensitive and problematic issues such as antisemitism and favorable references to Nazism. Speakers [could employ] a variety of euphemistic codes and phrases..., but their real meanings were crystal clear to their target audiences....In such a political culture Grass and Sebald could easily be interpreted as confirming the extreme right's claim that any talk of German suffering, or of injustices inflicting on the Germans, had been proscribed...The Allies were said to have imposed these rules of political correctness on Germany. This served 'foreign interests' (a familiar euphemism in these circles for 'international Judaism'). And these rules are still in force, the right contends. (pp. 267, 268)

Sebald did see an additional dimension in what these victims could not speak, something more than a myth of silence.

> For if anything first set off the immeasurable suffering that we Germans inflicted on the world it was language of [Jewish conspiracy]...The majority of Germans today know, or at least it is to be hoped, that we actually provoked the annihilation of the cities in which we once lived...Hitler [imagined] the total destruction of [London by] incendiary bombs of an entirely new type...This intoxicating vision of destruction coincides with the fact that the real pioneering achievements in bomb warfare...were the work of the Germans. [A]s early as August 1942...the city of Stalingrad, then swollen (like Dresden later) by an influx of refugees, was under assault from 1200 bombers, and...40,000 people lost their lives. (Sebald, p. 104–5)

Sebald not only spoke for a recognition that the Germans had brought devastation on themselves but also was stuck by the remarkable revival of normal life as a seemingly non-reaction to the destruction (p. 41), and of reminiscences that 'quickly revert to the harmless, conversational tone... so strikingly disproportionate to the reality of the time' (p. 85), as if they had not taken it in. They could avoid their helplessness and defeat and confirm their indestructability by simply negating their perceptions and magically reconstructing their destroyed cities—more an undoing than a rebuilding. The Mitscherlichs' thesis (1967/1975) gains importance in such a controversy. At the core of it was a new, different resource: the *clinical* observation that Germans had blocked out the capacity to mourn. Mourning restores the emotional and cognitive bond with reality. Germans, they argued, could not bear the loss of the narcissistic illusion of the Nazi nation, personified in the *Führerbindung*, nor the recognition of the horrendous attack on the Jews (as, in my analysis, the good object). Their perception matches Sebald's: both speak of detachment, not of literally not speaking.

I would add a point that is strongly implied, but not brought out as clearly as it might: that, whatever the mix of myth and actuality, shocked silence about German suffering suggests, in addition to the trauma of unbearable horror, a forbearance in adversity. In this scenario, it was now time to break the silence, heroically born so long by the Germans, and to allow the rightful assertion of victimhood. Germans could say, 'We have suffered enough guilt, done enough to compensate our victims and to assuage our guilt: it is time to move on.' Such an underground current of injustice and resentment, stifled and waiting to burst into the open, has blunted any purity of purpose in establishing site of remembering and mourning.

Recently, there has been a decided criticism of memorialization because it is seen to serve the purposes of repetitive ritual and complacency, rather than genuine recognition of the suffering inflicted by Germany in the Nazi period. Assmann (2013) distinguishes between *Vergangenheitsbewahrung* and the common expression for coming to terms with the past, *Vergangenheitsbetwältigung*. The former refers to a confirmation, in which memory is kept alive in the present without assimilation and recovery. *Vergangenheitsbewältigung* is a 'social-therapeutic' process, 'directed towards reconciliation and social and national integration' (pp. 115–18, 192). I think this differentiation so clarifies an ambiguity in *Vergangenheitsbewältigung* itself. Some ambiguity remains, however, in that, although *Vergangenheitsbewältigung* has been used to speak of coming to terms with the past, it actually means to master the past, which suggests an avoidance. But Assmann's distinction fits with Klein's view, that '[a]s a result of the failure of the act of reparation, the ego has to resort again and again to obsessional and manic defences' (1940, p. 351).

Critics of memorialization see more *Vergangenheitsbewährung* than *Vergangenheitsbewältingung*—even a form of undoing rather than assimilation (Domansky 1993, p. 192). It has given rise to a counter-memorial project in the 1980s and 1990s (Lupu 2003). Detailed historical work has revealed the intense, politicized, struggles that have shaped memorialization, both in events and in establishing memorial sites. In the extreme case of Dresden, there has been sharp criticism—to the point of advocating the abolishing of memorials—of the whitewashed, romantic image of the innocent Florence of the Elbe (on this critical movement, see Abolish Commemoration; Jerzak 2015; Moeller 2006; Reinhard 2010).

But, as Quindeau (2008) points out, '[t]he concept of unconscious guilt offers the possibility of explaining these irrationalities, the conflicts in individual and collective analyses of the Holocaust' (p. 84). Perhaps mourning always expresses both currents of feeling: grief at the loss of a love object as part of recovering a good internal world, and a bellowing triumph over, and denigration of, a lost world, external and internal. These two extremes may be enacted by different, perhaps small and radically opposed groups, but many more people can join in with their discordant sentiments by identification. In less extreme cases, one can speak of an inherent ambivalence in mourning, which can be channelled into a good enough resolution through the restoration of a good internal world, or towards repetitive demonstrations of hate-filled triumph.

The illusion that mourning can been forestalled by triumph over loss, as in the Mitscherlich's thinking, is akin to Melanie Klein's definition of manic defence, a composite of '[denial of] *psychic reality*[, a] *sense of omnipotence* for the purpose of *controlling and mastering* objects [and] *disparagement of the object's importance and the contempt for it*' (1935, pp. 277–8; Klein's emphasis). Manic reparation looks the same as reparation in the conscious world, but they are antithetical in the unconscious: the former is a defence against recognition of damage to the good object, identification with the good object and consequent reparation to the good object (described in Chap. 9).

Mourning and Melancholia

Perhaps mourning and memorials always contains both reparation and manic reparation. We need to look more closely at the distinction between mourning and melancholia as a form of pathological mourning, and then to bring them into alignment with reparation, which accompanies mourning, and manic reparation, which accompanies pathological mourning.

For Freud (1917[1915]), normal mourning involved the work of detaching the ego from the lost object, step by step. It was a struggle between the love for the object and the desire to stay alive, a struggle joined by the reality principle against the pull towards dying with the lost object. Normally, as the libidinal attachment weakened, the ego gained freedom libidinally to attach to a new object.

Melancholia was similar to mourning, in the hard work of liberation from an attachment to a lost object, but it alternated with mania, and that revealed a decisive difference. The attachment that seemed so firmly to bind the ego to the object easily shifted to an attachment to the ego itself, causing it to inflate with grandiosity reminiscent of the previous attachment to the object, which was now denigrated next to the superiority of the ego. The key features of melancholia are *narcissism*, in which the object and a part of the ego formed a primitive identicality, and *ambivalence*, in which the object is hated as well as loved. The self-abasement, so characteristic of melancholia, but not of mourning, follows from this primitive identicality. It is a narcissistic identification, in which the self-abasement is really an accusation of the object, arising from ambivalence, in which grieving is replaced by disparagement. Freud put it as follows.

> Just as mourning impels the ego to give up the object by declaring the object to be dead and offering the ego the inducement of continuing to live, so does each single struggle of ambivalence loosen the fixation of the libido to the object by disparaging it, denigrating it and even as it were killing it. It is possible for the process in the *Ucs.* to come to an end, either after the fury has spent itself or after the object has been abandoned as valueless. (p. 257)

Thus, there are two ways in which the object is given up, and much of the difference between mourning and melancholia derives from the difference in the type of identification of the ego with the object that follows upon this giving up. In mourning, the object is assimilated into the ego. In fact, the ego is built up from multiple identifications, multiple instances of assimilating some features of an object, but neither ego nor object is swamped by the other. As Freud would later say, '[T]he character of the ego is a precipitate of abandoned object-cathexes and ... it contains the history of those object-choices' (1923, p. 29). One can catch a glimpse of the object, for example, in a moment of self-conscious recognition of a gesture or a figure of speech, which belongs to the object. In melancholia, the ego survives by dividing itself. One part is submerged in a primitive, total identification with the object. Another part is drawn back in narcissistic purity, forming an ego-critic [*Ichkritik*], the existence and aim of which is to maintain narcissistic purity by an attacking superiority over merged ego-object. It seems that the ego-critic comes into existence once the ego is otherwise sullied by its relationship to the object. From its position of manic inflation, '[t]he ego may enjoy...the satisfaction of knowing itself as the better of the two, as superior to the object' (Freud 1917[1915], p. 257). Bearing in mind that this ego-critic is really ego in identification with a superior critic, I will follow Freud (1914, p. 94) in referring to this dominating, superior, condescending part-ego as the 'ideal-ego'.

Freud suggests that the object in its own right does not figure in this distorted, melancholic form of mourning. A part of the ego bonds with a shadow, a wispy, indistinct, negative image of the object, while another, unbound part of the ego provides a refuge by its annihilating attack on the lost ego-object; that is, the ego that bonds to the object is denigrated along with the faithless object. The object is hidden in the self-abasement typical of melancholia, which follows from the primitive identification with it. When this ego-object is in the ascendancy, the melancholic suffers, but when it is projected, purifying the remaining ego into an ideal-ego, the melancholic swells with manic superiority.

Here, in the melancholic relationship of ego to object, is an early version of projective identification. Part of the ego enters the object to control it and use it as a repository for unwanted parts of the ego. The ego that remains detached from the identification, cleansed of its debased parts, tends towards a narcissistic purity that constitutes the ideal-ego; the more so, the more split the ego. In its melancholic phase, the ego is overwhelmed by the projective identification; in the manic phase, the splitting is more complete and the ego-object is projected into (identified with) an external object, to be hammered by the narcissistically pure, ideal-ego. This pure ego is freed of debasement by its now projectively identified parts. Clinically, one can see these swings from depressive mourning to icy hatred of others, who were, first, the idealized objects of aspiration, but now loathed, inferior beings. The moment of self-debasement noted by Freud vanishes as projective identification displaces the ego-object into an external object.

In melancholia, the object is not mourned, because it has been replaced by an ego-part, bound in identicality with the otherwise lost object and projected in hatred. The system as a whole—the object, the ego-identified-with-the-object and the ego-identified with-the-ego-critic (ideal-ego)—is a narcissistic delusion, maintained by excluding external reality. So while melancholia with its manic counterpart is like mourning, in its mitigation of grieving, its mode is totally different. In mourning, the ego eventually and painfully gives up the object by recognizing that it is lost in external reality, but retained in internal reality; not concretely or completely, but through introjecting its features. In melancholia, grieving has been replaced by triumph, in which the object is not missed because it has been discarded along with the part-ego that attached itself to the object. In place of grief is the catastrophic loss of the delusion of ideality. In post-war Germany, the grief of enormous loss has been laced with the catastrophic disillusionment of the collapse of the Hitler delusion of a pure community of the people (*Volksgemeinschaft*).

In Freud's analysis, mourning is fundamentally a loving process, while melancholia is an ambivalent, but fundamentally hating process. Mourning is reality-orientated and acknowledges the separate existence of the object, which it holds in loving, partial identifications. Melancholia is narcissistic, takes the object's separateness to be a threat to its own existence, and holds the object in an identification that extinguishes it. Mourning and melancholia in Freud's analysis are at two polar extremes.

For Karl Abraham (1924), melancholia was a primitive form of mourning, in which the object is eliminated concretely by defaecation and magically restored to life by eating it. In both cases, the ideal-ego that remains, purified of this debased part, is a delusion of superiority. Melanie Klein (1940) went a step further. For her, melancholia was an essential stage in the process of normal mourning, which included psychotic anxieties, transient manic depression and triumphal feelings.

> In normal mourning early psychotic anxieties are reactivated ... [T]he subject goes through a modified and transitory manic-depressive state and overcomes it. [F]eelings of triumph are inevitably bound up even with normal mourning...When hatred of the lost loved object in its various manifestations gets the upper hand in the mourner, this not only turns the loved lost person into a persecutor, but shakes the mourner's belief in his good inner objects as well. (pp. 354–5)

Normal mourning calls out for reparation to re-establish a secure inner world of good objects in relation to reality, but can be overtaken by a manic defence, in which inner objects are hated and controlled in a state of 'manic omnipotence' (1940, p. 350). Objects turn into persecutors that have repeatedly to be controlled or killed and if the pressure is too great, the ego will be killed in the attempt to kill the object with which it is bonded. Klein said

> The desire to control the object, the sadistic gratification of overcoming and humiliating it, of getting the better of it, the *triumph* over it, may enter so strongly into the act of reparation…that the 'benign' circle started by this act becomes broken. The objects which were to be restored change again into persecutors, and in turn paranoid fears are revived. These fears reinforce the paranoid defence mechanisms (of destroying the object) as well as the manic mechanisms (of controlling it or keeping it in suspended animation, and so on). The reparation which was in progress is thus disturbed or even nullified—according to the extent to which these mechanisms are activated. (p. 351; Klein's emphasis)

Normal mourning achieves its loving aim by working through the melancholic urge to dominate and destroy the object in order to continue to live. Small steps of reparation recreate an inner environment that, in its gradually restored benevolence, supports the ego's confidence in its goodness, reparative capacity and reality, which further restores the inner world of good objects, in a benign circuit. In pathological mourning, hatred and a hardening, persecutory inner environment break down a benign circuit and replace it with the aim to control and destroy the inner object world, to the extent of delusion. In both cases, repeated projection and introjections bind internal and external object relations together, each reinforcing the other, for good or ill. Mourning and melancholia are two distinct states, but with a common core and mechanism.

Ambiguity in Public Mourning

Earlier I distinguished mourning (in public) from public mourning. In the former, a memorial can be an occasion for private mourning, empathically supported. In the latter, group processes intrude and incorporate individuals into it. In this case, we can speak of group subjectivity as an abstraction, defined, not by an experience of a putative group mind, but by the way it functions. If a group mourns, the reference is not to a majority of the population, but to a group process, the function of which is to protect the individuals from an intrusion of psychotic anxiety, driven by ambivalence and guilt towards the lost object.

As I argued in Chap. 3, this formulation provides an adequate answer to the charge that we cannot attribute feelings—or an aspect of subjectivity—to a group, but only to an individual. We need to do so, or we lapse into pop psychology or simply nebulous ersatz equivalents to such attributions, such as 'It was thought that…'; 'Public opinion supported…'. But we also need to do so because it provides a more complete explanation: because social groups do function as groups and clinical experience has supported the idea that they act as a unit in a way that allows individual to act and feel as if they were not individually responsible for thoughts, feeling and behaviour. Freud formulated this idea in psychoanalytic terms by proposing a mechanism whereby the individuals in a group shared an ego-ideal in common, invested in a leader, and identified with each other in their egos (1921, pp. 105–16). Freud speaks of the protection of the individual from neurosis by the formation of a group (Freud 1921, p. 142). Later psychoanalytic research has developed this idea into the concept of a 'social defence system' (Hinshelwood 1987, pp. 157–214; Hinshelwood and Skogstad [eds] 2000), and the 'Social Unconscious' (Hopper 1996).

If individuals do not work through the ambivalence that, Hannah Segal reminds us, is inherent in all object relations, they regress into their psychotic cores, in which they overcome the guilt of ambivalence by projecting it, thereby creating hateful, threatening and aggressive enemies, over which they need 'legitimately' to triumph. They are tempted to opt for a manic solution, which confirms their omnipotent control over psychic pain. Groups take on this psychotic core by acting in a mad way, often megalomanic and omnipotent, which restores the sense of normality to group members. In a formulation, attributable to the historian of the Nazi period, Ian Kershaw (1999), the German people worked 'towards Hitler'; that is, psychoanalytically speaking, they lived in the thrall of an ego-ideal in which the madness and criminality of the regime was lodged and which they supported. The group psychosis—in this case the use of enemies in order to assert a delusional superiority over guilt—protects their citizens from madness. They feel realistically aggressive or frightened, not crazy.[3] Hannah Segal (1995), for example, thought the policy of mutually guaranteed annihilation, which, it was argued, held the threat of nuclear war in check, was such a group psychosis. One could add that each individual might have felt frightened, perhaps terrified at times, but not psychotic. Each citizen of the Soviet Union or the United States 'knew' that the threat of extinction came from outside and could be realistically, if hopelessly, confronted.

What happens if a group—say, a nation—does not have an enemy? Without such an enemy, individuals are again threatened by their psychotic cores and will create sub-groups, such as extremist factions, whose psychotic behaviour towards each other will protect them. The members of factions will be 'normal', while the factions madly create and attack enemies. Although war most powerfully evokes defences against guilt, anything that stirs up ambivalence will have the same effect. It could be abortion, immigration, social welfare, economic hardship, religious symbols.[4]

I am proposing that memorialization includes public mourning. It is a group process that protects individuals from reality and the mourning that accompanies any encroachment into reality. The group can slip easily into a melancholic/manic-depressive state of psychotic dimensions in its denial of reality and mindless enactment of an anti-mourning state. It can do so because groups easily consolidate their identity by homogenizing themselves in opposition to other groups; that is, by splitting and projecting any internal disharmony into the other group. A group's ideology, around which it coheres, becomes a shared ego-ideal, its sacred core. Any alternative ideology is absolutely different and debased because the ego-ideal is absolute: there are no gradations of perfection (see Chaps. 4 and 5; Figlio 2006; Freud 1921). While mourning involves facing and working with guilt, which drives reparation, the pathological mourning of melancholia/manic depression dispels guilt and fosters manic reparation, which aims to square the circle of embracing recognition and responsibility for the victims of one's aggression and its repudiation. The group fosters defences, in which hatred, aggressiveness, disparagement and ultimately violent attack replace mourning with a clamorous demonstration of righteous protest and self-regard.

I have argued that an occasion and a site for public mourning is vulnerable to traduction into pathological mourning. We can make a connection to the Mitscherlichs' thesis. They argue that the Germans mourned in a particular way, which actually was a defence against mourning. Instead of mourning their actual losses or the damage inflicted on others, they were shocked by the collapse of their collective ego-ideal. It was a catastrophic implosion of an identity based on identifying with the ego-ideal, which could not be tolerated and which fed into resurgent nationalism and a delusion of instant recovery.

The heroism shown and evoked in war memorials conveys such a current, and can be caught up in what George Mosse (1990) calls 'the myth of the war experience', and the myth can then take off on its own and provide an aggressive shield against mourning. The heroic figures in the second Vietnam memorial look onto the inconceivable loss represented by the Wall. Overall, the memorial suggests the tragedy of war for the soldier. The sculptures represent the horror of war and the heroism of bearing up under it, more so because of their positioning overlooking the plain, first memorial, with its staggering listing of individual names of soldiers who died. They evoke compassion for the soldiers thrown into such a horrendous situation (see note 1 on the ambiguity in the three soldiers memorial). But the *nation* did release enormous violence against a liberation movement, misrepresented as an enemy threat, and created an enormous burden of mourning for the 'enemy', as well as for the soldiers it remembers.[5] In this context, the heroism of the figures supervenes in the occasion for mourning of both Americans and Vietnamese, and confirms a national defence against guilt for sending individual people into such danger, both the US soldiers and the Vietnamese.[6] In a similar memorial pair, the Hamburg memorials analyse the ambivalence of memorials by confronting the commemoration of a violent regime with a counter-memorial that reveals the atrocity of it. I will now turn to Dresden, not only a city of many monuments, but itself a memorial.

Dresden: The Innocent City of Culture

In Dresden, ambivalence at a memorial site stands out starkly in the form of (1) an event, the annual commemoration of the bombing of Dresden on 13–14 February 1945; (2) a site, the *Frauenkirche* in the town centre, along with the *Heidefriedhof* (Heath Cemetery) on the outskirts of the city; (3) a monument, to the victims of the bombing in the *Heidefriedhof*. Polarization is often extreme, so that the nature of the ambivalence becomes even clearer. The bombing caused a firestorm and completely destroyed the centre of the city. There are debates about the justification of the attack. The attack killed approximately 25,000 people, an estimate in the 'Final Report' of the Dresden police, based on their established figure of 18,375. It has continued to gather complex and conflicted motives around it ever since the Nazis added a '0' to this figure. The killing of 250,000 people supported the accusation that the Allies aimed to destroy Germany and that the charge of atrocity lay with them (Evans 2002, pp. 157–92; Overy, pp. 377–409, specifically, pp. 390–7).

Every year, thousands of people gather to remember their loss, an event that, since 1949, has included a performance of Rudolf Mauersberger's *Dresdner Requiem*.[7] But a requiem, though mournful, also elevates the destruction of the city, along with the destructiveness of the Nazis, to a spiritual plane, creating an ambiguous atmosphere of tragedy. Along with mourning the victims of Nazi atrocity and of Allied bombing, the Nazi past erupts in an annual neo-Nazi invasion of the commemorations, which is redolent 'of the scenes portrayed by Leni Riefenstahl in *Triumph of the Will* (1934): the hooded tops with slogans such as *Weisse Wille* (the will of whites); the banners referring to the "bombing holocaust"; or indeed the red, white and black flags waved during the Third Reich' (Pidd 2012).

Part of the *Heidefriedhof* has been redesigned and dedicated to those who died in the attack. It contains several memorials: one is a slightly curved wall of plain stone, resting on a flagstone base at the end of a long pathway (Fig. 10.5). One can walk towards it from a distance and stand in front of it in silent remembrance. A poem by Max Zimmerling—a

228   10 Remembering, Memorialization and Reparation

Fig. 10.5 Heidefriedhof memorial wall, Dresden

poet who fled both Nazi and Soviet persecution but returned to the GDR—is inscribed on the wall. The dedication reads:

> How many died? Who knows their number?
> In your wounds we see the agony
> Of the nameless who here burned
> In a hellfire wrought by man
>
>   In memory of the victims
>   Of the air attack on
>   Dresden 13–14 February 1945
>
> WIEVIELE·STARBEN? WER·KENNT·DIE·ZAHL?
> AN·DEINEN·WUNDEN·SIEHT·MAN·DIE·QUAL
> DER·NAMELOSEN·DIE·HIER·VERBRANNT
> IM·HÖLLEN FEUER·AUS·MENSCHENHAND

Survivors and their succeeding generations come to this memorial, many in quiet mourning. Many lay wreaths. The memorial, as well as the city of Dresden, has become a memorial shrine. While the bombing was horrific, late in the war and of questionable strategic importance, Dresden did not stand out from many other German cities (see Overy 2013 for a detailed analysis). Perhaps it has become a memorial site because, along with its being a site for mourning, it has gathered conflicted sentiment, beginning with anti-Allied Nazi and GDR propaganda, then opposition from the anti-Nazi peace movement.[8] Shortly after the end of the war, albums of photographs of Dresden and other cities, showing the city before and after the war, began to appear. Some of these books (e.g., Fritz Löffler's *Das alte Dresden*; see Fuchs 2012, pp. 21–69; Peter 1949) had extensive and multiple print runs, suggesting an intense interest. This genre of 'rubble photography' portrayed the utter devastation of Dresden, but, in its visual factuality, removed from its historical context, it created a trans-historical, nostalgic, forlorn, mournful sense of loss. But the loss could immediately be transformed, through photographs of a reconstructed Dresden, into a future in an ambiguous relationship with the past: was loss to be continuously re-evoked? Was it to be forgotten, having been overcome by progress, as if by magic or by the will of the people? Was it to be politicized as part of the anti-Westernism of the socialist German Democratic Republic? Dresden became, and remains, a symbol that condenses motivations that run from the peace movement at one extreme to neo-Nazism at the other.[9]

In an analysis of Friedrich's (2002) best-selling book, which portrayed in detail the bombing of German cities, Moeller (2006, p. 127) makes the point that his documentation of the extensive bomb damage of Dürer's house in Nuremberg creates a story that fits his account. 'But Freud, Saxl, Panovsky, Warburg and the institute that bears his name, Jewish philanthropy, exile, the immeasurable enrichment of the intellectual life of England and the United States and the loss to Germany do not fit…He is left with the story only of the bombs that fell on Germany, not those that destroyed parts of Germany's heritage transported to England, and with a "*Wir*" [we] in which Saxl and Warburg have no place.' Here is an eloquent example of the denial of mourning. The loss of the Jews does not fit.[10] Unfortunately, Moeller, while he lists Freud as one of the losses to German culture, turns away from Freud's analysis of mourning and melancholia because he too easily thinks it does not apply to the Germans because they do not demean themselves. The manic swing, which I have described, answers his criticism.

In an ambiguous combination, the two processes of reparation and manic reparation are at work. The public commemorations offer an occasion not only for individual mourning, with its base in reparation, but also for a group process, one that reinforces nationalism and triumphalism. The public commemorations at the Dresden memorials on the 13th and 14th of February each year offer occasions for individual mourning, but also for public mourning.

The poem on the commemorative wall reads, 'In *your* wounds we can see the agony', using the personal, singular form of 'your' (*An deinen Wunden*). But the individuals of 'who knows their number' become the mass of 'the nameless who here burned'. The poem moves from individual to abstraction in which individuals merge into a nameless, incinerated mass of people and the rubble of buildings. In this detritus, the beautiful city and its people, including the Jews, vanish. Loss is repudiated, despite the memorialization. The mourned object and mourners completely merge, but as a melancholic object, to be judged, even killed, by the Allies as the critical agency of 'Mourning and melancholia'. The ego's self-abasing plaint is seen in the rubble and in the *Dresdener Requiem*. In this mode, mourners are victims. In a manic swing, by an unconscious identification with nationalism and in neo-Nazi groups, they triumph over the demeaned victims of the Holocaust and of the bombing.

The primitive, complete identification of mourner with the object of mourning, and the narcissistic superiority that shows through the mourning, are group phenomena. The individual citizens become the nameless victims of Allied burning, disintegrating into a mass, losing any trace of individuality. We then remember that the multitude of people who were first made nameless by incineration were the victims of the Holocaust. There is no mention of them.[11] We further glimpse an undercurrent of this pathological mourning in the substantial gathering of right-wing, including neo-Nazi, groups that, with their bellowing triumphalism, try to invade and possess the peaceful, remembering mourners. If successful, this group process, comprising mourners and pathological mourners, would eliminate mourning this loss.

Thousands of people come to the remembrances, many with the aim of marginalizing the right-wing groups. *Individuals* can remain aware of the context of the mourning, but they have to grapple with ambivalence and guilt. In 2011, the city's deputy mayor, Detlef Sittel, said

Dresden: The Innocent City of Culture

When we remember [those whose final rest is in the Heidefriedhof] today, we do it in the knowledge of the nights and days in which, previously, Warsaw, Rotterdam and Coventry were turned to rubble and ash by German bombers…[I]n these hours, 66 years ago, the Gestapo rounded up the few remaining Dresden Jews, to be transported to a death camp. In these hours, 66 years ago, in Dresden, yet always more young Germans were drilled for the war, weapons [and] instruments of war, grenades, were produced…That remains unforgotten. And it demands that we oppose every extremist attempt to make political capital from the fate of our city. Fanaticism, hate songs and hollow slogans shame the memory of the dead…[R]ight here, at the graves of the victims, we declare: Dresden wants reconciliation and Dresden lives reconciliation.

The success of mourning depends on an ability to manage these memories and the guilt that they would evoke. It includes an identification with the lost object in which love and the capacity to live together predominate. What I call public mourning and manic reparation, as aspects of pathological mourning, give into the ambivalence; the world becomes persecutory, filled with retaliatory objects that have to be killed, and killed again to avoid another round of guilt. Ambivalence is clear in the rubble photography. One of these books, *Gesang im Feuerofen. Köln: Überreste einer deutshen Stadt* (Song in the Fire Oven. Cologne: Remains of a German City), for example, promulgates a redemptive myth based on identifying the German people with the Jews (Claasen 1947). It asserts German victimization by equating Allied bombing with the Nazi attempt to exterminate the Jews, *while appropriating the Jews' invincibility through their God in referring to the Old Testament Book of Daniel, in which Jews survive the fiery oven* (Fuchs, pp. 32, 226, n. 32; Fuchs' emphasis). Not only was German suffering equated to Jewish suffering: more concretely, the incinerated German was the incinerated Jew; the invincible German replaced the invincible Jew, taking the envied nature of the Jew and eliminating the impurity of the German. Contempt and annihilation rise again in the unconscious to quell the loss and call for another attack on the object of mourning.

The site for public mourning provided by the Dresden memorial evokes the unspoken equation in which Nazi aggression is replaced by

Allied aggression—a common feature of memorialization in Germany, which functions to avoid guilt. The intrusion into the Dresden commemorations by neo-Nazis aims to turn mourning with its undercurrent of ambivalence and guilt into a call to arms. They march with banners that speak of never forgetting, but it is the triumphalism of the manic position that is not, for them, to be forgotten. Their narcissistic zeal does not mourn lost lives, cities and pride, nor aim for reparation, but instead brings back the nationalistic superiority of the Nazis. With commemoration comes the inclination, either to find a way to live with the past in mourning and reparation or a manic avoidance, which resembles mourning and reparation but remains triumphal over them.

Notes

1. George Mosse (1990) shows how compellingly sites of mourning can also serve to celebrate heroic sacrifice, which reinforces a 'Myth of the War Experience'. The contrast between private and public mourning is more distinct in the views of politicians, presumably believing they also represent the public. The three soldiers memorial was commissioned amidst controversy over whether the Memorial Wall sufficiently commemorated the sacrifice of soldiers (Gallagher nd). The sculptor nonetheless intended to capture the sort of ambiguity and existential threat, which the politicians' bravado of heroism hides.

    Perhaps the politicians saw in it something more clear-cut than the desperate situation inflicted on the soldiers, to which the sculptor, Frederick Hart, was alert. In a press release for the unveiling of the sculpture, Kathleen Keenan (1984) says

    > The figurative sculpture that stands before you, three fighting men caught in a moment of watchful awareness, addresses the endless confrontation of man and his own mortality. These veterans stand in solitary repose, viewing from afar the long, dark wall that recounts the 58,022 names of those who have died or who are missing in battle… On one face there is an expression of grave incomprehension; on another, anguish and anxiety; on a third, almost angry defiance. Their faces mirror the turbulent passage from innocence to experience, from boyhood to manhood, and their individual reactions are reflective of

the men who have passed before them…Frederick Hart, sculptor of the statue, explains the expression he sought…'I wanted,' he said, 'to get the youth and to some degree the sense of psychology of what took place, the fact that there is a kind of shadow that passes over these young faces that will never go away. I wanted to capture them at that moment when that shadow passed…The statue I created is meant to elevate the veteran, to say something about their experience to them, to help them be acknowledged and understood.' (pp. 1–2, 6)

In this way, the reparative use that citizens have made of the Wall, the angry resentment of the politicians, and the attempt by the sculptor of the second memorial to represent tragedy inflicted on youth highlight the ambiguity of memorialization. The memorial pair is a site for remembering, mourning and reparation, but, in the politicians' ire and the absence of recognition of the delusional enemy as innocent victims, also an object that patches over guilt for the damage inflicted on the good object.

2. The monument bears an inscription from a poem by Heinrich Lersch: *Deutschland muss leben, auch wenn wir sterben mussen* (Germany must live, even if we must die). In the aftermath of the devastation of Germany, including the area in which the monument remained standing, it seemed a mockery and an affront to the war dead (Young, pp. 37–8).

3. There is some survey evidence that suggests a normalization of a group ideal within everyday, unexceptional terms. Johnson and Reuband (2005) carried out interviews and surveys in the 1990s. 'Sympathy for National Socialism', based on aggregated figures for several attitudes in four German cities was rated at 56% (49% weighted for the demographics in 1938). But 'What the People Liked Best about National Socialism' were 'Fight against Unemployment', 'Less Crime' and 'Construction of the Autobahns' (p. 341) (an ideological project more than a response to car ownership; Evans 2015, pp. 179–90). These memories of the Nazi period are ordinary expectations of government. The fury unleashed by this same government seems a million miles away, as does any delusion of Nazi supremacy or dread of collapse of the delusion.

4. Segal (1995) argues that the loss of the Soviet Union as an enemy, after its disintegration, to nations in the West, entailed the loss of delusional superiority over a dangerous enemy and the need to find another enemy, in order to avoid collective guilt. The guilt of Vietnam provoked the Gulf war, and in agreement with Fornari, so, says Segal, are all wars provoked by the unresolved guilt from previous wars. Groups become

psychotic to make the individuals in the group normal, perhaps normally frightened rather than mad. Without an enemy of a nation, individuals are again threatened by their psychotic cores and will create sub-groups, factions whose psychotic behaviour will protect them.

5. The retrospective admission of misrepresenting the threat from North Vietnam to the United States, and the guilt and recognition of tragedy that the war would evoke, is profoundly revealed in the filmed interview with Robert McNamara, screened as *The Fog of War* (Morris and McNamara 2003).

6. Such a distinction is recognized in German, in there being two words for a memorial. A *Denkmal* provides an occasion for thinking, a *Mahnmal* for an exhortation. The former encourages reflection; the latter induces a response: one should feel: accused, chastened, warned.

7. Rudolf Mauersberger also composed a mourning motet, based on the Book of Lamentations, 'Wie liegt die Stadt so wüst?' ('Why does the city lie in such despair?'), which also raises the fate of the city to a level of spiritual questioning.

8. Recently, this ambiguity has been renewed by the so-called PEGIDA (acronym for *Patriotische Europäer gegen die Islamisierung des Abendlandes*—Patriotic Europeans Against the Islamisation of the West) movement. Also this movement started in Dresden, where, since October 2014, it has organized demonstrations against immigration to Germany, appropriating the legendary 'Monday demonstrations' from 1989, in which citizens protested peacefully against the GDR regime, to articulate ethnocentric sentiments. As Krüger (forthcoming) points out, the movement, whose core is strongly conservative with leanings to the far right, struggles with a kind of patriotism that is as haunted as it is fascinated by German Nazism (note supplied by Steffen Krüger).

9. Moeller (2006) argues that, for Jews, captive workers, Soviet soldiers facing fierce resistance on the Eastern front, and other victims of the Nazis, the Allied bombing was salvation. Just as a symptom in psychoanalytic thinking binds contradictory currents of motive and feeling, and is consolidated as a psychic organization because it does just that, perhaps Dresden has been forced into symbolic status for the same reason. Jerzak (2015) gives a detailed account of the 'memory politics' of Dresden and Hamburg, showing how the myth of Dresden as the innocent Florence on the Elbe developed and the dissatisfaction among different groups whose voices were not adequately represented by the monuments or the commemorations.

In Johnson and Reuband's (2005) survey, Dresden scored the highest of the four cities in 'Belief in National Socialism, Admired Hitler and Shared Nazi Ideals' (Table 11.1, p. 330). While this result may suggest various interpretations, it supports the idea of the innocent city of culture as a myth.
10. Röder and Strauss (1980–1983) have collected data on a range of Jewish emigrants of people with a public profile, such as scientists, doctor, writers. They give at least a glimpse of denied loss to Germany, and it does not include the much greater number who were killed.
11. And as historians take up and re-present these aspects of the events as memory, so do they enact a conflict between partial memories, such as the Allied bombing, abstracted from a complex history that embraces context and divergent memories (Berger 1995; Herf 1997; Moeller 2006)

References

Abraham, K. (1924) Manic-Depressive States and the Pre-genital Levels of the Libido. In *Selected Papers of Karl Abraham*. London: Grant Allen, 1927, pp. 418–501.
Assmann, A. (2013) *Das neue Unbehagen an der Erinnerungskultur: eine Intervention*. München: C.H. Beck.
Berger, S. (1995) Historians and Nation-Building in Germany After Reunification. *Past & Present* 148: 187–222.
Church Times. (2013) https://www.churchtimes.co.uk/articles/2013/12-april/news/uk/thatcher-clashed-with-church,-despite-her-faith. Accessed 8.3.2017.
Claasen, H. (1947) *Gesang im Feuerofen*. Köln: Überreste einer deutshen Stadt.
Culpepper, M. (2014) Remembrance Day: The War Memorials of Ernst Barlach. https://shrineodreams.wordpress.com/2014/11/11/remembrance-day-the-war-memorials-of-ernst-barlach/. Accessed 27.10.2016.
Domansky, E. (1993) Die gespaltene Erinnerung. In Köppen, M. (ed.) *Kunst und Literatur nach Auschwitz*. Berlin: Erich Schmidt Verlag, pp. 178–96.
Evans, R. (2002) *Telling Lies About Hitler: The Holocaust, History and the David Irving Trial*. London/New York: Verso.
Evans, R. (2015) *The Third Reich in History and Memory*. London: Little, Brown.
Figlio, K. (2006) The Absolute State of Mind in Society and the Individual. *Psychoanalysis, Culture and Society* 11(2): 119–43.

Fornari, F. (1966) *The Psychoanalysis of War*. Bloomington/London: Indiana University Press, 1975.
Freud, S. (1914) On Narcissism: An Introduction. *The Standard Edition of the Complete Psychological Works of Sigmund Freud* 14: 68–102.
Freud, S. (1917[1915]) Mourning and Melancholia. *The Standard Edition of the Complete Psychological Works of Sigmund Freud* 14: 237–58.
Freud, S. (1921) *Group Psychology and the Analysis of the Ego. The Standard Edition of the Complete Psychological Works of Sigmund Freud* 18: 65–144.
Freud, S. (1923) *The Ego and the Id. The Standard Edition of the Complete Psychological Works of Sigmund Freud* 19: 1–66.
Friedrich, J. (2002) *Der Brand: Deutschland im Bombenkrieg 1940–1945*. Berlin: Propyläen.
Fuchs, A. (2012) *After the Dresden Bombing: Pathways of Memory, 1945 to the Present*. Basingstoke: Palgrave Macmillan.
Gallagher, E. (n. d.) The Vietnam Wall Controversy. Lehigh University Digital Library. http://digital.lib.lehigh.edu/trial/vietnam/about/. Accessed 27.10.2016. Brief overview, with list of sources.
Glover, E. (1947) *War, Sadism and Pacifism*. London: Allen & Unwin.
Hass, K. (1998) *Carried to the Wall: American Memory and the Vietnam Veterans Memorial*. Berkeley/Los Angeles/London: University of California Press.
Herf, J. (1997) *Divided Memory: The Nazi Past in the Two Germanies*. Cambridge, MA/London: Harvard University Press.
Hinshelwood, R. D. (1987) *What Happens in Groups: Psychoanalysis, the Individual and the Community*. London: Free Association Books.
Hinshelwood, R. D. and Skogstad, W. (eds.) (2000) *Observing Organizations: Anxiety, Defence and Culture in Health Care*. London/Philadelphia: Routledge.
Hopper, E. (1996) The Social Unconscious in Clinical Work. In *The Social Unconscious: Selected Papers*. London: Jessica Kingsley, 2003, pp. 126–61.
Jerzak, C. (2015) Memory Politics: The Bombing of Hamburg and Dresden. In Gerstenberg, K. and Nusser, T. (eds.) *Catastrophe and Catharsis. Narratives of Disaster and Redemption in German Culture and Beyond*. Rochester, NY: Boydell & Brewer Ltd, pp. 53–72.
Johnson, E. A. and Reuband, K.-H. (eds.) (2005) *What We Knew: Terror, Mass Murder, and Everday Life in Nazi Germany – An Oral History*. London: John Murray
Keenan, K. (1984) A Vietnam Vision: The Making of the Memorial Statue. https://commons.wikimedia.org/w/index.php?title=File%3APress_Release_From_Three_Servicemen_Statue_Dedication_11_Nov._1984.pdf. Accessed 19.05.2017.

Kershaw, I. (1999) 'Working Towards the Führer': Reflections on the Nature of the Hitler Dictatorship. In *Hitler, the Germans, and the Final Solution.* Jerusalem: International Institute for Holocaust Research, Yad Vashem; New Haven, [Conn.]: Yale University Press, 2008, pp. 29–48.

Klein, M. (1935) A Contribution to the Psychogenesis of Manic-Depressive States. In *The Writings of Melanie Klein*, vol. 1. London: The Hogarth Press and the Institute of Psychoanalysis, 1975, pp. 262–89.

Klein, M. (1940) Mourning and Its Relation to Manic-Depressive States. In *The Writings of Melanie Klein*, vol. 1. London: Hogarth and the Institute of Psychoanalysis, 1975, pp. 344–69.

Lupu, N. (2003) Memory Vanished, Absent, and Confined: The Counter-Memorial Project in the 1980s and 1990s. *History and Memory* 15(2): 130–64.

Mitscherlich, A. and Mitscherlich, M. (1967/1975) *The Inability to Mourn: Principles of Collective Behaviour.* Munich: Piper & Co. Verlag; English translation, New York: Grove Press.

Moeller, R. (2006) On the History of Man-Made Destruction: Loss, Death, Memory, and Germany in the Bombing War. *History Workshop Journal* 61: 103–34.

Money-Kyrle, R. (1951) *Psychoanalysis and Politics.* London: Duckworth.

Morris, E. and McNamara, R. (2003) *The Fog of War.* New York: Sony Pictures Classics.

Mosse, G. (1990) *Fallen Soldiers: Reshaping the Memory of the World Wars.* New York/London: Oxford University Press.

Overy, R. (2013) *The Bombing War: Europe 1939–1945.* London: Allen Lane.

Paterson, P. (Lieutenant Commander, U. S. Navy) (2008) The Truth About Tonkin. *Naval History Magazine* 22(1): no page numbers. http://www.usni.org/magazines/navalhistory/2008-02/truth-about-tonkin. Accessed 3.11.2016.

Peter, R. (1949) *Eine Kamera klagt an.* Dresden: Desdener Verlagsgesellschaft.

Pidd, H. (2012) Germany's Far Right Marches Out of the Shadows. *The Guardian*, February 23, p. 25.

Quindeau, I. (2008) Umgeschriebene Erinnerungen. Psychoanalytische Anmerkungen zu den Erregungen der Erinneringskultur. In Brockhaus, G. (Hg.) *Ist 'Die Unfähigkeit zu trauern' noch actuell? Eine interdisziplinäre Diskussion. Psychosozial* 31nr 114 (4): 79–87.

Reinhard, O. (2010) *Braucht die Erinnerung 19000 Namen? Sächsische Zeitung (SZ-Online.De)* 7.10.2010 http://www.szonline.de/nachrichten/braucht-die-erinnerung-19000-namen-107193.html. Accessed 27.10.

Richards, B. (1987) Military Mobilisations of the Unconscious. *Free Associations* 1: 11–26.

Röder, W. and Strauss, H. A. (eds.) (1980–83) *Biographisches Handbuch der deutschsprachigen Emigranten nach 1933 (International Biographical Dictionary of Central European Emigrés 1933–1945)*, 4 vols. München/New York/London/Paris: K.G. Saur.

Sebald, W. G. (2003) *On the Natural History of Destruction*. London: Hamish Hamilton.

Segal, H. (1995) From Hiroshima to the Gulf War and After: Socio-Political Expressions of Ambivalence. In *Psychoanalysis, Literature and War: Papers 1972–1995*. London/New York: Routledge, 1997, pp. 157–68.

Sittel, D. (2011) *Rede des zweiten Bürgermeister Detlef Sittel auf dem Dresdner Heidefriedhof.* https://www.sachsen-fernsehen.de/? s=detlef+sittel. Accessed 19.05.2017

Wangh, M. (1968) A Psychogenic Factor in the Recurrence of War. *International Journal of Psychoanalysis* 49: 319–23.

11

Conclusion

In this book, I have explored a way in which a dialogue between history and psychoanalysis might be developed. They share an interest in human beings as subjects as well as objects, and in the motivations and intentions of subjects. They share an interest in how the individual becomes the member of a group, and whether the individual retains an identity while participating in forming a group identity. They share an interest in what Freud called the 'genetic' aspect of explanation: not based on genes, but on the laying down of strata imbued with the continuous revision, which Collingwood called 'historical consciousness' and Freud called *Nachträgrichkeit*—later upon earlier, in which each informed the other.

Historians involve themselves in the lives of others and speak of general currents of thinking and of actions that reasonably follow from them. I say 'reasonably', because their themes are narratives. They are accounts that might arouse doubts that drive objections or press for other evidence, but they nonetheless flow as continuous—hopefully engaging—'remembering true' stories that are intelligible to participants in

---

I have included citations only for quotations or where clarification is needed. All other references are clear either from context or from prior usage.

historical thinking, whether practitioners or audiences. Historical narrative based on historical research and writing frames a field of enquiry. Doubt about these narratives and the evidence for them is compatible with historians' debates inside the frame of the field. Cynicism about them is not compatible with the exercise of the historian's skill and integrity.

Looking from the opposite pole, psychoanalysts also create narratives. Their narratives cast the internal world, dynamically alive and intriguing, as a 'remembering true' story of the struggles of the psyche. Their accounts, like those of the historian, might also arouse doubt, which drives objections or presses for further evidence; but, just as in history, the core of debate is intelligible both to practitioners and to audiences. Psychoanalytic cases and theory, like historical cases and theory, frame a field of enquiry. Here, too, doubt about the psychoanalytic narrative is compatible with debate within respect for psychoanalytic research and writing. Cynicism is not compatible with psychoanalytic debate.

I contrast cynicism with the doubt that calls for more evidence or refined theorizing, in order to bring out a difference in intention. Doubt aims for convergence of understanding; cynicism aims to undermine evidence and thinking, and to triumph. It is, in effect, a form of action, even if only spoken. It may pretend to engage in debate, but actually avoids debate. One tries to gain a mental grip, but encounters only a slippery surface. A problem arises when the cynicism is not as obvious as it is, for example, in blatant prejudice. In less flagrant cases, it can be hard to discriminate between a real debate, in which the terms are intelligible to participants and their audiences; and a false debate, in which the aim is to eliminate an enemy. In such a case, the intention can be hidden inside an *apparently* reasonable, conceptual and empirical disagreement.

Various contemporary examples spring to mind: intelligent design in 'debate' with evolutionary theory; climate change denial in 'debate' with environmental physics and chemistry. Perhaps the most telling example in historical studies is Holocaust denial. Deborah Lipstadt (1994) has written on the insidious importation of anti-Semitism into apparently legitimate historical debate based on apparently legitimate historical journals, such as the *Annals of Historical Revisionism* and in apparently legitimate research institutes, such as the Institute for Historical Review, in fact backed by anti-Semitic partisans. Her publisher, and herself through her publisher, was sued by David Irving, an established historian and Holocaust denier (recounted in Evans 2002 and Lipstadt 2006). Irving was defeated by intensive, detailed historical research that undermined his falsified evidence. There was no debate between Lipstadt and Irving. She refused to engage in a contrived dialogue, because there would not be a conferring, but a debasing of the very idea of truth-seeking. The significance of the Holocaust as the essential core of genocide, its rootedness in Nazism, its anti-Semitism, its racism—the crux of serious debate—could not be encompassed in a sham discussion, which could take place only by ignoring the lie of Holocaust denial, a lie undone by demonstrable fact.

I have drawn attention to this discrete episode in which an apparently historical debate was in fact not a debate at all, but a conflict that was brought to a decisive conclusion by a victory in court (though, no doubt Holocaust denial will continue), in order to sharpen a much vaguer, but nonetheless important, borderline debate. In Chap. 6, I reviewed the not so obvious *Historikerstreit* of the 1980s. In that case, no one was accused of falsification. Habermas objected to what he saw as a strand of apologetics inside Germany historiography, and historians divided between those who agreed with him and those who saw his reaction as a moralistic intervention into the professional field of history by a non-historian. One might speak of an ideology inside a profession acting with integrity, looking for a scientific foundation, not of a cynical breach of integrity.

I emphasized two main points about the *Historikerstreit*: (1) that the very terms of reference for historical research could carry the ideological bias to which Habermas referred. In particular, the reputable historian, Anreas Hillgruber, advocated the methodological demand that the historian empathize with the historical actors—the well-known principle of *Verstehen*, enunciated by Dilthey. But Hillgruber, in using it as a premise of historical research, also isolated a particular phenomenon, the dilemma of soldiers in the last days on the eastern front. The narrowing and sequestering of the field of enquiry could itself generate a bias if the methodology did not go on to reconnect the phenomenon with its historical place; this contextualization was in doubt; and (2) the matter was complex and subtle, because it included the Holocaust, which was deeply emotional, drawing historians into strongly held positions. The exchange of letters between the eminent historians, Martin Broszat and Saul Friedländer, aimed to bring out their underlying differences, but despite their respectful and determined intention, it did not establish clear points of difference.

I agree that empathy is a fundamental methodological principle. It goes, psychoanalytically, with an internal world, with identification and with the range of affect and affect-driven phenomena. We need them to understand the social world, just as we do in understanding the individual. I argued in Chaps. 2 and 3 that the reluctance to follow this line of thinking was based on misunderstandings that could be cleared up. I have tried to show by the example of reparation that historians take us right up to the skin around the internal world. A psychoanalytic approach allows an extrapolation into the social world, imaginatively slipping into it. Conversely, I think that psychoanalysis has no substance without the social world, which brings the experiences that one can describe. Moreover, the social world brings out clearly—sometimes savagely—an actuality that gives expression to the internal world. What psychoanalysis speaks of *really happens*. Both sides need to take on the full meaning of *really happens*.

It follows that history and psychoanalysis need each other. With respect to their shared focus on memory and on the collective memory of history, I have hypothesized that they are driven by tolerable and intolerable relationships to the past, where toleration depends on managing affect, particularly guilt, and that guilt drives reparation. Reparation, in this way of thinking, is a historical force. 'Remembering true' is a form of reparation and 'remembering false' is a form of manic reparation. I stick to these two judgements because they can be given these meanings as two forms of reparation within psychoanalysis. The psychoanalytic concepts can be refined and confirmed within psychoanalysis, then reflected back on memory in a way that clarifies what I mean by true and false. 'True' confronts defences, which can also be defined, and tolerates the consequences of living in reality. 'False' reinforces defences and enacts them in relation to groups that have been cast out—created in order to be cast out, as enemies in a delusional world.

11 Conclusion

The nucleus around which history and psychoanalysis might cohere is the idea of an internal world in society as well as in the individual. This internal world can be defined psychoanalytically. It is a virtual place in which the inhabitants relate to each other through a complex mixture of wish, phantasy, omnipotence, recognition, concern, self-concern, ambivalence—the list goes on. In some ways it is easier to discern the power of this internal world in groups than it is in society. Groups enact it by constantly creating factions, then rebuilding them in different configurations.

But that is also why self-reflectiveness, including psychoanalytic reflectiveness, is often rejected. To see oneself or one's group alive in front of one's own eyes in scenes, both internal and external, can be intolerable. It drives division and the creation of repositories of projection against which action can be taken. It thereby impairs thinking and self-reflection. It is facilitated by group dynamics and by fascination with the assault on thinking. This sort of process has taken hold in the recent surge of populism in contemporary politics. Politicians claim to be speaking to and for 'the people'—the people who have not been heard or regarded until now. 'The people' also say this claim is true. People of different persuasions seem to agree that *people*—maybe not themselves in particular—have at last been heard and their legitimate claims for recognition will be met. This relationship between leader and the people may rest on little evidence, but it does call out the deepest wishes, satisfactions, accolades, disappointments, prejudices, grievances and punishment.

The unconscious, affective driver of populist appeal is, in my view, closer to a thrall than to rationality. That is what excites the triumphalism and the denigration of dissenters, which so tarnishes these movements. Freud thought that what we call pathology was only an extreme phenomenon, which could sharpen the appearance of the normal. The analysis of the thrall of the Nazi regime gives us a glimpse at a malignant extreme of populist thrall. Bearing the analysis of the Nazi thrall in mind, I have argued that the denunciation of dissent is driven by an intimation of catastrophe. The catastrophe would be the collapse of the differentiation between the world of phantasy and the world of external reality; in other words, a psychotic breakdown. I think this dread reinforces the desire to credit the rationality of 'the people', on which politicians make a case for fulfilling the expressed wish of 'the people'. To speak of a dread of psychotic breakdown would seem to accuse rational people of mental illness, and in a very condemning way, just as mental illness is treated as an unspeakable plague. My view is the opposite: that it would bring politics alive with self-reflective, informed, democratic debate instead of the repetitive, exciting, but deceptive fostering of illusions, of allegiances, of likes and dislikes.

One of the dilemmas in historical scholarship, which it shares with psychoanalysis and with a self-reflective, informed democratic politics, is the conflict between aiming to pull out the truth from hidden depths and the dread of accusation that one is really revealing support for unconscionable crimes. Nowhere is this dilemma more prominent than in trying to assess what happened to the Nazi past in post-war Germany. The word on which one's fingers will be burnt is guilt. Who was responsible for Nazi atrocities? Who knew of them? To what degree did this knowing make them perpetrators or complicit in perpetration? Who are the apologists? Why are they apologists—were they complicit? I argued in Chap. 4 that the Jewish 'enemy' was a delusion. How many 'ordinary' enemies are actually delusions masquerading in rational clothes? Where do we stand today, in reconstructing the history of traduced responsibility?

One contribution that psychoanalysis can make to this dilemma is to define guilt and the defensive processes that surround it. Guilt is a feature of the depressive position. It accompanies recognition of the object and concern for damage to the object. It involves a capacity and openness to identify with the object. It distinguishes between identification with, and incorporation of, the object, and therefore between a relationship to the object and an identicality with the object. It recognizes loss to the object by perpetration, loss of the object and loss of oneself as an agent. These recognitions are not competitive: recognizing one's own loss does not replace the damaged object as the victim but enables the subject better to identify with and accept the object on its own terms: to allow it to have a voice. The aim of the depressive position is to recognize reality and to accept a reparative attitude towards it. All this is part of guilt. It does not jibe with the typical use of the word to signify an accountability that deserves punishment.

11 Conclusion

You can see the relevance of this confusion of meanings around guilt to post-war Germany and to the way the Germans remember the Nazi period, whether from personal experience, from family accounts, from school or from the media; and it intrudes into the assessment of the Nazi period by historians.[1] Already in 1946, the philosopher, Karl Jaspers, delivered a lecture series on 'The Question of German Guilt', in which he divided the forms of guilt into four categories: criminal guilt, political guilt, moral guilt and metaphysical guilt. They roughly divide into two larger categories: external (criminal and political), in which one is held to be culpable; internal (moral and metaphysical), in which one is witness to oneself or to oneself in identification with humanity, embracing the full meaning of being part of humanity. Jaspers says to his audience, that he, of the perpetrator generation (though living abroad), and they, of the student generation, are different from each other. They need to communicate with each other, in a way that is simultaneously an internal conversation; that is, that humanity, beyond just existing, is a self-reflective communication among participants, which not only adds up to humanity, but is humanity.

Can history be written without Jaspers' second broad—internal—category? I think not, and this book is based on the premise that it cannot. So we must include guilt at the heart of our enquiry. Hannah Segal's understanding of war speaks directly to this necessity. She argued (1995, p. 165), from a point made by Fornari (1966), that the guilt that cannot be assimilated and worked through is beaten away by another round of aggression, in the same way as an individual might stave off guilt and persecution by projecting phantasized aggression into another person and righteously attacking that person. An occasion for mourning turns into a triumphal repudiation of mourning, in which a society's internal unease is projected into an enemy and quelled. An incitement to war builds on unassuaged guilt from the destructiveness of a previous war.

If we pursue this line of thinking, we come to the conclusion that the reality of history depends on the conviction of its truthfulness, and this conviction originates in its immediate aliveness for each of us. That is what the historian's narrative aims to convey: not just the veracity of events but their reality as a conviction of their truthfulness. Conviction is an experience in the internal world. It is not necessarily pleasant or self-affirming, but it rings true. Fornari (1966) connects the belief that there could be a nuclear war and that it would destroy the world with the melancholic non-mourning of one of his patients.

> I was able to trace the contents of her delusion [that no more children would be born and that spring would never return, and that she was to blame] to unconscious fantasies of destructive attacks against her mother; the spring that would never again arrive pointed to the symbol of the mother (earth) robbed of all her children…Thus we find ourselves confronted with an unforeseen situation, leading to the following hypothesis: *In order to be able to perceive the catastrophic situation as a real historical situation, each of us must somehow associate himself with an illusory catastrophic situation relating to our sadistic attacks against our love object.* (pp. 159–60; Fornari's emphasis)

I think this extreme formulation applies to assessing post-war German conviction about the reality of the Nazi period. But bearing in mind that 'reality' refers necessarily to the veracity of documentation and to belief and sense of conviction, a version of Fornari's hypothesis is inherent in the reality of all historical situations.

The general conclusion towards which I am moving is to say that the themes covered in this book, organized as pairs of opposites that can seem to be the same—remembering true and remembering false, reparation and manic reparation, guilt and persecutory anxiety, commemoration and repetition—are also forms of thinking and non-thinking. I mean an intention, mostly unconscious, towards an identity built either on convergence or, by contrast, on divisive triumph. This line of argument owes a lot to Hannah Arendt's (1978) ideas on thinking. She argues that thinking is a form of internal discussion, which is then also pursued with interlocutors. It always aims for a convergence among the internal—and, therefore, external—interlocutors. If a dissonance among interlocutors is sustained, the process is not thinking. I think of Habermas' (1998, pp. 239–52) ideas on deliberative politics, a democratic politics built on self-reflective interlocutors, as equivalents to Arendt's thesis in the social arena. Self-reflection, for Habermas, is an internal process that aims for honesty in an internal consistency and, in doing so, does not rest with schisms. In this sense, Arendt and Habermas are speaking (though I make no case for their agreeing with me on this point) of the psychoanalytic concept of defence and of working through. Defence preserves a schism; working through aims to repair it.

Charles Maier holds a similar view of the work of the historian. He says that '[t]he writing and reading of history must rest upon intellectual sociability,' a common effort that can overcome ideological partisanship (1988, p. 63). He believes that the self-reflection required is equivalent to the psychoanalyst's own analysis. I would add that the psychoanalyst's enquiry into defensive 'forgetting' must work together with the historian's investigation of the 'multiple restorations' of memories, proposed by Herf (1997, pp. 10–11). One could say that the topic of this book—reparation and manic reparation—is also, in light of the above, the process of both history and psychoanalysis. Both aim to converge on 'remembering true' and on reality as a harmony between external and internal–psychic–reality, in narrating and understanding the subjective objects of their study. Both seek this convergence in their subjective objects and in themselves and in analyzing the falsifying aim to triumph over it.

I want to close by mentioning two areas of convergent research that are implied in this study but are not developed. They stem from the theme of this book—memory, history, reparation—and they are contemporary. The first is the gender dynamics of the Third Reich and its collapse. Gender relations figure in all object relations, historical and individual, but were especially expressive in the Third Reich. The second is the counter-memorial movement in Germany, which aims to overcome the tendency in memorialization towards repetitive enactments of static memories, whether evoked by stone monuments or by commemorations. Enactment can undermine the reparative, often mournful, aim of remembering.

I turn first to the gender dimension. The end of the war was a loss, not only in the military sense but also of the thrall of the Nazi regime. They were really collapses of structures. The Mitscherlichs (1967/1975) observed, on clinical observation, that 'the inability to mourn' followed from an inability to assimilate a collapse that was both internal and external. Their observation chimes with the assessment of historians of the structure of Nazi power. It was enthralling and its defeat was a collapse, and it was enthralling in its grandiose anti-Semitism and in its implosion into emptiness. In addition, the aggression towards, and demeaning of, women, needs to be put along with the Nazi treatment of the Jews. They are not the same—there was no aim to eliminate women—but are unconscious convergent themes.

Shortly after the war, a diary kept in the final days of the war by an anonymous woman living in Berlin, was published in English (Anon. 1954/2004), and later in Germany, where it was controversial. In his introduction to the diary—a diary that he judges to be both authentic and exceptionally astute—Antony Beevor draws out a gender dimension of collapse.

> 'These days I keep noticing how my feelings towards men are changing,' she writes as Hitler's regime collapses. 'We feel sorry for them; they seem so miserable and powerless. The weaker sex. Deep down we women are experiencing a kind of collective disappointment. The Nazi world – ruled by men, glorifying the strong man – is beginning to crumble, and with it the myth of "Man". That has transformed us, emboldened us. Among the many defeats at the end of the war is the defeat of the male sex.' Her optimism proved sadly premature. The late 1940s and the 1950s, after the men returned from prison camps, were a sexually repressive era in which husbands reasserted their authority. Women were forbidden to mention the subject of rape as if it somehow dishonoured their men who were supposed to have defended them. It remained taboo until the late 1980, when a younger generation of women started to encourage their mothers and grandmothers to speak about their experiences. (p. 11)

What this diarist and Beevor bring out is the gender dimension of the delusional state of Nazi authority and the calamitous nature of the loss of such a structure: not loss, but catastrophe, collapse. Hitler, National Socialism, dramatic politics, thrall, man, collapse together.

These observations suggest a psychoanalytic complement. The diarist reports a disappointment among women in the men who, defeated by other men, seemed, to the women, diminished from their previous state. To these women, the soldiers were identified with the grandiose Nazi empire. The defeat of the German army was not just a defeat, but an implosion of the illusion of a reborn, invincible Reich, created by the Nazis and the people; and simultaneously an implosion of the Man. Two entwined myths collapsed together. She implies that both had been built on denigration of an object expelled from the heart of Nazism and masculinity: the Jew and the woman. Though she speaks of woman now able to see the sorry state of Man once this inflation at her expense collapsed, one can extrapolate it to include Jews now able to see the sorry, collapsed, state of the Nazi regime.

Her self-reflective apprehension of the collapse as a collapse of the man in the woman's mind is born about by extensive interviews with men and women, who, pre-war, belonged to youth groups, some of whom reconnected after the war to form the 'Free German Circle', seeking the restoration of the collective spirit of those days. Both men and women spoke of a demoralization that hit the men harder than the women, who had achieved substantial independence during the war, and who were more at ease with themselves. Along with the restoration of relationships, there was also the meeting of strong women with, in the eyes of both, defeated men, men also blamed as Nazis. Kohut (2012) interviewed many members of this circle and provided detailed accounts and analyses of them (with respect to the returning men, see pp. 181–236; for other details relevant to these points, see pp. 182–3, 188, 206–9, 212–13, 224–30).

We can take the implication of the woman's view (including her circle and women generally) further in a psychoanalytic direction. Their association of 'Man' with 'Nazi' suggests an incomplete oedipal scenario as much as it suggests the defeat of the Nazi regime. In an oedipal scenario, a wife/mother—the object of desire and control by Man (father and son)—gains an unfazed view of masculinity as a masquerade when she comprehends the source of his violence towards her. He had the physical power to attack her sexually, but in doing so, unmasked a fragility in male identity. The (enemy) father who defeated her striving boy revealed to her the mechanics of male development as a persisting oedipal failure. The boy never completed an identification with the father through love, following oedipal rivalry. That boy was also the father who did not complete an oedipal resolution and visited the continuing aggression on the son, but also on the mother who had the power to seduce him and encourage a belief in his power and importance beyond what he could securely achieve (Chasseguet-Smirgel 1985, pp. 24–34). His oedipal insecurity left the boy prey, not only to the other man (father or son) but also to her disappointment in him. Freud (1910, 1912) is eloquent on the male's perplexity and insecurity in the light of the 'unfaithful' woman who is both mother to him and sexual partner to another (father). The returning soldier comes home to an 'unfaithful' wife/mother (albeit not of her choosing), and, as Beevor points out, re-establishes his authority. I would add that he does this through recovering oedipal mastery.

There has been some psychoanalytic work on male sexual violence as inherent in masculinity, albeit provoked into the open under the stresses of military discipline and of danger in war. Army discipline, certainly in the German and Russian armies, created a masculine carapace identified with an illusion of national prowess, instilled by a toughening severity. Beevor noted that '[m]any [Soviet] soldiers had been so humiliated by their own officers and commissars during four years of war that they felt driven to expiate their bitterness' (Anon. 1954/2005, p. 9). It was a severity that demeaned the soldier, who was then also pressed into dangerous situations. Noro (2014) studied male sexual violence in warfare. She based her analysis on the extreme brutality of the sexual violence, which suggested a deeply personal, even intimate, oedipal and pre-oedipal dimension. She also related it to severe, degrading, feminizing, military discipline, which was managed by projecting the degraded identity into women whom soldiers demeaned as they were demeaned.

Noro brings out an oedipal dimension underlying this brutality. The combination of the seductiveness of illusion and the threat to survival drew the male into the treachery of oedipal seduction and threat: the wish to have mother and replace father; the belief that mother prefers the son; the accompanying need protect mother from father, be father, defeat father—also to love him: a maelstrom of conflict. These intricacies of the phantasies of relationship are easily overlooked when dealing with the mass destructiveness of war, including rape.

Margarete Mitscherlich-Nielsen (1983) argued that anti-Semitism is a male illness. She grounded her analysis in the male oedipal scenario, in which the formation of the male ego-ideal tends towards illusion, the loss of secure reality testing as the boy's anxiety grew at being left with, and made anxious by, an anxious mother in the absence of a secure paternal presence. The boy unconsciously attributed his unfulfilled oedipal wishes, not to his immaturity, but to an internal, rival father. But this father, after the war, was also de-idealized and devalued, while also remaining a rival, and mother was envied as well as desired. Mitscherlich-Nielsen linked the Jew with the woman as available objects of denigration into which the swirl of oedipal conflict could be projected and attacked. 'Again the defence mechanisms of displacement and projection are implemented: not the father or the man himself is guilty, much more would the guilt be attributed totally to the Jew, who could be reviled and persecuted without anxiety' (p. 46, following Wangh 1962); 'not only suppressed hatred for the father but also the envy of the mother can be directed at the Jews' (p. 47).

Wieland has developed two themes with respect to masculine identity and to the exaggerated form it took in the Nazi regime. In one study (2000), she developed the concept of 'primitive masculinity'. Rather than emerging from oedipal resolution in a mature relationship, this uncompleted masculinity oscillated between a phallic repudiation of the mother in a matricide, which created an 'undead' internal mother, and oedipal conflict. In another study (2015), she postulated a fascist group formed in a state of mind that combined feminine and masculine through a male embodiment of the envied mother, triumphally absorbed into his 'masculine womb'.

The direction of this psychoanalytic research points the need to delineate a male identity composed in the midst of unresolved oedipal and pre-oedipal conflict, bearing also a confusion of phantasy and reality, with the temptation towards belief in an illusory reality represented by an early ego-ideal. It helps in understanding the enormity of internal and external collapse, as opposed to a recognition and mourning of a lost reality. It leads us back to the Mitscherlichs' notion of the 'inability to mourn'; that is, an immersion in the loss of an ideal, as a preoccupation with narcissistic injury. This narcissistic absorption obstructs the coming to terms with the past as a reality, including the perpetration of the Holocaust. I have explored the forms of delusion and unreality, the defences against 'remembering true' and the ambivalence in reparation. The connection with a masculinity created against the woman/mother adds an important dimension to the theme of this book.

There are, of course, specificities to 'Jew' and 'woman', each as an object of desire and contempt, and I have offered an interpretation with respect to the Jew as enemy in the course of this book. But in my concluding remarks, I aim only to bring out a common theme. In the case of the Nazi regime, this kinship does make sense, in that part of the hated of the Jew was the hatred of his feminization in Nazi phantasy, a theme explored by Stephen Frosh (2005). Anti-Semitism goes with anti-feminism.

If we add the dimension of male identity as a repudiation of the female as the bearer of male projections, then reparation becomes reparation to the female as a damaged object and to himself in enrichment by this regenerated object. The recognition of her reality installs her in his unconscious as a benefactor and beneficiary of her enrichment through reparation. That cannot happen without her becoming other to him, a renewal which entails the recognition of perpetration and 'remembering true'. Freud shows how difficult this process is through describing the powerful defence of disavowal, in which one does not know what one knows. He based it on fetishism, in which the mind divided itself, one part recognizing the reality of the female as female, the other part omnipotently erasing and replacing her with a phantasy of a man-woman. Remembering 'true' as reparation means the recognition of reality, and it is typically undone and disavowed. It brings us back to Melanie Klein's classic work, 'Love, Guilt and Reparation' (1937). Here Klein situates reparation squarely in the relationship between male and female in maturational development.

Turning to the second theme for further convergent analysis, I want to mention a current in thinking about reparation, which one might call 'post-memorializing'. Recently, there have been signs of an antipathy towards memorializing because of its tending towards stasis and repetition. I think this counter-memorializing current reflects a dismay and frustration at the obstruction of 'remembering true' by 'remembering false' and the undermining of reparative wishes that accompany them. Counter-memorialism calls into question the idea of a memorial that confines one's emotional reaction. Young (1993) speaks of a 'new generation of contemporary artists and monument makers in Germany [who probe] the limits of both their artistic media and the very notion of a memorial' (p. 27). He describes a range of constructions that interrupt any frozen ideas of memorializing: monuments that disappear, unfinished; dialogue between memorials, as in Hamburg; or suddenly and unexpectedly catch the attention of a passer-by. The *Stolpersteine* catch one unprepared and bring right into awareness a victim of persecution. In not knowing that person, but in being stopped in one's tracks by his or her fate, one is brought into a mournful state of mind.

Apart from criticisms of memorialization, and the construction of sites that draw one out of a stereotypical reaction in order to elicit a more inward response, people have sought more of a living engagement with the past through bringing opposing groups together—participants in conflict, their successors and others who feel drawn into this arena. They take the form of reconciliation as an ongoing process in the form of face-to-face meetings between opponents, including Germans and Jews. They also take the form of 'group relations' workshops, which are psychoanalytically structured meetings. The aim of both is to hold people together for an extended time, in the hope that their continuous meeting will bring a convergence of recognition of each other and of a sufficiently common reality, in which entrenched hatred can ease.

I will mention four initiatives. Locally, in the shrine city of Dresden: (1) the Antifa Recherche Team Dresden (ART DD) confronts neo-Nazi demonstrations (see https://www.addn.me/tag/art/); (2) Abolish Commemoration: Critique of the Discourse Relating to the Bombing of Dresden (abolishcommemoration.org). With respect to perpetration, primarily of the Jews: (1) Björn Krondorfer (1995) runs educational workshops with third-generation non-Jewish Germans and Jews; (2) The 'Nazareth-Conference' brings Israelis and Palestinians together in a psychoanalytically informed meeting (Davids 2016; Erlich et al. 2009). Group relations conferences put one into living confrontation between opponents, including those who bear a heritage, like it or not, of perpetration or victimization. The tough, often unconscious, foci of resistance and persistent hatred and prejudice come to the fore. The broader brief of this group is clear in its name Partners in Confronting Collective Atrocities (see their website www.p-cca.org).

These recent initiatives lead back to the spine of the book: reparation. Memorializing memory, as in monuments and commemorations, is ambivalent. It is both reparative and manic reparative. This ambivalence in remembering as reparation is inherent in reparation. The recent currents in counter-memorializing aim to enliven memorialization and to catch ambivalence as it surfaces, especially in its embedded, unconscious dimension.

Notes

1. Roger Frie (2017) unfolds a deeply engaging personal account of his discovery of his grandfather's Nazism and its impact on him as a German born well after the war, within a framework structured by the unusual experience of being a psychoanalyst, historian and philosopher. Bringing together personal, subjective and objective dimensions, deepened by intensive clinical analyses of Jewish and German patients, he addresses not-knowing, the shock of discovery and the complexity of post-war German history.

References

Abolish Commemoration. http://www.abolishcommemoration.org
Anon. (1954/2005) *A Woman in Berlin*. London: Virago Press.
Arendt, H. (1978) *The Life of the Mind*. New York: Harcourt.
Chasseguet-Smirgel, J. (1985) *Creativity and Perversion*. London: Free Association Books.
Davids, M. Fakhry (2016) Psychoanalysis and Palestine-Israel: A Personal Angle. *Psychoanalysis, Culture and Society* 21(1): 41–58.
Erlich, S., Erlich-Ginor, M. and Beland, H. (eds.) (2009) *Fed with Tears, Poisoned with Milk*. Giessen: Psychosozial Verlag.
Evans, R. (2002) *Telling Lies About Hitler: The Holocaust, History and the David Irving Trial*. London/New York: Verso.
Fornari, F. (1966) *The Psychoanalysis of War*. Bloomington/London: Indiana University Press, 1975.
Freud, S. (1910) A Special Type of Choice of Object Made by Men (Contributions to the Psychology of Love I). *The Standard Edition of the Complete Psychological Works of Sigmund Freud* 11: 163–75.

Freud, S. (1912) On the Universal Tendency to Debasement in the Sphere of Love (Contributions to the Psychology of Love II). *The Standard Edition of the Complete Psychological Works of Sigmund Freud* 11: 177–90.

Frie, R. (2017) *Not in My Family: German Memory and Responsibility After the Holocaust*. NY: Oxford University Press.

Frosh, S. (2005) *Hate and the 'Jewish Science': Anti-semitism, Nazism and Psychoanalysis*. Houndmills, Basingstoke: Palgrave Macmillan.

Habermas, J. (1996/1998) *The Inclusion of the Other: Studies in Political Theory*. Cambridge, MA: Massachusetts Institute of Technology; Cambridge, Polity Press, 1999.

Herf, J. (1997) *Divided Memory: The Nazi Past in the Two Germanies*. Cambridge, MA/London: Harvard University Press.

Klein, M. (1937) Love, Guilt and Reparation. In *The Writings of Melanie Klein*, vol. 1. London: Hogarth and the Institute of Psychoanalysis, 1975, pp. 306–43.

Kohut, T. A. (2012) *A German Generation: An Experiential History of the Twentieth Century*. New Haven/London: Yale University Press.

Krondorfer, B. (1995) *Remembrance and Reconciliation: Encounters Between Young Jews and Germans*. New Haven/London: Yale University Press.

Lipstadt, D. (1994) *Denying the Holocaust: The Growing Assault on Truth and Memory*. New York: The Free Press.

Lipstadt, D. (2006) *History on Trial: My Day in Court with David Irving*. New York: Harper Perennial.

Maier, C. (1988) *The Unmasterable Past: History, Holocaust, and German National Identity*. Cambridge, MA/London: Harvard University Press.

Mitscherlich, A. and Mitscherlich, M. (1967/1975) *The Inability to Mourn: Principles of Collective Behaviour*. Munich: Piper & Co. Verlag; English translation, New York: Grove Press.

Mitscherlich-Nielsen, M. (1983) Antisemitismus – eine Männerkrankheit? *Psyche – Zeitschrift für Psychoanalyse* 37(1): 41–54.

Noro, T. (2014) *A Study on the Motivation of Sexual Violence in WWII: The Conflict of Masculinity in Warfare* (PhD thesis). Colchester: University of Essex.

Segal, H. (1995) From Hiroshima to the Gulf War and After: Socio-Political Expressions of Ambivalence. In *Psychoanalysis, Literature and War: Papers 1972–1995*. London/New York: Routledge, 1997, pp. 157–68.

Wangh, M. (1962) Psychoanalytische Betrachtungen zur Dynamik und Genese des Vorurteils, des Antisemitismus und des Nazismus. *Psyche – Zeitschrift für Psychoanalyse* 16: 273–84.

Wieland, C. (2000) *The Undead Mother: Psychoanalytic Explorations of Masculinity, Feminintiy and Matricide*. London: Rebus Press.

Wieland, C. (2015) *The Fascist State of Mind and the Manufacturing of Masculinity*. London/New York: Routledge.

Young, J. (1993) *The Texture of Memory: Holocaust Memorials and Meaning*. New Haven: Yale University Press.

References

Abolish Commemoration. http://www.abolishcommemoration.org
Abraham, K. (1922) Letter from Karl Abraham to Sigmund Freud, March 13, 1922. *The Complete Correspondence of Sigmund Freud and Karl Abraham 1907–1925*, pp. 452–4.
Abraham, K. (1924) Manic-Depressive States and the Pre-genital Levels of the Libido. In *Selected Papers of Karl Abraham*. London: Grant Allen, 1927, pp. 418–501.
Adorno, T. (1959) The Meaning of Working Through [*Aufarbeitung*] the Past. In *Guilt and Defense: On the Legacies of National Socialism in Postwar Germany*. Cambridge, MA/London: Harvard University Press, pp. 213–28.
Alford, C. (2006) *Psychology and the Natural Law of Reparation*. Cambridge: Cambridge University Press.
Allison, R. (2000) Doctor Driven Out of Home by Vigilantes. *The Guardian*, August 29.
Anderson, B. R. O'G. (1983) *Imagined Communities: Reflections on the Origin and Spread of Nationalism*. London: Verso; revised edition 2006.
Andrade, V. (2007) The 'Uncanny', the Sacred and the Narcissism of Culture: The Development of the Ego and the Progress of Civilization. *International Journal of Psychoanalysis* 88: 1019–37.
Anon. (1954/2005) *A Woman in Berlin*. London: Virago Press.
Anon. [Ferenczi] (1933) Ontogenesis. *Psychoanalytic Quarterly* 2: 365–403.

Anzieu, D. (1975) *The Group and the Unconscious*. London: Routledge & Kegan, 1984.
Arendt, H. (1978) *The Life of the Mind*. New York: Harcourt
Arlow, J. (1992) Aggression and Vorurteil: Psychoanalytische Betrachtungen zur Ritualmordbeschuldigung gegen die Juden. *Psyche* 46: 1122–32.
Assmann, A. (2013) *Das neue Unbehagen an der Erinnerungskultur: eine Intervention*. München: C.H. Beck.
Bajohr, F. and Wildt, M. (2009) *Volksgemeinschaft: neue Forschungen zur Gesellschaft des Nationalsozialismus*. Frankfurt am Main: Fischer.
Bartov, O. (1992) Time Present and Time Past: The *Historikerstreit* and German Reunification. *New German Critique* 55: 173–90.
Bartov, O. (1998) Defining Enemies, Making Victims: Germans, Jews, and the Holocaust. *The American Historical Review* 103(3): 771–816.
Beattie, A. (2006) The Victims of Totalitarianism and the Centrality of Nazi Genocide: Continuity and Change in German Commemorative Politics. In Niven, B. (ed.) *Germans as Victims: Remembering the Past in Contemporary Germany*. Houndmills: Palgrave Macmillan, pp. 147–163.
Benz, W. (2001) Anti-semitism and Philosemitism. In Klessmann, C. (ed.) *The Divided Past: Re-writing Post-war history*. Oxford/New York: Berg, pp. 149–70.
Berger, S. (1995) Historians and Nation-Building in Germany After Reunification. *Past & Present* 148: 187–222.
Bergmann, W. (1997) Antisemitism and Xenophobia in Germany Since Reunification. In Kurthen, H., Bergmann, W. and Erb, R. (eds.) *Antisemitism and Xenophobia in Germany After Unification*. New York/Oxford: Oxford University Press, pp. 21–38.
Bion, W. R. (1957a) Differentiation of the Psychotic from the Non-psychotic Personalities. *International Journal of Psychoanalysis* 38: 266–75. In *Second Thoughts: Selected Papers on Psycho-Analysis*. London: William Heinemann, 1967; Karnac, 1984, pp. 43–64.
Bion, W. R. (1957b) On Arrogance. *International Journal of Psychoanalysis* 39: 144–6. In *Second Thoughts: Selected Papers on Psycho-Analysis*. London: William Heinemann, 1967; Karnac, 1984, pp. 86–92.
Bion, W. R. (1958) On Hallucination. *International Journal of Psychoanalysis* 39: 341–9. In *Second Thoughts: Selected Papers on Psycho-Analysis*. London: William Heinemann, 1967; Karnac, 1984, pp. 65–85.
Bion, W. R. (1962) A Psycho-Analytic Study of Thinking. *International Journal of Psychoanalysis* 43: 306–10; A Theory of Thinking. In *Second Thoughts: Selected Papers on Psycho-Analysis*. London: William Heinemann, 1967; Karnac, 1984, pp. 110–19.

Bion, W. R. (1970) *Attention and Interpretation: A Scientific Approach to Insight in Psycho-Analysis and Groups*. London: Tavistock.

Bleger, J. (1967) Psycho-Analysis of the Psycho-Analytic Frame. *International Journal of Psychoanalysis* 48: 511–19.

Bleger, J. (1967/2013) *Symbiosis and Ambiguity: A Psychoanalytical Study*. London/New York: Routledge.

Bleger, J. (1974) Schizophrenia, Autism and Symbiosis. *Contemporary Psychoanalysis* 10: 19–25.

Blok, A. (1998) The Narcissism of Minor Differences. *European Journal of Social Theory* 1(1): 33–56.

Blok, A. (2001) *Honour and Violence*. Cambridge: Polity.

Bohleber, W. (1992) Nationalismus, Fremdenhass und Antisemitismus: Psychoanalytische Überlegungen. *Psyche* 46: 689–709.

Bohleber, W. (1995) The Presence of the Past – Xenophobia and Rightwing Extremism in the Federal Republic of Germany: Psychoanalytic Reflections. *American Imago* 52: 329–44.

Bohleber, W. (1997) Die Konstrucktion imaginärer Gemeinschaften und das Bild von den Juden – umbewusste Determinanten des Antisemitismus in Deutschland. *Psyche* 51: 570–605.

Britton, R. (1989) The Missing Link: Parental Sexuality and the Oedipus Complex. In Britton, R., Feldman, M. and O'Shaughnessy, E. (eds.) *The Oedipus Complex Today: Clinical Implications*. London: Karnac Books, pp. 83–101.

Britton, R. (2015) *Between Mind and Brain: Models of the Mind and Models in the Mind*. London: Karnac.

Brockhaus, G. (2008) Die Unfähigkeit zu trauern als Analyse und als Abweher der NS-Erbshaft. In Brockhaus, G. (Hg.) *Ist 'Die Unfähigkeit zu trauern' noch actuell? Eine interdisziplinäre Diskussion*. *Psychosozial* 31, nr 114 (4) (special issue), pp. 29–39.

Broszat, M. (1970) Soziale Motivation und Führer-Bindung des Nationalsozialismus. *Vierteljahrshefte für Zeitgeschichte* 18(4): 392–409.

Broszat, M. and Friedländer, S. (1988) A Controversy About the Historicization of National Socialism. *New German Critique* 44: 85–126.

Brunkhorst, H., Kreide, R. and Lafont, C. (Eds.) (2009) *Habermas Handbuch*. Weimar: J. B. Meltzer and C. E. Poeschel.

Burrin, P. (2005) *Nazi Anti-semitism: From Prejudice to the Holocaust*. New York/London: The New Press.

Chasseguet-Smirgel, J. (1985a) *The Ego Ideal: A Psychoanalytic Essay on the Malady of the Ideal*. London: Free Association Books.

Chasseguet-Smirgel, J. (1985b) *Creativity and Perversion*. London: Free Association Books.
Church Times. (2013) https://www.churchtimes.co.uk/articles/2013/12-april/news/uk/thatcher-clashed-with-church,-despite-her-faith. Accessed 8.3.2017.
Claasen, H. (1947) *Gesang im Feuerofen*. Köln: Überreste einer deutshen Stadt.
Collingwood, R. G. (1946/1993) *The Idea of History*. Oxford/New York: Oxford University Press.
Confino, A. (2014) *A World Without Jews: The Nazi Imagination from Persecution to Genocide*. New Haven/London: Yale University Press.
Culpepper, M. (2014) Remembrance Day: The War Memorials of Ernst Barlach. https://shrineodreams.wordpress.com/2014/11/11/remembrance-day-the-war-memorials-of-ernst-barlach/. Accessed 27.10.2016.
Dahmer, H. (1982) In Memoriam Alexander Mitscherlich. *Psyche – Zeitschrift für Psychoanalyse* 36: 1071–2.
Davids, M. Fakhry (2011) *Internal Racism: A Psychoanalytic Approach to Race and Difference*. Houndmills: Palgrave Macmillan.
Davids, M. Fakhry (2016) Psychoanalysis and Palestine-Israel: A Personal Angle. *Psychoanalysis, Culture and Society* 21(1): 41–58.
Diebow, H. (1941) *Juden in USA*. Berlin: Franz Eher Verlag.
Domansky, E. (1993) Die gespaltene Erinnerung. In Köppen, M. (ed.) *Kunst und Literatur nach Auschwitz*. Berlin: Erich Schmidt Verlag, pp. 178–96.
Eley, G. (1988) Nazism, Politics and the Image of the Past: Thoughts on the West German *Historikerstreit* 1986–1987. *Past and Present* 121: 171–208.
Eley, G. (2004) The Unease of History: Settling Accounts with the East German Past. *History Workshop Journal* 57: 175–201.
Erdheim, M. (1984) *Die gesellschaftliche Produktion von Unbewusstheit: Eine Einführung in den ethnopsychonalytischen Prozess*. Frankfurt aM: Suhrkamp.
Erlich, S., Erlich-Ginor, M. and Beland, H. (eds.) 2009 *Fed with Tears, Poisoned with Milk*. Giessen: Psychosozial Verlag.
Evans, R. (2002) *Telling Lies About Hitler: The Holocaust, History and the David Irving Trial*. London/New York: Verso.
Evans, R. (2015) *The Third Reich in History and Memory*. London: Little, Brown.
Faimberg, H. (2005) *The Telescoping of Generations: Listening to the Narcissistic Links Between Generations*. London: Routledge.
Federn, P. (1936) On the Distinction Between Healthy and Normal Narcissism. *Imago* 22: 5–39. In Weiss, E. (ed.) *Ego Psychology and the Psychoses*; Karnac, 1977, pp. 323–64.

Figlio, K. (1998) Historical Imagination/Psychoanalytic Imagination. *History Workshop Journal* 45: 199–221.
Figlio, K. (2000) *Psychoanalysis, Science and Masculinity*. London/Philadelphia: Whurr/Brunner-Routledge, 2001.
Figlio, K. (2006) The Absolute State of Mind in Society and the Individual. *Psychoanalysis, Culture and Society* 11(2): 119–43.
Figlio, K. (2010) Phallic and Seminal Masculinity: A Theoretical and Clinical Confusion. *International Journal of Psychoanalysis* 91(1): 119–39.
Figlio, K. (2012a) The Hatred and Exclusion of Likeness. In Auestad, L. (ed.) *Psychoanalysis and Politics: Exclusions and the Politics of Representation*. London: Karnac.
Figlio, K. (2012b) Devaluing and Repairing the Internal World. *Psychoanalysis, Culture and Society* 17(1): 87–91.
Figlio, K. (2013) Projective Identification – An Overview. *Encyclopedia of Critical Psychology*. New York: Springer Verlag, 2013.
Firth, R. (1966) Twins, Birds and Vegetables: Problems of Identification in Primitive Religious Thought. *Man, New Series* 1: 1–17.
Fornari, F. (1966) *The Psychoanalysis of War*. Bloomington/London: Indiana University Press, 1975.
Freud, S. (1899) Screen Memories. *The Standard Edition of the Complete Psychological Works of Sigmund Freud* 3: 299–322.
Freud, S. (1909) Notes upon a Case of Obsessional Neurosis. *The Standard Edition of the Complete Psychological Works of Sigmund Freud* 10: 151–318.
Freud, S. (1910) A Special Type of Choice of Object Made by Men (Contributions to the Psychology of Love I). *The Standard Edition of the Complete Psychological Works of Sigmund Freud* 11: 163–75.
Freud, S. (1912) On the Universal Tendency to Debasement in the Sphere of Love (Contributions to the Psychology of Love II). *The Standard Edition of the Complete Psychological Works of Sigmund Freud* 11: 177–90.
Freud, S. (1913[1912–13]) Totem and Taboo. *The Standard Edition of the Complete Psychological Works of Sigmund Freud* 13: 1–165.
Freud, S. (1914a) On Narcissism: An Introduction. *The Standard Edition of the Complete Psychological Works of Sigmund Freud* 14: 68–102.
Freud, S. (1914b) Remembering, Repeating and Working-Through (Further Recommendations on the Technique of Psycho-Analysis II). *The Standard Edition of the Complete Psychological Works of Sigmund Freud* 12: 145–56.
Freud, S. (1915a) Instincts and Their Vicissistudes. *The Standard Edition of the Complete Psychological Works of Sigmund Freud* 14: 109–40.

Freud, S. (1915b) Repression. *The Standard Edition of the Complete Psychological Works of Sigmund Freud* 14: 141–58.

Freud, S. (1916) Some Character-Types Met with in Psycho-Analytic Work. *The Standard Edition of the Complete Psychological Works of Sigmund Freud* 14: 309–31.

Freud, S. (1917[1915]) Mourning and Melancholia. *The Standard Edition of the Complete Psychological Works of Sigmund Freud* 14: 237–58.

Freud, S. (1918[1914]) *From the History of an Infantile Neurosis. The Standard Edition of the Complete Psychological Works of Sigmund Freud* 17: 1–124.

Freud, S. (1918[1917]) The Taboo of Virginity (Contributions to the Psychology of Love III). *The Standard Edition of the Complete Psychological Works of Sigmund Freud* 11: 191–208.

Freud, S. (1919) The Uncanny. *The Standard Edition of the Complete Psychological Works of Sigmund Freud* 17: 217–56.

Freud, S. (1921) *Group Psychology and the Analysis of the Ego. The Standard Edition of the Complete Psychological Works of Sigmund Freud* 18: 65–144.

Freud, S. (1923[1922]) Two Encyclopaedia Articles: (A) Psychoanalysis. *The Standard Edition of the Complete Psychological Works of Sigmund Freud* 18: 235–54.

Freud, S. (1923) *The Ego and the Id. The Standard Edition of the Complete Psychological Works of Sigmund Freud* 19: 1–66.

Freud, S. (1924) The Loss of Reality in Neurosis and Psychosis. *The Standard Edition of the Complete Psychological Works of Sigmund Freud* 19: 181–8.

Freud, S. (1926) *Inhibitions, Symptoms and Anxiety. The Standard Edition of the Complete Psychological Works of Sigmund Freud* 20: 75–176.

Freud, S. (1927) Fetishism. *The Standard Edition of the Complete Psychological Works of Sigmund Freud* 21: 147–58.

Freud, S. (1930) *Civilization and Its Discontents. The Standard Edition of the Complete Psychological Works of Sigmund Freud* 21: 57–146.

Freud, S. (1933[1932]) *New Introductory Lectures on Psycho-Analysis. The Standard Edition of the Complete Psychological Works of Sigmund Freud* 22: 1–182.

Freud, S. (1939) *Moses and Monotheism. The Standard Edition of the Complete Psychological Works of Sigmund Freud* 23: 3–137.

Freud, S. (1940[1938]a) An Outline of Psychoanalysis. *The Standard Edition of the Complete Psychological Works of Sigmund Freud* 23: 141–208.

Freud, S. (1940[1938]b) Splitting of the Ego in the Process of Defence. *The Standard Edition of the Complete Psychological Works of Sigmund Freud* 23: 271–8.

Frie, R. (2011) Irreducible Cultural Contexts: German-Jewish Experience, Identity, and Trauma in a Bilingual Analysis. *International Journal of Psychoanalytic Self Psychology* 6: 136–58.
Frie, R. (2017) *Not in My Family: German Memory and Responsibility After the Holocaust*. NY: Oxford University Press.
Friedländer, S. (1978) *History and Psychoanalysis: an Inquiry into the Possibilities and Limits of Psychohistory*. New York/London: Holmes & Meier Publishers.
Friedländer, S. (1984) *Reflections of Nazism: An Essay on Kitsch and Death*. New York: Harper & Row.
Friedländer, S. (1993) *Memory, History and the Extermination of the Jews of Europe*. Bloomington/Indianapolis: Indiana University Press.
Friedländer, S. (1997) *The Years of Persecution: Nazi Germany & the Jews 1933–1939*. London: Weidenfeld & Nicholson/Phoenix.
Friedländer, S. (2000) History, Memory, and the Historian: Dilemmas and Responsibilities. *New German Critique* 80: 3–15.
Friedrich, J. (2002) *Der Brand: Deutschland im Bombenkrieg 1940–1945*. Berlin: Propyläen.
Frohn, A. (1991) *Holocaust and Shilumin: The Policy of Wiedergutmachung in the Early 1950s. (German Historical Institute Occasional Paper 2)*. Washington, DC: German Historical Instiute.
Frosh, S. (2005) *Hate and the 'Jewish Science': Anti-semitism, Nazism and Psychoanalysis*. Houndmills, Basingstoke: Palgrave Macmillan.
Frosh, S. (2010) *Psychoanalysis Outside the Clinic: Interventions in Psychosocial Studies*. Houndmills: Palgrave Macmillan.
Fuchs, A. (2012) *After the Dresden Bombing: Pathways of Memory, 1945 to the Present*. Basingstoke: Palgrave Macmillan.
Fulbrook, M. (1999) *German National Identity after the Holocaust*. Cambridge: Polity.
Fulbrook, M. (2016) Questionable Concepts: Trust, Distrust and Normalisation. In *Erfahrung, Erinnerung, Geschichtsschreibung: Neue Perspektiven auf die deutschen Diktaturen*. Weimar: Wallstein Verlag, pp. 62–110.
Gabbard, G. (1993) On Hate in Love Relationships: The Narcissism of Minor Differences Revisited. *Psychoanalytic Quarterly* 62: 229–38.
Gallagher, E. (n.d.) The Vietnam Wall Controversy. Lehigh University Digital Library. http://digital.lib.lehigh.edu/trial/vietnam/about/. Accessed 27.10.2016. Brief overview, with list of surces.
Girard, R. (1988) *Violence and the Sacred*. London: Athlone.
Glover, E. (1947) *War, Sadism and Pacifism*. London: Allen & Unwin.

Goldhagen, D. (1996) *Htiler's Willing Executioners. Ordinary Germans and the Holocaust.* New York/London: Alfred A. Knopf/Little Brown and Company.

Goschler, C. (2008) *Schuld und Schulden: Die Politik der Wiedergutmachung fur NS-Verfolgte seit 1945* (2nd edition). Gottingen: Wallstein Verlag.

Graeber, D. (2011) *Debt: The First 5000 Years.* New York: Melville House Publishing.

Greenberg, J. and Mitchell, S. (1983) *Object Relations Theory in Psychoanalysis.* Cambridge, MA: Harvard University Press.

Grubrich-Simitis, I. (1984) From Concretism to Metaphor – Thoughts on Some Theoretical and Technical Aspects of the Psychoanalytic Work with Children of Holocaust Survivors. *The Psychoanalytic Study of the Child* 39: 301–19.

Habermas, J. (1972) *Knowledge and Human Interests.* London: Heinemann.

Habermas, J. (1986a) A Kind of Settlement of Damages: The Apologetic Tendencies in German Historical Writing. Die Zeit, July 11; English translation in Knowlton, J. and Gates, T. (eds. and translators) *Forever in the Shadow of Hitler? Original Documents of the Historikerstreit, the Controversy Concerning the Singularity of the Holocaust.* Atlantic Highlands, New Jersey: Humanities Press, 1993, pp. 34–44; extended version in Habermas, J. One Sort of Compensation: Apologetic Tendencies in German Historiography. In *The New Conservatism: Cultural Criticism and the Historians' Debate.* London: Polity Press, 1989, pp. 212–28.

Habermas, J. (1986b) On the Public Use of History. *Die Zeit*, November 7. In Habermas, J. In *The New Conservatism: Cultural Criticism and the Historians' Debate.* London: Polity Press, 1989, pp. 229–40.

Habermas, J. (1988) *On the Logic of the Social Sciences.* London: Polity Press, 1990.

Habermas, J. (1989) *The New Conservatism: Cultural Criticism and the Historians' Debate.* London: Polity Press.

Habermas, J. (1998) *The Inclusion of the Other: Studies in Political Theory.* Cambridge, MA: Massachusetts Institute of Technology; Cambridge, Polity Press, 1999.

Hartman, G. (ed.) (1986) *Bitburg in Moral and Political Perspective.* Bloomington: Indiana University Press.

Hass, K. (1998) *Carried to the Wall: American Memory and the Vietnam Veterans Memorial.* Berkeley/Los Angeles/London: University of California Press.

Herf, J. (1997) *Divided Memory: The Nazi Past in the Two Germanies.* Cambridge, MA/London: Harvard University Press.

Herf, J. (2006) *The Jewish Enemy: Nazi Propaganda During World War II and the Holocaust*. Cambridge, MA/London: Harvard University Press.

Hillgruber, A. (1984) War in the East and the Extermination of the Jews. Yad Vashem. https://www.yadvashem.org/untoldstories/documents/studies/Andreas_Hillgruber.pdf. Accessed 31.5.2016.

Hillgruber, A. (1986) *Zweierlei Untergang: Die Zerschlagung des deutschen Reiches und das Ende des europäischen Judentums*. Berlin: Seidler.

Hinshelwood, R. D. (1986) The Psychotherapist's Role in a Large Psychiatric Institution. *Psychoanalytic Psychotherapy* 2: 207–215

Hinshelwood, R. D. (1987) *What Happens in Groups: Psychoanalysis, the Individual and the Community*. London: Free Association Books.

Hinshelwood, R. D. (1991) *A Dictionary of Kleinian Thought* (2nd edition). London: Free Association Books.

Hinshelwood, R. D. (1997) The Elusive Concept of 'Internal Objects' (1934–1943): Its Role in the Formation of the Klein Group. *International Journal of Psychoanalysis* 78: 877–97.

Hinshelwood, R. D. (2007) Review of Alford, C. (2006) *Psychology and the Natural Law of Reparation*. *Psychoanalysis, Culture and Society* 12(2): 199–202.

Hinshelwood, R. D. (2008) Repression and Splitting: Towards a Method of Conceptual Comparison. *International Journal of Psychoanalysis* 89: 503–21.

Hinshelwood, R. D. and Skogstad, W. (eds.) (2000) *Observing Organizations: Anxiety, Defence and Culture in Health Care*. London/Philadelphia: Routledge.

Hoffer, W. (1954) Defensive Process and Defensive Organization: Their Place in Psychoanalytic Technique. *International Journal of Psychoanalysis* 35: 194–8.

Hopper, E. (1991) Encapsulation as a Defence Against the Fear of Annihilation. *International Journal of Psychoanalysis* 72(4): 607–24.

Hopper, E. (1996) The Social Unconscious in Clinical Work. In *The Social Unconscious: Selected Papers*. London: Jessica Kingsley, 2003, pp. 126–61.

Human Rights Watch/Helsinki (1995) *'Germany for Germans': Xenophobia and Racist Violence in Germany*. New York and elsewhere: Human Rights Watch.

Ignatieff, M. (1994) *Nationalism and the Narcissism of Minor Differences*. Milton Keynes: The Open University.

Ignatieff, M. (1998) *The Warrior's Honor: Ethnic War and the Modern Conscience*. London: Chatto and Windus.

Isaacs, S. (1940) Temper Tantrums in Early Childhood in their Relation to Internal Objects. *International Journal of Psychoanalysis* 21: 280–93.

Jacoby, R. (2011) *Bloodlust: On the Roots of Violence from Cain and Abel to the Present*. New York/London/Sydney: The Free Press

Jager, J. (2002) Fotographie-Errinerungen-Identität.Die Trummeraufnahmen aus deutschen Stadten 1945. In Hillmann, J. und Zimmermann, J. (hrsg.) *Kriegsende 1945 in Deutschland*. München: Oldenberg Verlag, pp. 287–300.

Jaques, E. (1955) Social Systems as a Defence Against Persecutory and Depressive Anxiety: A Contribution to the Psycho-Analytical Study of Social Processes. In Klein, M., Heimann, P. and Money-Kyrle, R. (eds.) *New Directions in Psychoanalysis: The Significance of Infant Conflict in the Pattern of Adult Behaviour*. London: Tavistock Publications, pp. 478–98.

Jaspers, K. (1946) *The Question of German Guilt*. New York: Fordham University Press, 2000.

Jerzak, C. (2015) Memory Politics: The Bombing of Hamburg and Dresden. In Gerstenberg, K. and Nusser, T. (eds.) *Catastrophe and Catharsis. Narratives of Disaster and Redemption in German Culture and Beyond*. Rochester, NY: Boydell & Brewer Ltd, pp. 53–72.

Johnson, E. A. and Reuband, K.-H. (eds.) (2005) *What We Knew: Terror, Mass Murder, and Everday Life in Nazi Germany – An Oral History*. London: John Murray

Jokl, A. M. (1997) *Zwei Fälle zum Thema >Bewältigung der Vergangenheit<*. Frankfurt a.M.: Jüdischer Verlag im Suhrkamp Verlag.

Kansteiner, W. (2002) Finding Meaning in Memory: A Methodological Critique of Collective Memory Studies. *History and Theory* 42(2): 179–97.

Kaplan, T. P. (2009) *The Language of Nazi Genocide: Linguistic Violence and the Struggle of Jewish Ancestry*. Cambridge: Cambridge University Press.

Kauders, A. (2003) History as Censure: 'Repression' and 'Philosemitism' in Postwar Germany. *History & Memory* 15(1): 97–122.

Keenan, K. (1984) A Vietnam Vision: The Making of the Memorial Statue. https://commons.wikimedia.org/w/index.php?title=File%3APress_Release_From_Three_Servicemen_Statue_Dedication_11_Nov._1984.pdf. Accessed 19.05.2017.

Kernberg, O. (2009) The Destruction of Time in Pathological Narcissism. In Fiorini, G. and Canestri, J. (eds.) *The Experience of Time: Psychoanalytic Perspectives*. London: Karnac, pp. 155–74.

Kershaw, I. (1999) 'Working Towards the Führer': Reflections on the Nature of the Hitler Dictatorship. In *Hitler, the Germans, and the Final Solution*. Jerusalem: International Institute for Holocaust Research, Yad Vashem; New Haven, [Conn.]: Yale University Press, 2008, pp. 29–48.

Kershaw, I. (2011) *The End: Hitler's Germany, 1944–45*. London: Allen Lane.

Kershaw, I. (2014) *Volksgemeinschaft*: Potential and Limitations of the Concept. In Streber, M. and Gotto, B. (eds.) *Visions of Community in Nazi Germany: Social Engineering and Private Lives*. Oxford: Oxford University Press, pp. 29–42.

Klein, M. (1928) Note on the Preceding Communication. *International Journal of Psychoanalysis* 9: 255–58.

Klein, M. (1929) Infantile Anxiety-Situations Reflected in a Work of Art and in the Creative Impulse. In *The Writings of Melanie Klein*, vol. I. London: The Hogarth Press and the Institute of Psychoanalysis, 1975, pp. 210–19.

Klein, M. (1930) The Importance of Symbol-Formation in the Development of the Ego. In *The Writings of Melanie Klein*, vol. 1. London: Hogarth and the Institute of Psychoanalysis, 1975, pp. 219–32.

Klein, M. (1932) *The Psychoanalysis of Children*. London: Hogarth and the Institute of Psychoanalysis; revised edition 1975.

Klein, M. (1935) A Contribution to the Psychogenesis of Manic-Depressive States. In *The Writings of Melanie Klein*, vol. 1. London: The Hogarth Press and the Institute of Psychoanalysis, 1975, pp. 262–89.

Klein, M. (1937) Love, Guilt and Reparation. In *The Writings of Melanie Klein*, vol. 1. London: Hogarth and the Institute of Psychoanalysis, 1975, pp. 306–43.

Klein, M. (1940) Mourning and Its Relation to Manic-Depressive States. In *The Writings of Melanie Klein*, vol. 1. London: Hogarth and the Institute of Psychoanalysis, 1975, pp. 344–69.

Klein, M. (1945) The Oedipus Complex in the Light of Early Anxieties. In *The Writings of Melanie Klein*, vol. 1. London: Hogarth and the Institute of Psychoanalysis, 1975, pp. 370–419.

Klein, M. (1946) Notes on Some Schizoid Mechanisms. In *The Writings of Melanie Klein*, vol. 3. London: Hogarth and the Institute of Psychoanalysis, 1975, pp. 1–24.

Klein, M. (1957) Envy and Gratitude. In *The Writings of Melanie Klein*, vol. 3. London: Hogarth and the Institute of Psychoanalysis, 1975, pp. 176–235.

Klein, M. (1961) *Narrative of a Child Analysis: The Conduct of the Psycho-Analysis of Children as Seen in the Treatment of a Ten-Year-Old Boy. The Writings of Melanie Klein*, vol. 4. London: Hogarth and the Institute of Psychoanalysis, 1975.

Knowlton, J. and Cates, T. (eds.) (1993) *Forever in the Shadow of Hitler?: The Dispute About the Germans' Understanding of History, Original Documents of the Historikerstreit, the Controversy Concerning the Singularity of the Holocaust*. Atlantic Highlands, NJ: Humanities Press.

Kohte-Meyer, I. (1994) 'Ich bin fremd, so wie ich bin.' – Migrationserleben, Ich-Identität und Neurose. *Praxis der Kinderpsychologie und Kinderpsychiatrie* 43: 253–9.

Kohte-Meyer, I. (2000) A Derailed Dialogue: Unexpected Difficulties in the Psychoanalytic Work with Patients from East Germany. *Psychoanalytic Review* 87:417–28.

Kohut, H. (1971) *The Analysis of the Self: A Systematic Approach to the Psychoanalytic Treatment of Narcissistic Personality Disorders*. New York: International Universities Press.

Kohut, T. A. (2012) *A German Generation: An Experiential History of the Twentieth Century*. New Haven/London: Yale University Press.

Krondorfer, B. (1995) *Remembrance and Reconciliation: Encounters Between Young Jews and Germans*. New Haven/London: Yale University Press.

Kurthen, H. (1997) Antisemitism and Xenophobia in United Germany: How the Burden of the Past Affects the Present. In Kurthen, H., Bergmann, W. and Erb, R. (eds.) *Antisemitism and Xenophobia in Germany After Unification*. New York/Oxford: Oxford University Press, pp. 39–87.

Kurthen, H., Bergmann, W. and Erb, R. (1997) Introduction: Post-unification Challenges to German Democracy. In Kurthen, H., Bergmann, W. and Erb, R. (eds.) *Antisemitism and Xenophobia in Germany After Unification*. New York/Oxford: Oxford University Press, pp. 3–17.

LaCapra, D. (1997) Revisiting the Historians' Debate: Mourning and Genocide. *History and Memory* 9(1/2): 80–112.

Langer, L. (1991) *Holocaust Testimonies: The Ruins of Memory*. New Haven/London: Yale University Press.

Laplanche, J. and Pontalis, J.-B. (1980) *The Language of Psycho-Analysis*. London: The Hogarth Press and the Institute of Psycho-Analysis.

Lipstadt, D. (1994) *Denying the Holocaust: The Growing Assault on Truth and Memory*. New York: The Free Press.

Lipstadt, D. (2006) *History on Trial: My Day in Court with David Irving*. New York: Harper Perennial.

Longerich, P. (2006) *Davon Haben Wir Nichts Gewusst: die Deutschen und die Judenverfolgung 1933–1945*. Munich: Siedler.

Lüdtke, A. (1993) 'Coming to Terms with the Past': Illusions of Remembering: Ways of Forgetting Nazism in West Germany. *The Journal of Modern History* 65(3): 542–72.

Luppes, J. (2010) *To Our Dead: Local Expellee Monuments and the Contestation of German Post-war Memory* (PhD thesis). University of Michigan.

Lupu, N. (2003) Memory Vanished, Absent, and Confined: The Counter-Memorial Project in the 1980s and 1990s. *History and Memory* 15(2): 130–64.
Maier, C. (1988) *The Unmasterable Past: History, Holocaust, and German National Identity*. Cambridge, MA/London: Harvard University Press.
Mancia, M. and Meltzer, D. (1981) Ego Ideal Functions and the Psychoanalytical Process. *International Journal of Psychoanalysis* 62: 243–9.
Marcuse, H. (1997) *The National Memorial to the Victims of War and Tyranny: From Conflict to Consensus*. Paper presented to the German Studies Association Conference, September 25, 1997, Washington, DC. Retrieved from http://www.history.ucsb.edu/faculty/marcuse/present/neuewach.htm. Accessed 22.6.2011.
Margalit, G. (2010) *Guilt, Suffering, and Memory: Germany Remembers Its Dead of World War II*. Bloomington/Indianapolis: Indiana University Press.
McMahon, P. and Western, J. (2009) The Death of Dayton: How to Stop Bosnia from Falling Apart. *Foreign Affairs* 88: 69–83.
McNeill, W. (1995) *Keeping Together in Time: Dance and Drill in Human History*. Cambridge, MA: Harvard University Press.
Menzies Lyth, I. (1959) The Functioning of Social Systems as a Defence Against Anxiety. In *Containing Anxiety in Institutions: Selected Essays*, vol. 1. London: Free Association Books, 1988, pp. 43–88.
Mitchell, J. (2003) *Siblings*. Cambridge: Polity.
Mitscherlich, M. (1987) *Erinerungsarbeit zur Psychoanalyse der Unfähigkeit zu trauern*. Frankfurt aM: Fischer.
Mitscherlich, A. and Mitscherlich, M. (1967/1975) *The Inability to Mourn: Principles of Collective Behaviour*. Munich: Piper & Co. Verlag; English translation, New York: Grove Press.
Mitscherlich-Nielsen, M. (1983) Antisemitismus – eine Männerkrankheit? *Psyche – Zeitschrift für Psychoanalyse* 37(1): 41–54.
Mitscherlich-Nielsen, M. (1992) Die (Un)Fähigkeit zu trauern in Ost- und Westdeutschland.Was Trauerarbeit heissen könnte. *Psyche – Zeitschrift für Psychoanalyse* 46: 406–18.
Moeller, R. (2006) On the History of Man-Made Destruction: Loss, Death, Memory, and Germany in the Bombing War. *History Workshop Journal* 61: 103–34.
Mommsen, H. (1981) Die Stellung Hitler im nationalsozialistischen Hitler's Herrschaftssystem. In Hirschfeld, G. u. Kenttenacker, L. (Hg.) *Der 'Führerstaat': Mythos u. Realität: Studien zur Struktur u. Politik des Dritten Reiches*. Stuttgart: Klett-Cotta. English translation, Hitler's Position in the

Nazi System. In *From Weimar to Auschwitz: Essays in German History*. Cambridge: Polity, 1991, pp. 163–88.

Mommsen, H. (1983) Die Realisieren des Utopischen: Die 'Endlösung der Judenfrage' im 'Dritten Reich'. *Geschichte und Gesellschaft* 9(3): 381–420; English translation, The Realization of the Unthinkable: The 'Final Solution of the Jewish Question' in the 'Third Reich'. In *From Weimar to Auschwitz: Essays in German History*. Cambridge: Polity, 1991, pp. 224–349.

Money-Kyrle, R. (1951a) Some Aspects of State and Character in Germany. In *The Collected Papers of Roger Money-Kyrle*. Strath Tay: Clunie Press, 1978, pp. 229–44.

Money-Kyrle, R. (1951b) *Psychoanalysis and Politics*. London: Duckworth.

Morris, E. and McNamara, R. (2003) *The Fog of War*. New York: Sony Pictures Classics.

Mosse, G. (1990) *Fallen Soldiers: Reshaping the Memory of the World Wars*. New York/London: Oxford University Press.

Müller, J.-W. (2006) On the Origins of Constitutional Patriotism. *Contemporary Political Theory* 5: 278–96.

Müller, J.-W. (2008) A General Theory of Constitutional Patriotism. *I•CON* 6(1): 72–95.

Murer, J. (2010) Institutionalizing Enemies: The Consequences of Reifying Projection in Post-conflict Environments. *Psychoanalysis, Culture & Society* 15(1): 1–19.

Niven, B. (2006) The GDR and Memory of the Bombing of Dresden. In Niven, B. (ed.) *Germans as Victims: Remembering the Past in Contemporary Germany*. Basingstoke: Palgrave Macmillan, pp. 109–29.

Noro, T. (2014) *A Study on the Motivation of Sexual Violence in WWII: The Conflict of Masculinity in Warfare* (PhD thesis). Colchester: University of Essex.

O'Shaughnessy, E. (1981) A Clinical Study of a Defensive Organization. *International Journal of Psychoanalysis* 62: 359–69.

O'Shaughnessy, E. (1992) Enclaves and Excursions. *International Journal of Psychoanalysis* 73: 603–11.

Outhwaite, W. (2017) Reconstructing Social Theory, History and Practice. *Current Perspectives in Social Theory* 35: 211–23.

Overy, R. (2013) *The Bombing War: Europe 1939–1945*. London: Allen Lane.

Parin, P. (1977) Das Ich und die Anpassungs-Mechanismen. *Psyche – Zeitschrift für Psychoanalyse* 31(6):481–515.

Partners in Confronting Collective Atrocities. www.p-cca.org.

Paterson, P. (Lieutenant Commander, U. S. Navy) (2008) The Truth About Tonkin. *Naval History Magazine* 22(1): no page numbers. http://www.usni.org/magazines/navalhistory/2008-02/truth-about-tonkin. Accessed 3.11.2016.

Perels, J. (2015) *Die Nationalsozialismus als Problem der Gegenwart*. Frankfurt aM: Peter Lang.

Peter, R. (1949) *Eine Kamera klagt an*. Dresden: Desdener Verlagsgesellschaft.

Pew Research Center (2012) Global Religious Landscape. http://www.pewforum.org/2012/12/18/global-religious-landscape-jew. Accessed 9.5.2017.

Pick, D. (2012) *The Pursuit of the Nazi Mind: Hitler, Hess and the Analysts*. Oxford: Oxford University Press.

Pidd, H. (2012) Germany's Far Right Marches Out of the Shadows. *The Guardian*, February 23, p. 25.

Pók, A. (2006) The Politics of Hatred: Scapegoating in Inter-war Hungary. In Turda, M. and Weindling, P. (eds.) *Blood and Homeland: Eugenics and Racial Nationalism in Central and Southeastern Europe 1900–1940*. Budapest/NewYork: Central European Press, pp. 375–88.

Quindeau, I. (2008) Umgeschriebene Erinnerungen. Psychoanalytische Anmerkungen zu den Erregungen der Erinneringskultur. In Brockhaus, G. (Hg.) *Ist 'Die Unfähigkeit zu trauern' noch actuell? Eine interdisziplinäre Diskussion*. Psychosozial 31nr 114 (4): 79–87.

Rank, O. (1914) *The Double: A Psychoanalytic Study*. Chapel Hill, NC: University of North Carolina Press, 1971.

Reinhard, O. (2010) *Braucht die Erinnerung 19000 Namen? Sächsische Zeitung (SZ-Online.De)* 7.10.2010 http://www.sz-online.de/nachrichten/braucht-die-erinnerung-19000-namen-107193.html. Accessed 27.10.2016.

Rhode, E. (1994) *Psychotic Metaphysics*. London: Karnac.

Richards, B. (1987) Military Mobilisations of the Unconscious. *Free Associations* 1: 11–26.

Riviere, J. (1929) Womanliness as a Masquerade. *International Journal of Psychoaanalysis* 10: 303–13.

Röder, W. and Strauss, H. A. (eds.) (1980–83) *Biographisches Handbuch der deutschsprachigen Emigranten nach 1933* (*International Biographical Dictionary of Central European Emigrés 1933–1945*), 4 vols. München/New York/London/Paris: K.G. Saur.

Roper, L. (1994) *Oedipus and the Devil: Witchcraft, Religion and Sexuality in Early Modern Europe: Witchcraft, Sexuality and Religion, 1500–1700*. London/New York: Routledge.

Rosenfeld, H. (1952) Transference-Phenomena and Transference-Analysis in an Acute Catatonic Schizophrenic Patient. *International Journal of Psychoanalysis* 33: 457–64; In *Psychotic States: A Psychoanalytical Approach*. London: Hogarth, 1965, pp. 104–16.

Rosenfeld, H. (1964) On the Psychopathology of Narcissism a Clinical Approach. *International Journal of Psychoanalysis* 45: 332–7.

Rosenfeld, H. (1987) *Impasse and Interpretation: Therapeutic and Anti-therapeutic Factors in the Psychoanalytic Treatment of Psychotic, Borderline, and Neurotic Patents*. London: Routledge.

Rothe, J. (2009) *Das (Nicht-)Sprechen über die Judenvernichtung: Psychische Weiterwirkingen des Holocaust in mehreren Generationen nicht-jüdischer Deutscher*. Giessen: Psychozial Verlag.

Rothe, K. (2012) Anti-semitism in Germany Today and the Intergenerational Transmission of Guilt and Shame. *Psychoanalysis, Culture, and Society* 17(1): 16–34.

Rustin, M. (1991) *The Good Society and the Inner World: Psychoanalysis, Politics and Culture*. London/New York: Verso.

Sapisochin, G. (1999) 'My Heart Belongs to Daddy': Some Reflections on the Difference Between the Generations as an Organizer of the Triangular Structure of the Mind. *International Journal of Psychoanalysis* 80: 755–67.

Schlink, B. (2009) *Guilt About the Past*. St Lucia, Qld: University of Queensland Press.

Schulze, R. (2006) The Politics of Memory: Flight and Expulsion of German Populations After the Second World War and German Collective Memory. *National Identities* 8: 367–82.

Schwab, G. (2010) *Haunting Legacies: Violent Histories and Transgenerational Trauma*. New York: Columbia University Press.

Scott, J. (2012) The Incommensurability of Psychoanalysis and History. *History and Theory* 51: 63–83.

Sebald, W. G. (2003) *On the Natural History of Destruction*. London: Hamish Hamilton.

Segal, H. (1972) A Delusional System as a Defence Against the Re-emergence of a Catastrophic Situation. *International Journal of Psychoanalysis* 53: 393–401. In *Psychoanalysis, Literature and War: Papers 1972–1995*. London/New York: Routledge, 1997, pp. 49–63.

Segal, H. (1981) *The Works of Hannah Segal: A Kleinian Approach to Clinical Practice*. New York: Jason Aronson.

Segal, H. (1987) Silence Is the Real Crime. *International Review of Psychoanalysis* 14: 3–12. In *Psychoanalysis, Literature and War: Papers 1972–1995*. London/New York: Routledge, 1997, pp. 143–56.

Segal, H. (1995) From Hiroshima to the Gulf War and After: Socio-Political Expressions of Ambivalence. In *Psychoanalysis, Literature and War: Papers 1972–1995*. London/New York: Routledge, 1997, pp. 157–68.

Sittel, D. (2011) *Rede des zweiten Bürgermeister Detlef Sittel auf dem Dresdner Heidefriedhof.* https://www.sachsen-fernsehen.de/?s=detlef+sittel Accessed 19.05.2017.
Spillius, E. and O'Shaughnessy, E. (eds.) (2012) *Projective Identification: The Fate of a Concept.* London: Routledge.
Steiner, J. (1993) *Psychic Retreats: Pathological Organizations in Psychotic, Neurotic and Borderline Patients.* London/New York: Routledge.
Sternberger, D. (1979) Verfassungspatriotismus. *Frankfurter Allgemeine Zeitung,* May 23.
Strachey, J. (1934) The Nature of the Therapeutic Action of Psycho-Analysis. *International Journal of PsychoAnalysis* 15: 127–59.
Streeck-Fischer, A. (2000) Vergangene und gegenwärtige Traumatisierung – jugentliche Skinheads in Deutschland. In Opher-Cohn, L. et al. (eds.) *Das Ende der Sprachlosigkeit? Auswirkungen traumatischer Holocaust-Erfahrungen über mehrere Generationen* (2nd edition). Giessen: Psychosozial Verlag, pp. 51–70.
Vetlesen, A. J. (2005) *Evil and Human Agency: Understanding Collective Evildoing.* Cambridge: Cambridge University Press.
Volkan, V. (1986) The Narcissism of Minor Differences in the Psychological Gap Between Opposing Nations. *Psychoanalytic Inquiry* 6: 175–91.
Volkan, V. (2006) *Killing in the Name of Identity: A Study of Bloody Conflicts.* Charlottesville: Pitchstone Publishing
Wangh, M. (1962) Psychoanalytische Betrachtungen zur Dynamik und Genese des Vorurteils, des Antisemitismus und des Nazismus. *Psyche – Zeitschrift für Psychoanalyse* 16: 273–84.
Wangh, M. (1968) A Psychogenic Factor in the Recurrence of War. *International Journal of Psychoanalysis* 49: 319–23.
Weil, F. (1997) Ethnic Intolerance, Extremism and Democratic Attitudes in Germany Since Reunification. In Kurthen, H., Bergmann, W. and Erb, R. (eds.) *Antisemitism and Xenophobia in Germany After Unification.* New York/Oxford: Oxford University Press, pp. 110–42.
Wetzel, J. (1997) Antisemitism Among Right-Wing Extremist Groups, Organizations, and Parties in Post-unification Germany. In Kurthen, H., Bergmann, W. and Erb, R. (eds.) *Antisemitism and Xenophobia in Germany After Unification.* New York/Oxford: Oxford University Press, pp. 159–73.
Wieland, C. (2000) *The Undead Mother: Psychoanalytic Explorations of Masculinity, Feminintiy and Matricide.* London: Rebus Press.
Wieland, C. (2015) *The Fascist State of Mind and the Manufacturing of Masculinity.* London/New York: Routledge.

Williams, A. H. (1998) *Cruelty, Violence and Murder: Understanding the Criminal Mind*. London: Karnac.
Winnicott, C. (1980) Fear of Breakdown: A Clinical Example. *International Journal of Psychoanalysis* 61: 351–7.
Winnicott, D. W. (1949) Hate in the Counter-Transference. *International Journal of Psychoanalysis* 30: 69–74.
Winnicott, D. W. (1974) Fear of Breakdown. *International Review of Psychoanalysis* 1: 103–7.
Young, J. (1993) *The Texture of Memory: Holocaust Memorials and Meaning*. New Haven: Yale University Press.
Zimmermann, M. (2008) *Deutsche Gegen Deutsche: Das Schicksal der Juden 1938–1945*. Berlin: Aufbau Verlagsgruppe GmbH.

Index[1]

A

Abolish Commemoration (movement), 218, 253
Abraham, K. (on mourning *vs.* melancholia), 68n3, 222
Adenauer, K., 136, 148, 153, 168, 198, 199
  memory or democracy, 153, 168
  and normalization, 147–8
Adorno, T., 136, 137
agglutinated nucleus, 89, 104, 105, 113
Alford, C. F., 194
ambivalence, 22–4, 48, 63, 88, 92, 101–15, 119–21, 139n3, 147, 178, 200, 219, 220, 223–6, 230–2, 243, 251, 254
  primal, 91, 103, 104, 108, 109, 111, 112, 119, 166

Anderson, B. R. O'G., 52, 125
Annals of Historical Revision, 240
anonymous, 248
anonymous (Ferenczi), 84
anti-Bolshevism (communism), 63, 76, 171
anti-Nazism (fascism), 18, 136, 148
anti-reparative, 180, 200
anti-Semitism, 6, 14, 15, 63, 66, 73–82, 92–4, 112, 133, 134, 137, 146, 155, 166, 167, 174–6, 178, 180n1, 216, 240, 248, 250, 252
  gender and, 247–52
  redemptive (Freidländer), 15, 79, 155, 174
Anzieu, D., 69n4, 82, 112
Arendt, H., 14, 246, 247
Assmann, A., 139n3, 218

---

[1] Note: Page numbers followed by 'n' refers to notes.

B

Barlach, E., 211
Bartov, O., 93, 95, 126, 136, 137, 139n3, 147, 168, 176
Benz, W., 176
Berger, S., 125, 126
Bergmann, W., 175, 176, 180
Bion, W. R.
   agglomerated ego, 89, 90
   arrogance, 106
   connection with reality, 87, 192
   containment, 32–3
   nameless dread, 110
   primitive communication (projective identification), 33, 34, 40, 41, 111
   use of senory organs, 34, 102, 103, 107
Bleger, J.
   agglutinated nucleus, 89, 90, 104, 105, 113
   ambiguity, 110, 112
   catastrophe, 90, 104, 105, 112
   psychoic object, 96
   undifferentiation, 89, 90, 104
Blok, A., 87–8
Bohleber, W., 155, 157
Britton, R., 7, 27, 106
Brockhaus, G., 136, 139n3, 181n3
Broszat, M., 18, 63, 64, 75–9, 94, 127, 128, 134, 169, 242
Brunkhorst, H., 114, 125
Burrin, P., 73–5

C

catastrophe (narcissistic, primal), 19, 22, 61, 86, 93, 95, 96, 101, 138n2, 145, 146, 166, 169, 178, 180n3, 243, 248

Chasseguet-Smirgel, J., 64, 69n4, 77, 88, 147, 250
chiliastic leadership (Mommsen, H.), 78, 134
civilization (discontents), *see* Unbehagen
Claasen, H., 231
clinical cases, 2–5, 31–6, 52–60, 84–7, 108, 158, 159, 177, 191, 195–8
collapse
   masculine, 24, 248–50
   narcissistic, psychotic, 8, 19, 39, 63, 86, 88, 102, 105, 110, 138n2, 159, 173–8, 198, 222, 226, 233n3, 243, 251
Collingwood, R. G., 1, 2, 9, 239
community, *see* Volksgemeinschaft
Confino, A., 14, 15, 18, 66, 74, 75, 77, 79, 81–3, 94, 133, 134, 169
counter anti-memorial, 24, 212, 218, 226, 247, 252, 254
Culpepper, M., 211

D

Dahmer, H., 47
Davids, M. F., 58, 59, 61, 65, 253
Defensive organization, 112
   See also enclaves; psychic retreat; psychosocial; social defence system
delusional enemy, 22, 73–96, 119, 147, 166, 233n1
Denkmal/Mahnmal, 234n6
depressive, 86, 87, 121, 197–9, 221
   anxiety, 10, 108, 112, 145, 178, 193

position, 19, 23, 86, 104, 121, 125, 165, 193, 244
reparation, 200, 201
Diebow, H., 93
Dilthey, W., 241
disavowal, 5, 23, 121, 148, 156–61, 165–73, 252
   Freud on, 156–7
Domansky, E., 19, 161, 169–71, 180n2, 218
Dresden, 232
   bombing of, 153, 158, 217, 227–9
   and extremism, 234n9
   Heidefriedhof, 227, 228, 231
   innocent city of culture, 227–32
   memorialization, 231, 232, 234n8, 234n9, 253
   Requiem, 230, 234n7

E

ego-ideals, 30, 38, 39, 47, 49, 63, 64, 69n4, 77, 79, 81, 82, 88, 122, 157, 173, 174, 181n3, 221, 224–6, 250, 251
   See also Chasseguet-Smirgel, J.
Eley, G., 122, 124, 126, 127, 135–7, 139n3, 167, 173, 175
Erdheim, M. (social production of the unconscious), 54
Evans, R., 6, 63, 131, 133, 139n3, 227, 233n3, 241

F

Faimberg, H., 195, 196
Figlio, K., 80, 85, 86, 104, 225
Final Solution, 23, 64, 75, 76, 78, 79, 133

Fornari, F., 40, 213, 233n4, 245, 246
Freud, S., 22, 29, 81–5, 101, 102, 106, 146
   disavowal, 156, 252
   group psychology, 38, 56, 61, 69n4, 224
   guilt, 102
   internal world, 28–31
   mourning/melancholia, 16, 24, 201, 219–22
   Nachträglich, 2, 3, 9, 161
   narcissism, 67–8n3, 87
     primary, 29
     of small differences, 22, 81–5, 101, 102, 106, 146
   Oedipus complex, 106, 250
   primal ambivalence, 103, 109, 110
   reality ego, 89
   reparation, 9, 188, 189
   screen memories, 3
   structural model, 50, 55
   super-ego (ego-ideal), 30, 40, 49, 50
   taboo conscience, 188
   taboo of virginity, 83, 84, 157
   Unbehagen, 91, 96, 101, 119, 147
   undoing, 161
   Wolf Man, 4–5
   working through, 135
Frie, R., 56–8, 65, 67, 254
Friedländer, S., 15, 17, 20, 67n1, 76–9, 127, 128, 133, 139n3, 242
Frosh, S., 67n1, 252
Fuchs, A., 149, 153, 215, 229, 231
Führer
   regime, 63, 132
   working towards, 76, 81, 94, 134

Index

Führerbindung, 18, 95
Fulbrook, M., 138n1, 167, 169

G

Gallagher, E., 232n1
genocide, 13, 14, 241
Germans as victims, 17, 18, 126, 129, 135, 136, 139n3, 149, 150, 153, 157, 159, 168–71, 179, 215, 227, 228, 231
Girard, R., 88
Glover, E., 213
Goldhagen, D., 15
Goschler, C., 187
Graeber, D., 10
group (ego-)ideal, 39, 69n4, 81, 233n3
group formation, 3, 8, 9, 35, 38, 39, 41, 42, 48–53, 56, 61, 69n4, 80–2, 102, 105, 110–13, 146, 154–9, 172, 173, 223, 224, 239
  See also ego-ideal; group (ego-)ideal
Grubrich-Simitis, I., 64
guilt, 122, 124, 125, 136, 139n3, 148, 178, 216, 234n5, 244, 245
  and ambivalence, 102, 110, 219
  and capacity to mourn, 17, 225, 231
  defence against, 14, 29, 38, 40, 48, 51, 84, 110, 124, 165–70, 224–6, 233n1, 233n4, 251
  and depressive position, 121, 193, 244
  as a historical force, 21, 47, 57, 213, 218, 233n4, 242, 245

and internal worlds, 28
vs. persecutory (social)anxiety, 15, 246
and reparative urge, 11, 14, 23, 147
in society, 51, 52, 56

H

Habermas, J.
  (communicative) self-reflection, 46, 48, 63, 246
  constitutional patriotism, 114
  deliberative politics, 114, 246
  historians' debate (*Historikerstreit*), 62, 114, 124–6, 128, 129, 132, 135–7, 241
  historical liability, 123
  memory work, 62, 128
Hartman, G. (on Bitburg), 126, 179, 201
Hass, K., 208, 210, 213
Herf, J., 167, 168, 247
Hillgruber, A., 18, 140n6, 140n7, 153, 241
  and *Historikerstreit*, 127
Hinshelwood, R. D., 171, 172
historical consciousness, 1–5, 125
historicization, 77, 129
Historikerstreit, 6, 18, 22, 114, 119, 138–9n3, 169, 180, 199, 201, 241
  Habermas and, 62, 114, 124–6, 128, 129, 132, 135, 241
  Hillgruber and, 127–35
Hoffer, W., 108
Holocaust, 5, 6, 12–16, 18–20, 23, 47, 62, 75, 77, 95, 113, 114, 120, 125, 126, 128, 135–7,

140n5, 150, 152, 153, 156, 159, 160, 173–5, 218
denial and evasion, 6, 17, 127, 138–9n3, 179, 180n2, 240, 241 (*see also* not knowing)
singularity of, 129, 135, 150, 166, 174, 187, 193
survival, 57, 64, 125
victims, 126, 179 (*see also* Germans as victims)
Hopper, E., 52, 53, 65, 109, 110, 224
Human Rights Watch/Helsinki, 176

ideal, 4, 8, 17, 33, 37, 49, 56, 64, 74–9, 174, 176, 208, 210, 214, 233n3, 235n9, 250, 251
ideal-ego, 157, 221, 222
Ignatieff, M., 92, 174
imagined community, *see* Anderson, B. R. O'G
inability to mourn, 17, 138n2, 139n3, 180n3, 247, 251
Institute for Historical Review, 241
intellectual sociability, 12, 156, 247
internal world, 6, 7, 10, 18, 20, 21, 27–42, 45, 48, 62, 66, 107, 122–4, 177, 190, 196, 218, 240–3
introjection, 30, 36, 89, 95, 104, 105, 114, 121, 172, 178, 223
 forced, 56
introjective identification, 9–11, 16, 21, 23, 27, 186, 197, 198
 and reparation, 9–11, 15, 185–201
Irving, D., 6, 241
Isaacs, S., 85

J
Jacobson, E., 140n4
Jacoby, R. (violence and samemess), 88–91, 93, 96n2
Jager, J., 149
Jaspers, K., 245
Jerzak, C, 234n9
Jews as indistinguishable from gentiles, 93, 95, 137
Jokl, A. M., 85

K
Kaplan, T. P, 82, 133
Kernberg, O., 192
Kershaw, I., 18, 19, 63, 75, 76, 96, 131, 132, 134, 138n2, 224
Klein, M
 depressive (anxiety, position), 10, 23, 63, 121, 165, 166, 193, 194
 internal object, 40
 manic defence, 68n3, 219
 melancholia, 222, 223
 mourning, 68n3, 214, 215
 paranoid (anxiety, schizoid position), 41, 86–9, 108, 111, 112, 121, 193
 projective identification, 33, 86, 171, 197, 198
 reparation, 63, 185, 190, 191, 218, 252
 splitting, 23, 105, 165
Kohte-Meyer, I., 54–6
 social superego, 56, 58, 65
Kohut, H., 67n3
Kohut, T, 67n1, 249
Kollwitz, K., 150–2, 179
Krondorfer, B., 253

L

LaCapra, D., 139
Langer, L., 15, 140n5
leader-bond (*Führerbindung*), 18, 75, 95, 138n2, 217
Lipstadt, D., 6, 138–9n3, 240, 241
Longerich, P, 81
Luppes, J., 153
Lupu, N, 201, 218

M

McNamara, R., 213, 234n5
Maier, C., 11–13, 95, 122, 123, 126, 127, 156, 247
Mancia, M., 50
manic, 16, 17, 32, 68n3, 78, 88, 111, 192, 195, 198, 201, 219–22, 224, 225, 229–32
　defences, 48, 68n3, 218, 219, 222, 232
　depression, 39, 68n3, 193, 222, 225
　reparation, 3, 10, 11, 13, 16, 23, 24, 125, 179, 180, 185–201, 207, 218, 219, 225, 229–32, 242, 246, 247, 254
Marcuse, H., 152–3
Margalit, G., 215
masculinity, 67n1, 96n2
　and Nazism, 248–54
Mauersberger, R., 227, 234n7
melancholia, 188, 219–23
　and manic reparation, 16, 201
　and mourning, 24, 68n3, 230
　and public mourning, 24

Meltzer, D., 50
memorial(ization), 3–5, 20, 31, 138n1, 150–6, 175, 176, 201
　See also counter anti-memorial
　ambiguity of, 24, 153, 213, 223, 233n1
　and ambivalence, 24, 119, 120, 139n3, 186, 226, 227
　Berlin (*see* Kollwitz, K.)
　and conflicted feelings, 155, 156, 210–12, 229, 234n6
　and defences, 218, 219
　Dresden, 226–32
　Hamburg, 210–12, 226, 253
　and German victims, 37, 231
　and public mourning, 225, 230, 231
　and reparation, 16, 23, 152, 201, 207–35
　states of mind, 36, 153, 155
　Stolpersteine, 214, 253
　Vietnam, 208, 210, 213, 226
memory, *see* remembering
Mitchell, J., 87–8
Mitscherlich, A., 16–18, 47, 136, 137, 138n2, 139n3, 159, 167, 171, 178, 180n3, 217, 226, 247, 251
Mitscherlich, M., 17, 47, 64, 136, 137, 138n2, 139n3, 159, 167, 171, 178, 180n3, 217, 219, 226, 247, 251
Mitscherlich-Nielsen, M., 174, 178, 250
Moeller, R., 216, 229, 234n9
Mommsen, H., 75, 78, 79, 94, 134, 169

Money-Kyrle, R., 198
Mosse, G., 208, 210, 226, 232n1
mourning, 16, 47, 48, 51–3, 63, 77, 123, 138n2, 174, 201, 211–15, 217–27, 230, 231, 232n1, 234n7, 245, 246
  and melancholia, 219–23, 229, 230
  and memory, 47, 63, 139n3, 207, 233n1
  private, 24, 207, 232n1
  public, 24, 207, 208, 210, 214, 223–6, 231, 232n1
  and reparation, 47, 48, 139n3, 207, 232, 233n1
Murer, J., 91
myth(ic)
  collective national, 125, 248
  of Dresden, 234n9
  redemption, 231
  remembrance, 77
  of second guilt, 136
  of silence, 215–16
  of war experience (*see* Mosse, G.)

Inability to mourn, The, 17, 47, 138n2, 139n3, 180–1n3, 203n6, 247, 251
Nachträglich, 2, 3, 9
narcissism, 7, 8, 22, 29, 47–9, 64, 67–8n3, 81–4, 87–90, 97n2, 101, 102, 104, 106, 109, 111, 138n2, 146, 157, 159, 188, 194, 220
  and hatred, 89

  primary, 29, 49, 68n3, 88, 104, 111
  of small differences, 22, 81–3, 97n2, 101, 102, 106
  thin-skinned, 8
natural reparative law, 194
Noro, T., 250
not knowing, 5, 23, 137, 156
not-remembering, 5, 22, 23, 67n2, 137, 147

Oedipus complex, 88, 96n2, 106, 107, 188
O'Shaughnessy, E., 86, 108, 109
Outhwaite, W., 116n4
Overy, R., 228

paranoid-schizoid, 19, 86, 87, 165, 166
  anxiety, 112
  position, 86, 90, 107, 108, 121, 165, 193
  splitting, 23, 90
Partners in Confronting Collective Atrocities, 253
Patriotische Europäer gegen die Islamisierung des Abendlandes (PEGIDA), 234n8
persecutory anxiety, 11, 15, 24, 246
Peter, R., 229
Pidd, H., 227
populism, 8, 243

primal
  ambivalence, 91, 103, 104, 108, 109, 111, 112, 119, 121, 166
  catastrophe, 22, 93, 101, 102, 109, 111, 112
  communication, 32
  states, 3, 29, 35, 36, 38–41, 80, 88, 90, 104, 106–8, 111, 193, 197
  projections, 30, 36, 38, 39, 41, 48, 51, 60, 61, 64, 65, 76, 79, 80, 82, 86, 87, 89, 90, 95, 103, 105, 109, 114, 168, 172, 199, 223, 251, 252
  repositories for, 22, 74, 83, 112, 113, 172–4, 178, 180n1, 243
projective identification, 9, 20, 23, 27, 61, 62, 86, 88–90, 102, 105, 106, 111, 113, 119, 186, 221
  and manic reparation, 186
psychic retreat, 101, 109–13, 172
  See also defensive organization; enclaves; psychosocial; social defence system
psychosocial
  defence, 95
  enclaves, 29, 121, 145, 166, 171–8

Q

Quindeau, I., 218

R

Rank, O., 88, 88
regime
  Führer, 132

German Democratic Republic (GDR), 234n8
Hitler, 138n2
Nazi, 15, 18, 79, 80, 157, 168, 243, 247, 249, 251, 252
socialist, 130
remembering, 2, 3, 5–11, 13, 17, 18, 20, 22–5, 62, 95, 113, 115, 119–37, 139n3, 199–201, 207, 208, 210, 230–2, 233n1, 240
  'false', 11, 23, 24, 147, 179, 201, 242, 246, 252
  mastering (see Vergangenheitsbewältigung)
  neutralization of/exclusion of Jews from, 167–71
  as reparation, 9–25, 52, 115, 139n3, 201, 212, 254
  'true', 11, 23, 24, 147, 157, 179, 185, 201, 207, 239, 240, 242, 246, 247, 251, 252
reparation, 3–5, 9, 11, 13–19, 23, 24, 45, 47, 52, 107, 113, 120, 125, 137, 139n3, 147, 148, 150, 153, 167, 168, 179, 180, 201, 222, 223, 230, 242, 244, 246, 247, 252, 254
  and collective memory, 198–201
  and depressive concern for the object, 19, 125, 194
  and identification, 193–8
  introjective identification, 185–97
  manic (see manic)
  and reality, 188–9
repression, 5, 23, 51, 63, 64, 78, 107, 121, 124, 136, 170, 171

Rhode, E., 86–8
right-wing extremism, 51, 148, 166, 173, 175–7, 230
Riviere, J. (on restitution), 190
Roper, L., 67n1
Rosenfeld, H., 7, 68n3, 103
Rothe, K., 67n2, 158, 159
   and scenic understanding (Lorenzer), 67n2
rubble photography, 149, 229, 231
Rustin, M., 67n1

S

sameness, 21, 88, 91, 97n2
   dread of, 74, 75, 80–3, 89, 145
   phantasy of, 83–5
Sapisochin, G., 31–2
scientific history, 75, 77, 128, 129, 133
Scott, J., 67n1
screen memories, 3
Sebald, W. G., 149, 215–17
Segal, H., 47, 109, 207, 225, 233n4, 245
   war as a defence against guilt, 47, 213, 225, 233n4, 245
sensory organs
   motor use of, 102–3
Sittel, D., 230
sociability, 12
social defence systems, 29, 172, 224
social production of the unconscious, *see* Erdheim, M.
social subject, 21, 41, 42, 45–66, 102
social system, 38
splitting, 23, 33, 51, 55, 56, 90, 105, 112, 121, 148, 161, 167, 170–4, 180n1, 208, 221, 225
Steiner, J., 7, 96, 109, 112, 172

Stolpersteine, 213, 214, 253
Strachey, J., 65
Streeck-Fischer, A., 177
subjective, 2, 6–8, 20, 27, 77, 130, 148, 186, 187, 247
subjectivities, 2, 6–9, 21, 27, 113, 128, 223, 224
superego, 46–66, 101, 102, 106, 192
   social, 46, 52–66, 102, 122
superego-ideal, 50

T

taboo, 83, 84, 188, 216, 248
   conscience, 189
   sense of guilt, 189
   of virginity, 83, 84
thrall, 39, 50, 64, 75, 76, 79, 115, 132, 210, 224, 243, 247, 248
   See also chiliastic leadership (Mommsen, H.)
Totem and Taboo, 188, 189
transference, 29–32, 65, 158
   counter, 58, 108
   interpretation, 46, 53, 54

U

Unbehagen, 22, 91, 96, 101, 113, 119, 166, 177, 178
unconscious guilt, 218
unintegration, 104–5

V

Vergangenheitsbewältigung, 13, 120, 135, 136, 152, 174, 218, 251
   vs. Vergangenheitsbewahrung, 218

Volkan, V. (narcissism of small differences), 91
Volksgemeinschaft, 80, 81, 83, 114, 115, 133, 140n3, 170, 179

W

Wieland, C., 251
Winnicott, D. W., 104, 108, 109
Wolf Man, 4–5

world without Jews, *see* Confino, A.

Y

Young, J., 149, 154–6, 159, 201, 233n2, 252

Z

Zimmermann, M., 74, 133

GPSR Compliance

The European Union's (EU) General Product Safety Regulation (GPSR) is a set of rules that requires consumer products to be safe and our obligations to ensure this.

If you have any concerns about our products, you can contact us on

ProductSafety@springernature.com

In case Publisher is established outside the EU, the EU authorized representative is:

Springer Nature Customer Service Center GmbH
Europaplatz 3
69115 Heidelberg, Germany

www.ingramcontent.com/pod-product-compliance
Lightning Source LLC
LaVergne TN
LVHW020341260326
834688LV00045B/1476